The Two Thousand Mile War

W.E. Crosskill

Foreword by
Sir Richard Turnbull, G.C.M.G.

ROBERT HALE · LONDON

First published in Great Britain 1980

ISBN 0 7091 8591 X

Robert Hale Limited
Clerkenwell House
Clerkenwell Green
London EC1R 0HT

Photoset by
Specialised Offset Services Limited, Liverpool
and printed in Great Britain by
Lowe & Brydone Limited
Thetford, Norfolk

CONTENTS

LIST OF ILLUSTRATIONS

PICTURE CREDITS

Brigadier M.W. Biggs, C.B.E., 1; Mr John Hillaby, 2, 8; the Imperial War Museum, 3, 13, 14, 15, 17, 20, 22, 23, 26, 27, 29, 30, 33, 34, 47, 49; the Kenya Government Information Service, 4, 5, 6; Mrs Sylvia Seex, 7; *Springbok Victory*, Carel Birkby, 9, 10, 11, 24, 39, 44, 45; the South African Ministry of Defence, 12, 18, 40; *The Abyssinian Campaigns*, H.M.S.O. 1942, 16, 19, 21, 25, 28, 31, 32, 35, 36, 37, 41, 42, 43, 46, 48; the author, 38.

Foreword

by Sir Richard Turnbull, G.C.M.G.

This is a book that all East Africans, whether or not they played a part in the Somalia and Ethiopia campaign of 1940 and 1941, will read with the greatest interest and satisfaction. For Ted Crosskill brings to his account of the operations not only the eye of the Infantry Officer but the reflections of the student of political history and the judgement of the experienced farmer on the quality of the land through which the sweep of the campaign takes him; and the various aspects of his story are given sharpened point by the special roles that he was from time to time chosen to undertake, from Battalion Intelligence Officer in June 1940 and Brigade Intelligence Officer in the following month, to the successful completion of the Staff College Course at Haifa in September 1941. His narrative, presented in an agreeably clear and unpretentious manner, and frequently lit by flashes of humour, starts with his posting to the 1st Battalion of the King's African Rifles, then at Moshi, and his introduction there to the rigours and inconsistencies of military life; and moves on to describe his experiences in the Northern Frontier District of Kenya during the queer twilit periods between the declaration of war with Germany and the entry of Italy into the conflict, whilst being instructed in the arts of war by that immensely formidable character Brigadier Fowkes.

Then when the real war started — real for East Africa that is — Ted was closely and personally involved right from the Caproni raid on Wajir in the second week of June 1940, the first attack on Eil Wak, and the withdrawal from Moyale; then, in the advance from the Tana River leading to the capitulation of Kismayu, the crossing of the Juba, and the entry into Mogadishu. After that, he was selected for the Staff College course at Haifa, passing out of it six months later to become D.A.Q.M.G. to General Godwin-Austen's 12th Division at Addis Ababa — just in time to take an active part in the fighting around

Gondar where the closing engagement of the Ethiopian campaign was to be fought out. 'There,' he says, 'in the wild north-west corner of Abyssinia, General Nasi, a good soldier and a stern but just disciplinarian, elected to make the last stand.' And there the author concludes the personal part of his story.

In the book there is of course far more than individual reminiscences and individual accounts of the dangers and boredoms, the splendours and miseries of campaigning. His time at the Staff College gave him a much deeper insight into the science of war and the arts and crafts of military operations than the run-of-the-mill infantry officer, however gifted he might be, could ever manage to acquire; and, with this heightened perception, he has set down detailed and graphic accounts of the operations that were taking place at the same time as those in which his own battalion was engaged. He describes the defence of British Somaliland and the unhappy withdrawal from the Protectorate, the fierce fighting for Keren and the hardly-won victory, and the race by the 11th Division to get themselves to Addis before the weather wholly disrupted communications. He deals, too, with the battles fought *en route* – by the Nigerians for the Marda Pass, by the 5th Battalion of the K.A.R. at the Awash, and by the Transvaal Scottish at Hubeta Pass; and with the hardships that the 12th Division had to endure sitting out the rains in the south and around the Lakes until the weather allowed the advance to be resumed; then with the splendid achievements of the Gold Coast Brigade at Uadoara, and of the East Africans and the Nigerians at the two crossings of the Omo.

These narratives are not merely expanded chapters of the Regimental Histories of the campaign. They owe as much to first-hand reports from a score of friends and colleagues who themselves had taken part in the operations as they do to the official records; and they are further strengthened by the author's own experiences of the problems of fighting a war against the same enemy and in not dissimilar country. And excellent reading they make.

It is hard to think of anyone better equipped than Ted Crosskill for the authorship of a book of this sort. For close on a dozen years he farmed in northern Tanganyika, and in that time acquired a deep love of the country and an informed recognition of the problems, political, constitutional and economic into which the East African Territories, in common with most of the other colonial dependencies, were moving. And in his army days he was constantly aware of the way in which the cement of comradeship between Europeans and Africans would play an essential part in the building up of a nation.

After the war he disposed of his Tanganyika property and redeployed his farming enthusiasms in Kenya. But, before many years had passed, his need to be at the focus of events began to re-assert itself; and in 1952 he successfully fought the Mau constituency to become an elected member of the Kenya Legislative Council. He was re-elected in 1956; and in the following year was offered and accepted one of the Ministerial posts that the Lennox-Boyd constitutional changes had brought about. From 1957 until 1960 he was the Minister for Tourism, Forests, Game and Fisheries, and is remembered with gratitude and affection by all those who had dealings with those departments, or who took part in the Parliamentary Morris Dance of that tense and not very comfortable period.

In conclusion let me say what a pleasure it was to find, in the early chapters, the names of that fine pair of 'Somalophils' (to use the author's word for those who fall under the spell of these fascinating people), John Llewellin and Gualtiero Benardelli, each of them a master of the Somali tongue and of the complex inter-relationships of the Somali clans, and each of them a lively and courageous leader of Irregulars.

There are three more of the *dramatis personae* who, although not present on the stage, can, as it were, be sensed to be in the wings during the first act of the play, and without whom no work that takes in the N.F.D. and the world of the Somalis can be regarded as complete. They are Vincent Glenday, Gerald Reece, and Hugh Grant. Glenday, after close on twenty-five years in the N.F.D. and Turkana, during which time he managed to be present at every storm-centre as it arose, went in 1938 to British Somaliland as Governor; and it was he who had the melancholy duty of organizing the removal of the Civil Government at the time of the withdrawal from the Protectorate that is described in Chapter 4. Gerald Reece, the successor to Glenday and another great figure of the N.F.D. and Southern Ethiopia, was in charge of the Civil Administration of the Northern Frontier and of the Borana Province of Ethiopia throughout the campaign. A few years after the end of the war he, too, moved on to be Governor of Somaliland. As for Hugh Grant, that matchless *Hielan'man* – as Willie Keir, later to be killed by Ethiopian Shifta in a gallant action in defence of the local tribespeople's stock, used to call him – it was he who raised the Somali Irregular companies that did such valuable work in holding the Banda at arm's length before the advance into

Jubaland took place, when the gathering pace of the war dispelled the need for such auxiliaries. Hugh Grant commanded the northern of the two companies, and John Llewellin the one in the south. What splendid men we were privileged to be with in those days!

RICHARD TURNBULL

Preface

During the war years of 1939 to 1942 it was natural that the spotlight should be on the Western Desert in Egypt and Libya rather than on East Africa: it was nearer home and the stakes were high. Our prospects of winning the war in Europe depended on our first defeating the German and Italian armies in Africa, but it is not generally recognized that success in the Western Desert could not be achieved until the strong Italian forces in Eritrea, Abyssinia and Somalia, which constituted a threat to General Wavell's left flank, had been eliminated. My story tells how this was done.

The East African campaign, in its initial stages, was similar in several respects to that in the Western Desert: each was fought over vast areas of barren land where water was scarce and roads non-existent. Later on, however, conditions in the Abyssinian highlands were sometimes like those in the rain forests of Burma and, at others, reminiscent of the Pyrenees. The natural hazards of terrain and climate then made the task of supply both herculean and risky. On the other hand the Italians had no Rommel in East Africa and no German troops to stiffen their resistance. Although they fought well and stubbornly on occasions, their large, well equipped forces were soon defeated for reasons which will be told.

Just before Italy declared war in 1940 they had a force of a quarter of a million men in North Africa while we had only 36,000. We did have, in addition, 27,000 men in Palestine; but their task was elsewhere than in Egypt and, in any case, this figure included several, still horsed, cavalry regiments which could scarcely be used, as at Balaclava, against guns or, still less, against tanks. The Italian armies in East Africa were even stronger with 300,000 well equipped men. To oppose them we had a mere 10,000 men in Kenya, the Sudan and Somaliland. But, within a year, five British and Commonwealth divisions were fighting the Italians on four different fronts in East

Africa. The architect – Field-Marshal Lord Wavell.

It is nearly forty years since the incidents I relate took place: not so long that I have forgotten any of the fun, fears, friendships and excitement of the time, but long enough for the picture to have become clearer to me than it then was – when I was too near the trees to see the wood. It is written of happier days when people of all races in the British Commonwealth made common cause to ensure that neither their home-lands nor Britain would be dominated by a German or Italian dictator. Men from East, South and West Africa, from the Rhodesias, the Sudan, Britain, Cyprus, Australia and India, joined in mutual endeavour in this successful campaign. Since then inevitable and necessary winds of change have grown to gale force through lack of patience and under-standing and caused rifts which could have been averted had there been a greater appreciation of common interests, problems and human ties. I hope this tale of joint endeavour may assist in mending the cracks in the family structure which are so useful to our enemies.

"La Ginelle"   W.E.C.
France.
September 1979.

Acknowledgements

I am very grateful to Mr J.W. Howard for lending me a number of despatches and reports on the East African campaign, and to Mr W.D. Draffan, M.B.E., for information I obtained from the War Journal of the 5th King's African Rifles which he wrote in conjunction with the late Mr T.C.C. Lewin, O.B.E., M.C. They, all three, served with the 5th K.A.R. throughout the war and their personal knowledge and experience contributed a great deal to this story. I wish, too, to thank Mr J.S. Ross, M.B.E., for the information I gained from his *History of the 1/3 K.A.R.*

I am also grateful to Sir Richard Turnbull for his valuable guidance on several points and I am indebted to Messrs Frederick Muller Ltd for permission to quote some extracts from Kenneth Gandar Dower's book, *Abyssinian Patchwork*, and to Messrs Cassell & Co. Ltd for agreeing to my quoting briefly from Sir Winston Churchill's *History of the Second World War*.

To 'The Brigadier', the late Major-General C.C. Fowkes, C.B.E., D.S.O., M.C., whose indefatigability and swift variability between 'Stormy' and 'Set Fair' created an atmosphere of healthy apprehension which kept us all on our toes.

Chronological Table of Events

	ATTACK from SOUTH	ATTACK from NORTH	PATRIOTS
1939			
3 Sept.	War declared against Germany.		
Dec.	East African force to Northern Frontier.		
1940			
10 June	Italy declared war.		
14 July	Moyale evacuated.	Italians invade the Sudan.	
2 Aug.	Italians invade Somaliland.		
19 Aug.	Berbera evacuated.		
Sept.	Withdrawal to Wajir.		Brig. Sandford to Abyssinia.
Oct.	Marsabit reinforced.		
Nov.		Failure to recapture Gallabat.	
Dec.	Concentration, Tana River.	Italians withdraw from the Sudan.	
1941			
20 Jan.			Emperor into Abyssinia.
23 Jan.	Advance into Italian Somaliland.		
2 Feb.		Agordat & Barentu captured.	
3-14 Feb.		1st Battle of Keren.	Wingate's force invades.
14 Feb.	Kismayu occupied.		
25 Feb.	Mogadishu taken.		
4 Mar.			Battle of Burye.
15-26 Mar.		2nd Battle of Keren.	
16 Mar.	Berbera relieved.		
29 Mar.	Diredawa captured.		
1 Apr.		Asmara occupied.	
3 Apr.	Awash River.		
6 Apr.	Addis Ababa capitulated.		
8 Apr.		Massawa captured.	
17-26 Apr.	Battle of Dessie.		Battle of Dessie.
2 May	Uaddara and Fike.		All Italians out of Gojjam.
4-16 May	Amba Alagi.	Amba Alagi.	Amba Alagi.
22 May	12 Div. & 22 Bde meet at Uondo.		Battle of Agibar.
6 June	Omo River crossings.		
21 June	Jimma occupied.		
3 July	Debra Tabor taken.		
4 July	Gen. Gazzera surrenders.		
27 Sept.			Wolchefit surrenders.
13 Nov.	Kulkaber.		Kulkaber.
27 Nov.	Gondar captured.		Gondar captured.

Orders of Battle East Africa, 1940-41

(Principal formations and units only)

	British and Commonwealth Forces	Italian Forces

June '40
KENYA
	Six infantry bns:
	    1 & 2 K.A.R. (Nyasa.)
	    3 & 5 K.A.R. (Kenya)
	    4 K.A.R. (Uganda)
	    6 K.A.R. (Tanganyika)
	22 (Ind.) Mtn Bty
	1 (EA) Lt Bty
	(Total strength approx. 7,000 men
	in East Africa, 5,000 in the Sudan
	and 2,000 in Br. Somaliland.)
		300,000 men
		400 field and mountain guns
		200 aircraft(+)
		200 light and medium tanks
		100 armoured cars
		10,000 motor vehicles

July '40 **BR.** **SOMALILAND**	Somaliland Camel Corps 2 Black Watch 2 K.A.R. 3/15 and 1/2 Punjabi Regt 1 (EA) Lt Bty (Total strength approx. 6,000 men.)	Four Blackshirt bns Twenty Colonial bns Eleven Gps Irregulars Four Gps pack artillery 30 tanks, light and medium Two sections armoured cars (Total strength approx. 25,000 men.)
Aug. '40 **KENYA**	1 South African Brigade Group 21 (EA) Brigade Group 22 (EA) Brigade Group 23 Nigerian Brigade Group 24 Gold Coast Brigade Group (Total strength approx. 20,000 men.)	

Jan. '41
KENYA
	1 (S. African) Div.: {25 (EA) Bde
	                  {2 & 5 S.African Bdes
	11 (African) Div.: {23 Nigerian Bde
	                {1 N.Rhodesian Regt
	12 (African) Div.: {1 (S.African) Bde
	                {22 (EA) Bde
	                {24 Gold Coast Bde
	(Total strength approx. 75,000 men.)	

Feb. '41
JUBA RIVER
	12(A) Div.: Four motorized Bde Gps:
	    {1 (SA) Bde
	    {21, 22 & 24 (EA) Bdes
	Light tanks, armoured cars,
	Field and mtn artillery
		Six bdes regular tps
		(101 & 102 Divs)
		Six gps Irregulars
		Arty and armoured cars

Feb. '41 **KEREN**	4 & 5 (Ind.) Divs Arty & 'I' and light tanks (Total strength approx. 13,000 men.)	Total strength approx. 30,000 men and 144 guns

March '41
MOGADISHU-
ADDISABABA
	11(A) Div.:
	  1 (SA) Bde: {Transvaal Scottish
	             {R.N. Carbineers
	             {Duke of Edinburgh's
	  22 (EA) Bde: (5 & 6 K.A.R.)
	  23 Nigerian Bde
		Army of Somalia
		withdrawing from line
		of Juba River

March/May '41 SOUTHERN ABYSSINIA	12(A) Div.: { 21 (EA) Bde 24 Gold Coast Bde 25(EA) Bde 1 N.R.R.	Seven divs south of Addis Ababa 21, 22, 23, 24, 25, 26 and 101 Divs
Apr./July '41 THE LAKES	11(A) Divs.: 22 (EA) Bde:{ 5 & 6 K.A.R. 2 Nigerian Regt (Attached) { 1 N.M.R. and 1 F.F.B. (1 S.African Bde to Dessie.)	22, 23 and 26 Divs (Total strength approx. 40,000 men.)
Apr. '41 DESSIE	1 (SA) Bde (approx. half-strength or 1,500 men.) 14 guns	Twelve battalions 44 guns
May '41 OMO RIVER CROSSINGS	22 (EA) Bde: 5 & 6 K.A.R. and 2 Nigerians 23 (EA) Bde: 1 K.A.R. and 1 & 3 Nigerians	Remnants of divisions withdrawing from southern Abyssinia and the Lakes.
May '41 AMBA ALAGI	5 (Indian) Div.: 29 Bde: 1 Worcesters Garhwal Rifles F.F. Rifles Skinner's Horse Jewish-Arab Commando Sudan Defence Force (Total strength approx. 3,000 men before arrival of 1 (S.A.) Brigade	Total strength approx. 5,000 men including two battalions 211 Iuf., Savoia Grenadier M/G Bn and arty of Savoia Div.
Nov. '41 GONDAR	12(A) Div.: 25 (EA) Bde 26 (EA) Bde Southforce: 6 K.A.R. 1 (EA) Pioneer Bn 51 (GC) Light Bty D Coy. 1/3 K.A.R. (Total strength approx. 20,000 regular tps with 25 guns plus 6,000 Patriots.)	Total strength approx. 34,000 men (including 18,000 white troops) and 60 guns.

1

Clouds of War over Africa

SEPTEMBER TO NOVEMBER 1939

The snow-covered summit of Mount Kilimanjaro, rising above the early morning cloud, seemed to be floating in the air. But lower down, the vast forest, the deep valleys and the rocky crags were all distinctly visible in the crystal clear air as were, nearer at hand, the clusters of little farms and coffee plantations dotted about among the foothills. Far below, the plains of Africa stretched sun-baked and brown away to the horizon in a country of infinite space and variety.

But dark clouds were gathering over this peaceful part of Tanganyika in August 1939 – clouds of war. Hitler, by sheer force of oratory, had convinced his people that Germany was all powerful and could dominate the world.

The seed of this inspiration fell on fertile ground with the German community. This country, as German East Africa, had been their colony until they lost it after the war of 1914-18; now was their chance to regain it. Old flames of bitterness against the British which had disappeared with time, mutual interests and friendship were rekindled; attendance by all Germans at secret Nazi meetings was mandatory and young hotheads increased the tension by flying Swastika flags on their cars – only to have them torn off by the British in anger.

War seemed imminent. I and many of my friends, then living in Tanganyika, left our farms, professions and businesses to join the army, and were posted to the 1st Battalion of the King's African Rifles which was in barracks at the little town of Moshi on the slopes of Kilimanjaro. For most of us it meant learning a new trade from scratch and for week after week we marched, crawled and ran across country and were then drilled on the parade ground by the Regimental Sergeant Major.

In that testing time I shared my annoyances, exasperations and worries with Jock Mackie, a friend of mine who farmed near me at

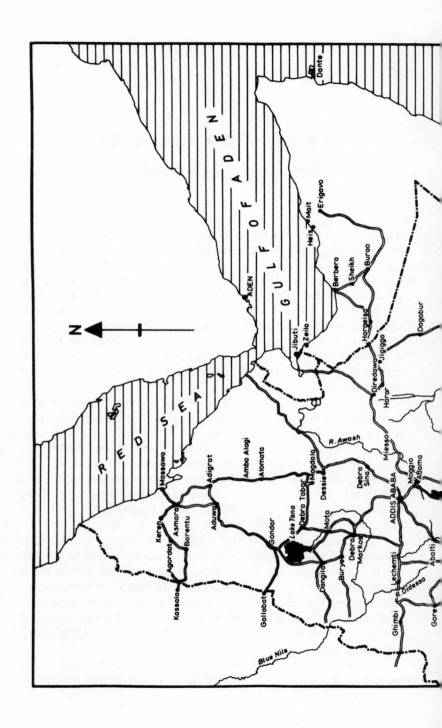

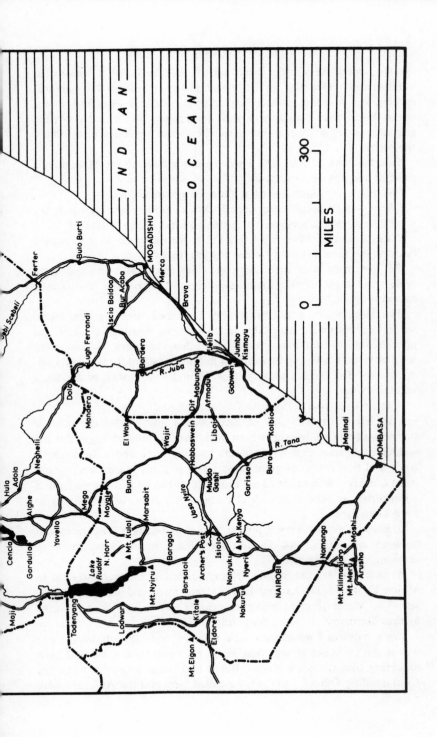

Arusha, some forty miles from Moshi. We both felt it was rather childish and 'infra dig' to be marched up and down the 'square', turning and wheeling, particularly when some of our African soldiers, our Askaris, were watching us with amusement. But if that was what our king and country required of us, the sooner we learnt how to do it the better.

One morning as Jock and I were walking back to the Mess after a difficult and not very successful bit of arms drill he said,

'What a lousy place and what a bloody waste of time.'

There was no point in arguing; Jock was hungry and so was I. We went into the Mess, took off our belts and sat down to breakfast.

Jock continued, 'You see I feel I'd be far more use to the country back on my farm. At least I know my job there.'

But just then a cheerful African waiter brought us bacon, eggs, coffee and toast. Jock's focus of interest changed and life became tolerable again.

The large room was comfortably furnished with big armchairs, several settees and a long table laden with the Regimental silver and piles of papers and magazines. Two other amateurs like ourselves were obviously listening to words of military wisdom from the second-in-command of the Battalion, Major Thornhill, who was, of course, a regular soldier.

'Yes sir, of course sir, I see, sir.'

I smiled to myself. One of them was a lawyer and the other a business executive, men to whom such humility was strange. But the sudden realization that we amateurs knew nothing about the soldier's trade and that it was of great importance that we should learn – and learn quickly – had made us all, though loath to admit it, as eager and competitive as schoolboys. And I knew that Jock, at heart, was as keen as anyone.

'I know I'm not very good at this drill business,' he remarked between mouthfuls, 'but did you see what a muck Gerry made of ordering and sloping arms?'

At that moment the Signals Officer hurried in and went straight to Major Thornhill. He handed him a signal form and said, 'It's come sir.' The Major grunted and then read it out to us: 'War declared against Germany.' It was 3 September 1939.

For a moment I felt slightly sick. It wasn't the eggs and bacon, nor was it the prospect of war that made me squeamish – we had been expecting that for some weeks. But it had come at a time when the Commanding Officer, the C.O. we called him, and the Adjutant were about 120 miles away making arrangements for interning some prospective enemy aliens who lived in a remote part of Tanganyika. I, as Battalion Intelligence Officer, had been told to stand in for the Adjutant. My knowledge of soldiering was almost nil. Would I be able to cope with the problems?

For two years Jock and I had been in the Reserve of the King's African Rifles and held the rank of lieutenant. This was the equivalent of being in the Territorials in Britain and only entailed attending a training-camp for two weeks each year. We enjoyed these as a pleasant change from the farm; they gave us plenty of opportunity for shooting both big game and for the pot. We certainly learnt to find our way about in the bush with a compass, stalk an animal and shoot pretty straight, but it had not taught me what an adjutant should do at the outbreak of war. In fact, at that moment, all I could really remember about my training was how to turn to the left and right on the march and how to put my puttees on so that they ended in the right place.

But to hell with such qualms. I knew there was a sealed envelope in the safe containing operation orders in case of war; these would tell us what to do. The envelope was taken from the safe and the orders read. They were perfectly clear. Ball ammunition was to be issued to the guards, patrols were to be sent out to three different places, road blocks were to be set up here and there and several people were to be arrested and brought into custody pending internment. Major Thornhill, now Acting C.O., called in all the company commanders, issued brief verbal orders and that was that. Everything was in motion. I sat back and wondered what there had been to worry about. Then I remembered to 'ack' the signal about the war.

Looking through the window at the plains below I began to think about the battles General von Lettow-Vorbeck had fought against us in the 1914 war. We had been re-fighting some of them recently on the original battlefields. They seem mainly to have been fought on the old principle of storming a strong-point only to find on reaching it that the wily enemy had disappeared after exacting a heavy toll from us. I hoped we should not be fighting that sort of war; and certainly not one in the wet, swampy country through which our men had plodded in southern Tanganyika in 1917 and 1918, hampered more by malaria, dysentery and hunger than by the enemy.

My reverie was interrupted. The Signals Officer dashed in saying,

'Where's the C.O.? Another signal has just come in saying there's no war after all.'

'Good God, let me see it,' I said. 'It must be a mistake. Where's it from?'

But it was the real thing all right. It was from Dar es Salaam and read: 'Ref. my 213 stop war not rpt not declared.'

I sent the clerk to find the C.O., an orderly to get messengers, telephoned to two outposts, wrote messages to others and wondered how many wretched people had been seized and interned and how much traffic had been dislocated by the road blocks. I then dashed down the stairs and over to the guard at the main gate. I waited for the sentry's salute, fearing that the resounding slap on the rifle might send one of the newly loaded rounds of .303 soaring into the sky, and then ordered him to unload.

With parade ground perfection he worked the bolt to and fro, then closed it and squeezed the trigger. The bullet hit the ground just by my foot. He had forgotten to count five when emptying the magazine and I had escaped being the first casualty of the war by inches.

I went back to the orderly-room and found that all was going smoothly. The cancellation messages had been received, the patrols were returning and the road blocks pulling in. This soldiering business was quite easy really. But I had thought too soon. The Signals Officer, now almost frantic, dashed in saying,

'The ruddy war *is* on after all. Look at this.'

He pushed a signal over to me. Yes, obviously authentic. We could only laugh – and then get everything moving forward again. I had read about the 'fog of war'; perhaps this was a special preliminary training for it.

Not until about two years later, when I was in another theatre of war altogether, did I hear how it came about that the contradictory signals were sent to us. It seems that the Governor's A.D.C. in Dar es Salaam had been listening to the BBC news from London and heard the announcement of the declaration of war. He, therefore, went to the Governor and asked permission to send out a number of prepared signals to the various key places in the Territory. H.E. agreed and off they went. A few minutes later the Governor saw the Chief Secretary, his 'chief of staff', and said,

'Oh, by the way, I've sent off those signals about the war.'

'Heavens alive, sir,' he replied, 'I don't think we should have done that: it hasn't been confirmed by the Colonial Office yet. May I cancel them?'

My historian could not quote His Excellency's exact reply: I do know, however, that the Chief Secretary had his way.

There followed two weeks of intense activity during which we were cursed, encouraged, praised, warned, re-equipped and reclothed. Until then officers, all of whom were British, had worn Wolseley helmets. These had been fashionable in the Boer War but were so no longer. The African Askaris had red tarbooshes for 'best' and silly little pill-box hats for everyday wear. Now, however, we were all to wear the more sensible Australian-type slouch hat.

In peacetime a battalion of the King's African Rifles (the K.A.R.) had seven British officers and a British regimental sergeant major; all the non-commissioned officers and private soldiers were African. Under a new War Establishment, however, the number of British ranks was increased to eighty and the extra men came to us from the Kenya Regiment, Kenya Defence Force and the K.A.R. Reserve, our Territorials.

The Africans were superb on the parade ground; their drill was almost, if not quite, up to Guards standard. To a few of them, however, drill and dressing up to impress the girls was the 'be all and end all' of army life and when war seemed likely they asked for leave on one pretext or another and disappeared. Good riddance, we thought. The remainder, in time, became good, tough soldiers.

My orderly, Jackson Ngoni, was one of the toughest of them. He was a soldier by profession as had been his father before him. As a small boy he had worked with an English farmer and his family. There he had learned to speak English, to cook a little and to enjoy the 'perks' of office such as cups of tea and slices of bread and jam. He also learnt to wash and iron clothes and took pride in doing this well. I was lucky to have him.

But, good soldier and excellent servant though he was, he had his Achilles heel − the female of the species. I did appreciate that, when a man has had two wives around the house for some time, it comes as a nasty shock when he loses both of them at once but, at the outbreak of war, the order had been given for all wives to return to their homes.

'Isn't there room for one of mine?' he pleaded. 'Fatima is very small.' But I had to point out that if he took a wife, every other man in the battalion would expect to do likewise. Camp-followers were just not on.

We had been ordered to move up to Kenya and, on the appointed day, our long line of trucks bumped and bounced along the road. Road? Well, the map called it that but it was really nothing but a track across the plains composed of a succession of potholes filled with volcanic ash. This, at least, had the advantage of making each driver keep his proper distance from the truck in front of his since no one wanted to drive in a blinding and suffocating cloud of dust.

We had a motley collection of vehicles. Most of them had been requisitioned from traders in the Moshi bazaar and were of different makes and sizes and of varying degrees of dilapidation. But they did look better than when we had taken them over. They had been camouflaged – or so Henry told us. Henry had come to us from Kenya and, on arrival, had said that his hobby was painting. So before he had had time to explain whether his medium was water or oils, he was detailed to paint the trucks. Camouflage, we now know, is a scientific business, but the subtler aspects of it were then unknown to us. Nevertheless Henry got to work and, after applying a base coat of green – a colour alien to us since the grass for hundreds of miles around was dried and burnt by the sun to a pale beige – he superimposed black and white blobs. I doubted whether this would be effective but Henry reassured me:

'Effective? Of course it's effective. Do you know I lost one of these trucks the other day and only found it when I bumped into it.'

Although artistic to his fingertips, Henry became a remarkable soldier. He cheerfully and willingly undertook any job however hard, difficult or dangerous. Angus was another improbable but very good soldier. He was the thin, pale manager of the local chemist's shop who later, when the fighting started, always took his night patrol deeper and farther into enemy country than most of us deemed wise or, let's face it, safe. Neither Henry nor Angus was fearless I am sure; they were too intelligent for that, but each was absolutely determined that, though water-colour painting or dispensing drugs was his first love, he was not going to be beaten by bombs or bullets. All this came to light later on.

My reverie was interrupted by the C.O. calling me over and telling me to go up the road to see how the convoy drill, new to our transport section, was working out in practice. There was to be a halt from five minutes to every hour to the clock hour. I found Budge Gethin, the Transport Officer, looking at his watch and ready to blow his whistle. When the signal was given all went well; truck after truck drew into the side and stopped. About the tenth one, however, came to rest in the middle of the road. Budge stormed back down the line and shouted to the man standing by the truck door,

'Hi, driver! *Peleka gari yako kando* [take your truck to the side].'

The man jumped into the driving seat and, in a moment, the truck began to move, rolled forward and continued to roll until it toppled over a small embankment and fell on its side. The African climbed out unscathed and said, 'Driver? Don't call me a driver, I'm a cook.' He had done his best. A score of laughing men with willing hands and strong arms soon had the truck back on the road and off we went on our way.

The next halt was a longer one and everyone sought the shade of a bush, sat down and ate his midday snack. We were well on our way to the night stopping-place, Namanga on the Kenya border. The sun was shining, the scenery wonderful and adventure before us. Across the plains, shimmering in the heat, I could just see the conical shape of Mount Meru.

When we set off on the last lap, herds of zebra and wildebeest watched us approach and then galloped away kicking their heels disdainfully in the air. Some Thomson's gazelle were more wary; they all wagged their black tails anxiously and waited for a signal from their leader to dash away to safety. Just as we came in sight of the ugly corrugated-iron buildings which constituted the Namanga shopping centre, it started to rain. Our luck was out. This was probably the first drop they had had for four or five months. A miserable welcome to Kenya.

Markers were waiting on the roadside to show each company commander his bivouac area and soon, amid intense activity, fires were lit and the men began to chatter away cheerfully. It was my job to find the biggest and most rainproof tree to shelter the C.O. and then to encourage the cooks to produce some tea. Meanwhile Jackson cut branches and quickly and cleverly made a frame to support my groundsheet. In this way we each soon had a mini-tent to huddle under at night.

Later, when we were all trying to get some sleep, my thoughts went out to the comfortable, warm, dry little hotel about half a mile away. So did Jock's. It so happened that it belonged to our transport officer.

'I'll bet Budge is O.K. in his own bed,' said Jock. But he wouldn't take a bet on it: we both really knew that Budge would be with his men – seeing that they were 'O.K.'

Just as I was dozing off I had a sudden disquieting thought – what about the elephant? Namanga was one of their favourite haunts and the strip of forest in which we were camping was quite their most favourite corner of it. But I was too tired to worry for long about this. In fact they did not come near us that night. Whether they were put off by our camp fires or by the smell of so many humans, I know not. We were left in peace – perchance to dream.

My dreams centred on how *dulce et decorum* it was supposed to be *pro patria mori*. If only I had had an efficient, modern, portable crystal ball in my haversack, I could have seen that ours was not to be the sort of war in which many had to die for their country; our opponents' policy, more often than not, was 'to run away and live to fight another day'.

I woke up next morning to a cheerful call from Jackson. '*Chai, bwana*, here's a mug of tea for you.'

The sun was rising, the rain was over and the camp was a hive of industry. We had to be on our mettle as we were to practise making war that day. The Northern Brigade from Kenya was deployed somewhere in front of us with the task of preventing our reaching the capital, Nairobi. The C.O. summoned his company commanders to a conference, described the somewhat obscure situation, ordered patrols to be sent out and small reconnaissance parties to climb the hills nearby to try and spot the enemy. The C.O. then went forward himself and established a command post and there, for the first of many times during the war, I experienced the boredom of having to wait; to wait for developments, wait for news, wait for action. There seemed to be no half-measures in war, one is either bored, excited, or frightened. So, to fill in time, I started to sketch the hills around us. This I did throughout the war, becoming an expert at drawing hills if nothing else – and, on several occasions, this proved very useful.

We were now passing through some lovely country; the hills were wooded and the valleys green after recent rain. (I made a mental note to apologize to Henry: his green camouflage was remarkably effective against this background.) It was Masailand at its best. Herds of sleek cattle were enjoying the lush grass each guarded by small Masai boys carrying spears who, I knew, were quite capable of driving off a lion if necessary.

The transport had now caught up with us and I walked back down the road to tell Budge that the C.O. wanted him to park the trucks under some big trees. As I did so I saw Jackson chatting to some Masai girls. It seemed that he had been carrying out a personal reconnaissance because he came up to me and said,

'*Bwana*, can I have an advance of two months pay?'

Apart, of course, from not carrying that sort of money about with me, I smelt a rat and asked what he wanted it for. He said that he was tired of his monastic life, or words to that effect, and an opportunity had arisen for changing it for the better.

'If I buy two of those cows over there,' he said, 'I could swop them for one of these girls.'

Several samples of these were giggling together across the road and, not being a misogynist myself, I had to agree that his first choice had many points in her favour – but not all.

I admitted to Jackson that she was buxom and cheerful but asked if he had noticed her peculiar aroma. This was an understatement because the cosmetic with which they daubed themselves was rancid sheep fat mixed with red ochre – and it stank to high heaven. I had won a point and followed up my advantage:

'Also, as she lives on nothing but blood and milk, she wouldn't cook you much of a meal. And, as she only wears skins, she couldn't even sew a button on your trousers. Furthermore I suppose you know that the Masai never cultivate the land so she certainly wouldn't be any use to you in that way.'

Jackson then realized that the prospective investment would not be so good as he had thought. He sadly said, '*Kweli, bwana*' and the matter was closed.

Then, at last, word came back from the patrols; the enemy was astride the road in considerable strength about two miles in front of us. What could we do about it? I knew this road to Nairobi well and I suddenly realized that we were on a new alignment and that the old road, which had been abandoned some time ago, lay over to the east and on the other side of the valley. If that, with its numerous drifts and bridges, was still passable, we could use it to get round the enemy's flank and capture their railhead at Kajiado.

We were able to pick out some stretches of the old road through our field-glasses. The C.O. sent a small party on foot to examine some of the bridges and, at the same time, ordered two 1-ton trucks to get over to the old road across country – laden with 'dynamite'. Luck was with us and the plan worked like a charm. The trucks got through without a hitch and without being spotted. The railway station was guarded by only two Askaris who were chatting to the stationmaster. Never were two prisoners of war more surprised. The battle was over.

The next day we moved into Nairobi where, quite clearly, we were an embarrassment to the staff of the East African Force Headquarters. They had nowhere to put us. When I managed to find an officer there of as low a rank as mine, I expressed myself freely:

'Here we are, travel-stained and tired, having come at your behest to defend you against attack by the Italians, victorious over your inexperienced Northern Brigade in battle at Kajiado, and you say you can't even put us up. A pretty poor show I must say.'

They solved the problem by sending us up to Uganda by train where there was a convenient shelf for us, the almost completed new barracks at Jinja.

Jinja was a splendid town, the lake is simply lovely — but so, unfortunately, were the local ladies who were to cause us so much anxiety in the days to come. After only two days Jackson again asked for an advance of pay.

'I have found a very pretty Uganda girl going cheap,' he said. I was at once apprehensive; things are not normally cheap in Jinja. He said she brewed the best beer in town and that her talent could enhance the amenities of our battalion. I had no doubt at all about this but I pointed out that whilst the capital cost of Uganda girls might be low, running expenses and maintenance were pretty high. I know he didn't believe me but, as luck would have it, we were forced to leave Jinja at short notice due to circumstances beyond our control and Jackson's freedom, and savings, were preserved.

Our sudden departure was entirely on account of the wholehearted hospitality extended to our troops by the aforesaid lovely ladies of the town which, including as it did, free beer, was irresistible. This created a major problem which started to raise its ugly head some three or four weeks after our arrival in Uganda. It could not be checked immediately and, at the end of two months, our battalion fighting strength was down to less than 50 per cent. For an army unit on a wartime basis at which not a single shot had been fired this is probably a world record, albeit not one of which we were proud. Headquarters in Nairobi took a practical and realistic step to remedy the situation: they moved the battalion back to Kenya and up to a desolate place in the Northern Frontier District where hospitality of that kind was nil, but where we should be more suitably located in the event of Mussolini declaring war and invading Kenya from Abyssinia.

2

The Northern Frontier District of Kenya

DECEMBER 1939 TO MAY 1940

The Northern Frontier District of Kenya always had a particular glamour of its own. Bronzed White Hunters told one about it in the bar of the Norfolk Hotel in Nairobi; the camel safaris, the elephant, lion and rhino they had shot — and the clients they had nearly lost. Then there were strange tales of Imperial pro-consuls who became extreme Somalophils, detested visitors and formed the Royal Wajir Yacht Club in a place where there was scarcely water to drink, never mind sail.

It held little glamour for us, however, and was just the proverbial 'miles and miles of bloody Africa'. This vast area of over a hundred thousand square miles extends from the Sudan border to the Indian Ocean and up to the Abyssinian boundary in the north — but there was not a road in it worthy of the name. Although two rivers, the Tana and the Uaso Nyiro, flow across it and there is a large lake, Lake Rudolf, in the north-west corner of Kenya fed by streams from the Abyssinian highlands, water is a scarce commodity. The rainfall is minimal and, apart from on the slopes of four small mountains which rise surprisingly from this otherwise flat semi-desert, little grows except thorn-bush in varying degrees of height and impenetrability. One particularly vicious species of this is aptly named the 'Wait a bit' thorn. Visibility in this thorn country is often no more than ten yards and to leave the road without a compass is asking for trouble. Several men lost their lives through going too far into the bush to 'spend a penny', losing direction, and then going farther from the road instead of back to it. This predatory place was destined to be our playground for the next year.

The four mountains are refreshing oases in this desert. The cool forest, green grass and sparkling streams are in astonishing contrast to the arid plains around them. Mount Marsabit is especially beautiful

with its several small crater lakes, one of which was made famous as
Lake Paradise by Martin and Osa Johnson in the 1920s. Elephant,
buffalo and greater kudu roam there freely and safely, grazing the
forest glades and open grassland. But around this isolated jewel there
is utter desolation. To the north and east lies a plain, the Dida
Galgalla, which resembles the parts of the moon that have recently
been photographed. It is probably more difficult to traverse than the
moon since it is covered with round volcanic lava boulders a little
smaller than footballs and spread with diabolical ingenuity at a
spacing just not suited to one's stride. On the other side, to the north-
west, lies the Chalbi Desert, a sandy waste which, almost overnight,
can be flooded and become a lake.

Lake Rudolf is as surprising an anomaly in its way as are the
mountains. Who would expect to find a sheet of water 200 miles long
in the middle of the desert? But there it is, in the north-west corner of
Kenya, an inland paradise for fishermen who like catching them up to
200 pounds in weight. To some, a place of strange beauty, to me, a
wild and surprising piece of majesty – but I prefer to do my fishing
where one is not frequently assaulted by a ninety mile an hour wind.
The last time I went there I flew in a small aircraft. The wind was
blowing faster than we could fly and the little aeroplane was literally
moving backwards when we touched down. It was only stopped by
several stalwarts on the landing-strip tackling it ruggerwise and
anchoring it to a truck.

Nevertheless, whilst the N.F.D. is certainly not everybody's cup of
tea, if there must be a war what more suitable place could there be to
have it? There is little natural beauty to destroy and very few humans
and animals to disturb. Furthermore the forbidding and inhospitable
nature of the country made it a formidable obstacle that the Italians
would have to overcome – if they decided to advance into Kenya. It
was not an area to be defended to the last man and last round; far
from it. The farther we could lure the Italians into this desolation, the
more difficult their task would become. But they must not be allowed
to get as far south as Nanyuki and Mount Kenya; that would interfere
with the polo and trout fishing!

Force Headquarters had now to decide how best to dispose the few
troops they had across this barrier. The length of the Kenya frontier
with Abyssinia and Italian Somaliland from the Sudan border to the
Indian Ocean is some eight hundred and fifty miles. Obviously our six
battalions could not be deployed along this front on the 'thin red line'
principle as this would mean our men would be more than three

hundred yards apart! So, instead, strong-points were established at Moyale, Marsabit, Garissa and Malindi with small garrisons at Wajir, Isiolo and on the western side of Lake Rudolf.

So far, so good. But I can imagine the General Staff marking these places in red on the map and handing it with ill-concealed glee to 'Q' Branch to deal with. For them it was a formidable task indeed. Every item of food had to be brought from Nairobi and carried over roads which were little better than tracks for distances of up to three hundred miles. To make things more difficult there were different scales and types of rations for Africans, Somalis, Indians and Europeans. It was sometimes even necessary to send water to them over long distances. On one occasion this had to be done for troops operating over a hundred miles from the supply, the Tana River at Garissa, and in old open-topped, four-gallon petrol tins stuffed with leaves to prevent some of the water, at least, from splashing out.

At the end of February 1940 we were still at Isiolo on the southern edge of the N.F.D. We had become accustomed to our sordid camp, the haunted and depressing collection of mud huts that had been built for the refugees from Mussolini's Abyssinian war three years before. But we were all, both Africans and Europeans, getting very bored. There was still no sign of war and we began to feel that we should be doing more good back on our farms. Two incidents, however, brought some relief and interest – a mutiny and the invasion of our parade ground by a herd of elephant.

At that time new infantry battalions were being formed and trained in Kenya, as were engineer and artillery units and also those very useful pioneer battalions who are able and willing, not only to fight, but make roads, bridges, concrete pill-boxes, wire defences and help the sappers generally.

Kenya farmers, both black and white, often live far from telephones and are, therefore, accustomed to improvising and getting a job done somehow: admirable material for these units. But it was a pioneer battalion that mutinied.

They had been ordered to move from Isiolo to another area but had refused flatly to do so and, like 'Albert', laid down their muskets. Signals were sent, wires hummed and conferences were held. The penalty for mutiny in wartime is shooting – but you can't shoot a whole battalion and there was no prison in the area capable of holding six hundred men. So an elderly and experienced officer with service in at least one other war was sent to investigate. A deputation of the mutineers was marched before him and the leader said,

'*Bwana*, we have all enlisted as soldiers, not as sweepers or porters. We are willing to fight when the "Kingi" wants us to do so, but we are ashamed of our dress and the other Askaris laugh at us. We want proper boots and hats.'

He then gave the old officer a salute that no guardsman would have been ashamed of and the deputation marched off.

It turned out that they had been issued with shoes instead of boots and hats of an old type until the severely pressed Ordnance Depot could replace these with the new pattern. Their pride was at stake. The requisition for new headgear and footwear must then have been marked RUSH because the battalion moved off proudly and in good order the next week. The mutiny was over.

Later in the war this battalion, commanded by Michael (now Sir Michael) Blundell, fought valiantly in the attack on Gondar, the last Italian strong-hold in Abyssinia.

The elephant did not cause such a stir as the mutiny but they certainly were a nuisance. Regularly at the time when the C.O. required us to do early morning P.T. they would wander at a leisurely gait on to the parade ground. They then appeared to hold a meeting, possibly to decide where they should go for a meal that day. There were miles and miles of elephant country but only this one little open flat space on which we could drill. When the C.O. asked what could be done about them I offered to shoot one. That, I said, should persuade the herd to move to a more convenient area. After proper reference to the civil authority, my offer was accepted.

I had never shot an elephant but, having hunted rhino and buffalo and possessing a double-barrel .470 rifle, I thought I could do so. I was very glad, however, when Sarel du Toit, a farmer friend of mine in the battalion, said he would come with me. I jumped at his offer.

The next morning we waited in the bush above the parade ground and soon heard the crack of breaking branches and the rumbling of large stomachs. As I pushed the safety catch forward a large elephant loomed up before me. I stepped from behind a bush and, when he was about fifteen yards away, aimed as I had learnt from a book, at the fourth wrinkle down his trunk and fired. He crumpled to the ground like a pricked balloon − and then all hell was let loose. There were elephant to the right of us and more to the left, squealing and stampeding. How elephant hunters avoid being trampled to death I know not: we were lucky. Anyway, the herd disappeared over the hills and far away to seek pastures new. Our mission had been accomplished.

About this time I was granted some leave which I spent partly on my farm and partly at Mombasa. Our farming community was highly cosmopolitan and our Farmers' Association included British, Greeks, Afrikaners, Germans, assorted Scandinavians, a Rumanian and a particular friend and prospective enemy of mine, an Italian called Count Davico di Quittengo. It was with him that I went to Mombasa and one evening while we were there he said,

'I have a feeling we shall be in the war very soon so I am going to get a lift up to Kismayu on an Italian ship which is here in dock.'

I laughed and said, 'I don't believe your "Duce" has any intention of fighting this time: he could do much better for himself by keeping out of it. Come back home with us and don't be damned silly.'

He did come back with us but I think he must have found a message there because he returned straightway to Mombasa and sailed away. Some two years later we met in Asmara, he as a prisoner of war on parole reorganizing agriculture in Eritrea, and I on the staff of the 12th (African) Division. When we celebrated at the local hotel he told me some interesting instances of his interception of our wireless signals – not to my advantage – about which more will be told later.

When the order came for us to move, in April 1940, it was like the end of an unhappy term at school. The Africans were cheerful and pulled each other's legs while we went about with quiet grins on our faces. Our battalion, less one company, had been ordered up to Wajir, some two hundred and twenty miles to the north, and the detached company was to go on up to Moyale on the Abyssinian frontier, a further one hundred and fifty miles. This was part of the general deployment of the East African force. The other two battalions in our brigade, the 22nd, were also to be in the Wajir area, and the 21st Brigade along the Tana River at Garissa and Bura.

The little township of Wajir lay mainly within the mud walls of a square fort, very like the Fort Zinderneuf of Foreign Legion fame. The camels and goats roaming around the countryside and the local people in their turbans and long burnous-like khanzus completed the Saharan picture.

This is the country of the Somalis who originally came from Arabia and have no Bantu connections or characteristics whatsoever. They are tall, slim, good-looking by European standards and proud to the extent of vanity. They dislike and disdain manual labour and live a leisurely pastoral life with their herds of camels and flocks of sheep and goats. Being fervent Muslims they have an inherent antipathy to dogs – and all other infidels including ourselves.

Some of our best administrators and soldiers have grown to like and admire the Somalis, not infrequently with an extravagance so often characterizing the admirable gentlemen who have been responsible for administering 'Pax Britannica' to millions in isolated parts of the Empire. They learnt the Somali tongue, got rid of their dogs, and came to believe that they were accepted as brothers by the Somalis, only to be disillusioned.

Our battalion was to camp several miles short of Wajir, at Arbo where a series of wells had been dug many years ago through a deep stratum of limestone. This achievement was, of course, admirable but the water was abominable. Besides being brackish it contained minute insoluble crystals which made passing water a painful process.

Every day we were out practising various tactical moves suited to the environment – the wretched thorn-bush. The Brigadier's favourite one was to tell our C.O. to send a platoon down the road with two other platoons keeping pace and direction with it but about one hundred yards off the road and in the bush. At some point, known only to the Brigadier, the platoon on the road, the cheese in the trap, was ambushed. At the sound of the blank ammunition some of the Askaris, who were good actors and loved this sort of thing, rolled over as if dead and others scampered off into the bush as the ambushers charged with bayonets fixed. Then came the 'denouement', the loose column of two platoons counter-attacked from their lair in the bush and carried the day. It was all good fun but, if one happened to be with one of the platoons off the road, it took time to remove the thorns from one's clothes – and flesh.

We became quite good at bushcraft but we were at least two decades behind the times in one important branch of training which we did not then appreciate. None of us was accustomed to explosions louder than the crack of a rifle so it took a little time to learn that the roar and crump of aerial bombardment, shells, mortar bombs and hand-grenades, which we were soon to experience, by no means portended imminent death – provided one kept one's head and, preferably, kept it down.

One day the C.O. told me to report to Brigade Headquarters to take over temporarily from the Brigade Intelligence Officer who was going on leave. Brigadier Fowkes, one heard, was not one of the easiest men to work for. There was certainly an aura of healthy apprehension around him which kept us all on our toes, but his bark was worse than his bite. A few days after I had joined him he told me to take a truck

and go to Garissa. This, I thought, would be splendid. It would be a
nice change and I should see some friends there. It was about two
hundred miles via Habaswein and Muddo Gashi so, unwisely, I said to
the Brigadier that I thought I could get there by lunch-time. 'Like hell,
you will,' he replied. 'I want you to go on a compass-bearing across
country. You young chaps have got to get off the roads and learn to
find your way about in the bush.' This was to be a greater change than
I had expected. I said, 'Of course, sir,' saluted and went off to look at
the map and get hold of a truck. This was not easy. In fact Sergeant
Rockett, the Transport Sergeant, was pretty wild. 'It takes me all my
time keeping the trucks going on these bloody roads, sir. If you go
mucking about in the bush in one, it'll never be the same again.' How
right he was. However, he did me proud and even offered me a Somali
driver. I certainly needed a guide and interpreter, so quickly said, 'Yes
please.'

My general direction from Arbo was to be due south and the map
showed a promising camel track marked in red going more or less on
this line. As the crow flies, and I was expected to travel crow-wise, it
was one hundred and forty-five miles to Garissa. I should be able to
do it in the day but it would be safer to take enough food, petrol, and
water for two. Mohamed, the Somali driver, checked the tools, extra
oil and petrol, water, spade, axe, pangas, spare fanbelt, and puncture
repair outfit. Jackson and I saw to the food, whisky and ammunition.

We were off early next morning, corkscrewing and twisting through
the bush. Occasionally a turn was so acute that we had to reverse and
take another bite at it and, sometimes, we had to crash through the
bush and flatten it with the bumper bar. Then a puncture. Never mind,
it was quite time to stop for breakfast in any case. We changed the
wheel, Mohamed mended the puncture and we all had a bite to eat.
This took us an hour.

We had seen nothing that looked like a camel track although we
had tacked to port and then to starboard across the line shown on the
map. Later I learnt that camels filter through the bush from water-hole
to water-hole and any tracks they leave are soon covered over with
blown sand. At that moment we felt another puncture. We stopped
and found we were wrong, we had two. As, perforce, we were
continually running over thorn tree branches, and some of the thorns
were as big as two-inch nails, this was not surprising.

However, the country might change for the better. We mended and
replaced the two wheels. This took us well over an hour as by then it
was getting pretty hot. During this process Jackson made some highly

uncomplimentary remarks about unthinking higher authority sending
us on madcap journeys through the bush when there were some
perfectly good roads. But, as his criticism was impersonal and general,
I decided not to regard it as seditious.

During this stop I had been wondering whether it would be wiser to
return to camp and call the expedition off: we should obviously run
out of tyres pretty soon. But I decided to go on and, when we had
another puncture, remove the tube and stuff the outer cover with grass
and leaves instead of air.

When we were on our way again I asked Mohamed how well he
knew this country.

'Not at all,' he said. 'I was born in Nanyuki and have never been so
far away before.' I had the feeling that he added quietly to himself,
'and never want to again.'

I could have kicked myself for not having asked this question before
we left Arbo. But at least he could speak the language – if ever we saw
anyone to speak to. It was then we had a bit of luck; quite by chance
we came to a water-hole. Some camels were drinking and, better still,
a real Somali was herding them. I told Mohamed to go over and have
a chat with him. It seemed silly to ask him the way to Garissa. For
one thing he had probably never heard of the place and, anyway, this
was no way to get there so he couldn't reply like a good English
'Bobby': 'Yes, sir. Go right down this street and take the last on the
right.' The only sensible answer would be 'Get back to the road, you
fool.'

After a good quarter of an hour of continuous chat I asked
Mohamed what he had found out. He replied, 'This man welcomes
you to his water-hole.' All right so far as it went, but it wasn't getting
us on our way and I decided that a drastic step had to be taken –
kidnapping.

I told Mohamed to tell the stranger to get into the truck. Jackson
and I 'helped' him in and off we went. Mohamed was explaining to
him that we would release him with a good reward when he had taken
us to the next water-hole in approximately the direction we wanted to
go, due south. The poor chap was obviously very frightened but
Mohamed said,

'He's only afraid of the motor car, *bwana*, not of you. He's never
been in one before.'

About five o'clock I began to think there could be no water-holes
between us and the Tana River. By then all four tyres had been stuffed
with vegetation of various sorts. Doing this was a slow job because it

soon broke down into a kind of mushy chopped hay and more had to be added and rammed in about every half hour. It was getting dusk when we did reach a water-hole. Mohamed and our guide grinned, rather smugly I thought. We proceeded to fill up all our drinking-water containers from those brought from camp for the truck as that was pretty clean stuff. Then we topped up all the rest with the dirty water from the muddy pool.

Other animals besides ourselves, possibly unfriendly ones, might be interested in the water-hole during the night so we drove on about half a mile before selecting a camp-site.

The first task was to make a fire so we looked around for dead branches and pulled them near to the place we had chosen for our beds while Mohamed chopped them up with his panga. Although we were in semi-desert country and only about six hundred feet above sea level, the nights were chilly and we were glad to sit round the crackling fire waiting for the kettle to boil.

The sun went down and the perennial enchantment of the African night made us forget the trials and tribulations of the day. I sat with a mug of tea laced with whisky watching the dancing flames of the camp-fire and trying to find some blessings to count. It was difficult. The speedometer told me that we had covered only fifty-two miles since morning – and speedometers don't lie. As we had zigzagged so much in the bush, we were perhaps only about forty miles from home – as a crow should have flown – and, if so, we had not yet done a third of the distance to Garissa.

From the map it looked as though we might reach Lak Dera next day. This would be recognizable because a Lak is caused by a stratum of limestone on which the bush can't grow and, as water can't seep through it, it could be swampy, particularly as this one was an extension of the Lorian Swamp, famous for its herds of elephants.

I got myself another drink. Jackson was busy by the fire and there was a pleasant smell of cooking. I knew what the menu would be. First, tomato soup, perfected through years of trial and error by Mr Heinz, followed by tinned sausages and, if Jackson had been enterprising, a couple of eggs. I must shoot something for the pot tomorrow or we should be on short rations. Just then a lion started grunting nearby. They too must be hungry and on a kill. I told Mohamed to put some more wood on the fire.

I slept fitfully and I know Mohamed did no better. I expect he was wondering what the Transport Sergeant would say when we returned the truck to him, battered, buckled and bruised. The only really happy man was our erstwhile hostage. He slept soundly with a full stomach, a handful of shillings and the knowledge that he would be returning to his water-hole on the morrow.

The next day we were off soon after dawn. In a few minutes we spotted the lion we had heard in the night. He and his mate were still on the kill. But we had other things on our mind and left them to their meal.

The going was no better and we had to bulldoze through the lighter bush and turn and twist around the tougher stuff. At the first stop for 'blowing up' our tyres I shot a brace of partridge and, later in the day, a duiker. Our larder looked a little healthier – and Mohamed and Jackson much happier. We found no more water that day but we still had plenty on board. About four o'clock in the afternoon the picture became rosier; the bush suddenly became thinner and we then soon ran into open country. This must be the promised lak. We camped down for the night.

As we struggled along on the third day our trusty steed was obviously tiring. The water in the radiator boiled continuously despite our blowing the grass seeds out of it periodically; I fear the muddy slush from the water-hole had done it no good. The bush was now no problem but the ground was more difficult with occasional channels running across our route which had to be negotiated by digging drifts. I had hoped to reach the Tana River that night and find the Garissa road running along its northern bank, but I was disappointed. We found it next morning, but this was not the last of our problems: the road provided another one. We had no means of knowing whether Garissa was east or west of us. However, an army truck came along shortly and I asked the driver this vital question. He, assuming that if we hadn't come from Garissa we must know we were going towards it, thought we were mad and looked rather apprehensively at us. But when he asked where we had come from and I waved my hand vaguely towards the north, he was relieved, told us where we were and off we went on the last lap.

I walked into the Officers' Mess at Garissa to be greeted by a storm of cheerful abuse.

'Where the hell have you been? Why didn't you telephone?'

'We've just received a signal from Force to send out a patrol to look for you.'

'An aircraft is on its way here.'

I said we had only done this to test their readiness for war – and that we were now ready for breakfast.

The ingenuity and resources of the Brigade R.E.M.E. people were taxed to the full that day in making our truck roadworthy. They did a remarkable job because when we got back home the next day, by a more conventional route, Sergeant Rockett gave us a warm welcome.

On my return I found that the Brigadier had thought up a number of other exercises for the battalions to practise in the bush and we were kept very busy. But you can't keep a bad man known. Jackson had, somehow, managed to carry out another personal shopping reconnaissance, this time in Wajir and one day, to my horror, he brought the girl in question to the camp for me to see. Knowing that Mohammedans have very special feelings about their girls and harems, I looked anxiously around to see whether an angry father or brother had followed them, knife or scimitar in hand. If so they would certainly assume that Jackson had brought the girl to me! I was furious. But this seemed not the time to tell him so as the slim, lovely houri was obviously very frightened and, if she started to scream, there really would be hell to pay. She had the natural grace and dignity of the Somali people as well as the shy smile of the Mona Lisa. For a moment I found myself envying Jackson — but *force majeure* prevailed over *amour impropre* and I said we would discuss the matter in the morning.

I knew I was on a poor wicket next day when I advanced an argument which caused me considerable trouble a couple of months later.

'When wars are won,' I told him, 'there are spoils, booty and loot, and these always include women. Don't pay out good money now when, shortly, you'll be able to get what you want for free.'

I know he wasn't convinced that this nebulous prospect was better than today's certainty — nor was I — but, luckily, the Italians solved the problem by declaring war and, for some time we had other things on our minds.

3

Mussolini Declares War

Nine months after the declaration of war against Germany the Italians were still sitting on the fence. They were shrewdly waiting until they felt quite certain that the Germans were going to win. By the end of May 1940 the German army had plunged through the Low Countries into France, the British forces had been evacuated through Dunkirk and the French army was on the verge of collapse. Yet Mussolini, the Italian dictator, still hesitated. On 22 May General Wavell, our Commander in Chief, wrote the following lines summing up the position:

'Italy still seems to be hesitating on the brink, but I think must take the plunge soon. Musso looks to me rather like a man who has climbed up to the top diving-board at a swimming-pool, taken off his dressing-gown and thrown a chest to the people looking on. I think he must do something; if he cannot make a graceful dive, he will at least have to jump in somehow; he can hardly put on his dressing-gown and walk down the stairs again.'

He hesitated until 10 June and then took the plunge, convinced that Germany would win the war in a matter of weeks.

During the nine months from September 1939, little progress had been made towards making us into a modern fighting force. Our total resources of manpower at that time were six battalions of infantry and our artillery consisted of a mountain battery from India and a light battery being formed and trained in Kenya. The only automatic weapons we had were a few old Vickers machine-guns and some older Lewis guns, and our ancient motor transport vehicles were obsolete. We had heard, however, that the railway workshops in Nairobi were making us some armoured cars and that one of the infantry battalions, the 3rd K.A.R., was being converted into a machine-gun battalion.

That was all. Britain had more important and urgent commitments than equipping us; she was even talking of fighting on the beaches of England with museum-pieces and shot-guns.

As against this the Italian military strength in Abyssinia was formidable. Mr G.L. Steer, an expert on Italian East Africa at that time, made the following assessment in May 1939:

> Italy has in Abyssinia today a garrison of two hundred thousand men with the artillery requisite for a Western war; two hundred aeroplanes, a string of aerodromes running north-west from the sea beyond the Kenya frontier; and efficient motorization calculated at nine thousand or ten thousand military vehicles in bases behind the great road that she has built through Eritrea to the boundary of the Anglo-Egyptian Sudan; enough petrol and food for a smashing offensive; interior lines.

Later he added:

> In the case of a war in which she was involved against Britain, Italy would not only have the means to attack us with success, she would be bound to do so for her own security.

Their choice must, therefore, be to attack us now, very soon, or never.

In these very unpropitious circumstances General Dickinson, the commander of the East African forces, had to plan the defence of Kenya. Luckily for us the attack, when it came, was on a far smaller scale than the Italians could have mounted and he succeeded in countering it by using the Northern Frontier District as a barrier, by checking their advance at point after point and making them fight for every mile. At the same time he gradually withdrew his forces farther into Kenya so making the Italian task of supply more difficult – and his own easier. This strategy gained time, and time was needed to build up our strength. Men and *matériel* were coming to our aid from Nigeria, the Gold Coast and South Africa.

At the time of the declaration of war by Britain against Germany, Kenya had only small administrative and police posts on the northern frontier, at Moyale and Mandera, and a larger one at Wajir where there was also a company of the 5th K.A.R. The East African Defence Scheme provided that on the outbreak of war the district commissioners at Moyale, Mandera and Wajir, and the police detachments at those stations should be prepared to withdraw to

Isiolo; and the K.A.R. garrison at Wajir be ready to move to positions on the south side of the Uaso Nyiro River. It must have seemed to the planners of that day, and, indeed, to most thinking people, virtually inevitable that the Italians would have no hesitation in accompanying the Germans into hostilities; and, as a result, very little attention appears to have been given to the situation that would arise if the Italians, instead of entering the fray with their senior partners, chose to sit upon the sidelines. In the event, although the Italians were making no overt signs of being about to take part in the war, the Kenya government decided that the proper course was to proceed with the evacuation of the forward stations and the administrators of Moyale and Mandera received instructions direct from Nairobi to withdraw. Evacuation plans had been drawn up for Wajir, but it was felt in Nairobi that the distance of that station from the northern and eastern frontiers of Kenya was so great, and the international situation so uncertain, that no immediate withdrawal was necessary.

The vacuum created in the forward areas of the N.F.D. by the departure of the British from Moyale and Mandera caused considerable concern to the Italian Administration who, quite naturally, were apprehensive of general unrest in North Kenya, and the spread of inter-tribal feuding and cattle-raiding into their territory; and there can be no doubt that the formal request they made to Kenya for Frontier administration to be resumed helped to persuade the Kenya government to reopen Moyale and Mandera with a minimum of delay. The Italians, for their part, gave practical and effective assistance at both stations in tracing and recovering private and government property which had been looted by the local people.

The Kenya boundary with Abyssinia, generally speaking, follows the line of a steep escarpment which rises from the Northern Frontier District plain and runs approximately east and west. Kenya had, in Moyale, a precarious foothold on this cliff. It was a healthy, quiet station in peacetime, ideally suited to any district officer who was not keen on telephones, paper-work and interference generally by senior officials. Half a mile away, across a valley, was its Abyssinian counterpart, Moiale. The only difference between the two lay in the spelling because I am certain the Italian administrative officers had similar inclinations: they were always willing to come over for a chat and a whisky and then ask one back for a further gossip and a glass of wine.

But life there had barely returned to its normal bucolic, peaceful tenor after the alarm and excursion of September 1939 when war really came. History records that the Italian foreign secretary, Count Ciano, summoned the British ambassador in Rome on the afternoon of 10 June 1940 and informed him, at 4.45 p.m., that Italy would consider herself at war with Britain as from 1 a.m. the next day. It seems, however, that the Italian garrison commander across the valley had not been informed that hostilities should not start until the 11th and he 'beat the gun'. Two men from the British side, the superintendent of police and a friend, who had probably not even heard at the time that war was declared, went for their customary evening stroll on the 10th and were promptly taken prisoners. So, with this political and social solecism, relations with the Italians were broken off. Their planes bombed Moyale on the 12th but no great damage was done and no attack on the ground was attempted.

Towards the end of May we had had a very pleasant and, as it turned out, opportune surprise. A flight of Hawker Hart planes arrived from Rhodesia. We were very proud of the three little aircraft standing in a row on the Wajir airfield beside the new corrugated-iron building in which some eight thousand gallons of aviation spirit were stored, all laboriously brought up from Nairobi by road.

The day after the declaration of war the Brigadier told me to go to Wajir before dawn next day to ask the Flight Commander to do a reconnaissance for him: he wanted to know if there was any troop movement around Moyale. I was there as the sun rose and found him in his camp-bed on top of one of the flat-roofed houses. As I was pointing out to him on the map some of the key places to look at, we heard the unmistakable whirr-whirr-whirr of a three-engined plane and, looking up, we saw two Caproni bombers flying straight towards us. I leapt from the roof to the ground and dived into a convenient and comforting slit trench as the bombs began to burst around us. One of the pilots was not so quick as I was and got the blast of one of them in the face which blinded him for a time. The main targets, of course, were the petrol store and the aircraft, and the Capronis went in one behind the other dropping their sticks of bombs. The store burst into flames and two of the Harts were damaged but not set on fire.

I rushed over to the aircraft with the Rhodesians to see what could be done. Whatever it was would have to be done quickly as the Capronis, finding three sitting-ducks and no opposition, might be on their way back to have another shot. Three of our Askaris who had been guarding the planes lay headless on the ground. One of the aircraft was, miraculously, undamaged and the pilot taxied it over to a hiding-place in the bush. We towed the other two there behind our trucks.

The petrol store burnt for two days. Every now and again a drum would burst and the top fly off, whirling into the air like a quoit. We had learnt a bitter lesson: the peacetime era of whitewashed stones to mark out the cantonment and trucks neatly parked in rows was over. In future aircraft, petrol, ammunition, food and men must all be dispersed and either hidden away or put into slit trenches.

In the meanwhile our first battle of the war was being planned to take place a few days later, just a little one for two companies. The object was twofold: to show the Italians that we intended to take the offensive and to test our fighting ability. A convenient objective was the little post of El Uach on the Italian Somaliland border some sixty-five miles north-east of Wajir. It was reported to be manned by only a few Italian Irregulars known as Banda. This was to be, so to speak, a dress rehearsal for the larger shows we hoped to put on later. Like so many dress rehearsals of even the most successful shows it was a flop.

To mark the boundary with Somaliland a strip had been cleared out of the bush as broad as a road and in a dead straight line for scores of miles. Running parallel to this there was a road on the Italian side. Two other roads cut across these at right angles joining the Italian village of El Uach to the British one, El Wak. The result was a pattern of roads through the bush like the framework for a game of noughts and crosses and the visibility, except along one of these avenues, was restricted by the bush to about twenty yards.

These topographical difficulties had been appreciated and guides accompanied the troops on the appointed day. But for some reason they were late. A Hawker Hart that was timed to arrive on the scene after the ground attack had gone in, came before it and, in order to fill in time, swooped and soared around. In the process it collected a bullet or two in the fuel tank and had to make a forced landing on one of the tracks.

When the Italian troops in the little fort saw the aircraft they expected to be bombed and took to the bush. Consequently when our troops arrived a few minutes later they found the place abandoned, concluded they had won the day and proceeded to search for maps, documents and souvenirs and have a nice chat generally. They were more than surprised, therefore, when the Italians, seeing that the enemy had taken possession of their fort, made a spirited counter-attack. It was then our turn to take to the bush — which our Africans did somewhat over-enthusiastically – leave a few British to fight a rearguard action.

After consolidation and reorganization the commander of our force sent out two patrols to locate the aircraft. So did the Italians, and these small, armed parties kept catching glimpses of each other from time to time along one or other of the noughts and crosses lanes with mutual consternation and surprise – rather like the appearance of several assorted couples at the various bedroom doors in a French farce.

One of these patrols, luckily one of ours, found the aeroplane. The pilot was making strenuous endeavours with his gunner to carry out repairs but, as this proved impossible, the plane was towed away. Its wheels, however, unaccustomed to such rough treatment, seized up and it had to be set on fire and abandoned.

Many lessons were learnt from this expedition and many mistakes were corrected during the next few weeks. Operations in thick bush must be simple and not reliant on split-minute timing; the tough fight put up by the Italian garrison who, as we found out later, had been reinforced by some regular Colonial troops, was instructive to our Askaris; and the maps we had were not accurate enough: for all future operations new maps were made from aerial photographs.

After this practice battle our main attention was focused on to the vulnerable and isolated little post at Moyale. For many weeks before the Italians declared war there had been great activity there: it had unostentatiously been converted into a small fort. The mud walls of all the houses on the perimeter had, under the guise of repair and redecoration, been reinforced internally with concrete. The whole area, some six hundred yards by two hundred, had been surrounded by triple Dannert wire, a system of trenches dug and concrete pill-boxes built from which this could be covered by rifle and machine-gun fire. In addition an underground command post and a field dressing station were constructed.

Our garrison consisted of one company of my battalion, the 1st K.A.R., plus a platoon from the 3rd K.A.R., which was a machine-gun battalion, and a detachment of sappers from a field company, a total of one hundred and eighty men. Our weapons were not quite museum-pieces but the Lewis guns should, perhaps, have been on their way there. However, we did have a few brand-new Boyes .50 anti-tank rifles, some 4-inch mortars, and a lot of those most useful things in our sort of little war, Mills hand-grenades. But our Achilles heel was the water-supply: the wells were outside the perimeter and we had to refill our storage tanks when the Italians were not looking.

As for the opposition, we had been told that the Italian garrison at the outbreak of war was three thousand strong, that they had some guns and, possibly, a few light tanks and armoured cars. If true this was certainly formidable. The Italians started the ball rolling by dropping some bombs on the fort on 12 June, but these did no serious damage and there was very little warlike activity after that for some days.

As Battalion Intelligence Officer I was sent to join the garrison with the first supply convoy to go there since the declaration of war. It was a seventy-mile journey from our battalion position at Buna and we knew that Italian patrols had been operating along most of that distance so we had a strong escort. The Italian guns had been shelling the road sporadically between the top of the escarpment and the fort and were obviously on the look-out for us, but we reached the fort without incident.

My main jobs in Moyale were to try and locate and deal with snipers who were firing occasional shots at us from nearby trees – real bird-watching; to teach the Askaris not to wander about in the open; and to dissuade some of the British N.C.O.s from lying on the grass to sun themselves. We had a notice put up – 'North for Sunshine, South for Safety.'

We had a patrol roster and each night two of us blacked our faces, put on dark-blue sweaters and, armed with pistols, Mills bombs and compasses, went out with four Askaris to locate the Italian positions. This is where Henry the Painter and Angus the Chemist came into their own. I, privately, used to hope that I wouldn't be drawn to go with either of these over-intrepid soldiers.

'Yes,' they would say, 'we know that old post – and the pit near it; there are always a few "Itis" there. But, if we creep round to the right of them, we should be able to find the next line of defence.'

But, normally, having reached a point somewhere near where we believed the Italians to be, we would fire a shot or two to wake them up and draw their fire, register their positions as nearly as we could and return home for a mug of hot cocoa. Occasionally a hyena would let out a howl and put the wind up us, and sometimes we ran into some wretched ponies who stampeded when they got our scent and gave the show away. The Askaris were not very keen on these night patrols at first but, when they saw that we never seemed to have any casualties, they entered into the spirit of the thing.

The Italian guns opened up on us in the fort for the first time on 28

June. They were only small pack-animal type Howitzers and many of the shells, being left-overs from their 1936 war, were duds. There were no casualties and it was a useful, instructive and encouraging baptism of fire for us. There could have been quite a number of casualties at one point during the night, however. I had just gone to the command post to make a report to the company commander, Captain Drummond, when one of our, then civilian, African servants walked in carrying one of the dud shells.

'*Nini hi, bwana?*' (What is this?) he said. When I said hastily 'Take it away' he threw it on the ground, disgusted at our lack of interest. It still didn't go off!

No attempt was made at a ground attack either that night or the following one but, on 30 June, we saw a good deal of troop movement across the valley and, when some Italian Savoia bombers came over that evening and gave us a real pounding, we knew we were in for it. There was only sporadic shelling during the first part of the night but, before dawn, this became intense and, shortly afterwards, the ground attack came in on all sides. Several attempts were made to cut our wire defences but, with the aid of Verey Lights, our rifle and machine-gun fire prevented any serious breach being made.

We were using mortars, as were the Italians. Every time we fired one it seemed that one of theirs landed near us. The Askaris thought the wind was blowing ours back and wanted to stop using them! The main attack was called off at about 8 a.m. but was stubbornly continued against our northern side until mid-morning.

In addition to the fairly heavy bombs dropped on us from the air, hundreds of shells were fired into the fort area as well as thousands of rounds of S.A.A. from rifles and machine-guns. It was an unpleasant night but, almost incredibly, we had only four casualties and the only major material damage was to three of our trucks which were set on fire.

Of less consequence, though of considerable inconvenience to me, two shells went clean through my bedroom. 'Clean through' is, perhaps, the wrong expression because everything I possessed was covered with dirt and dust. This was too much for my servant who left Moyale on foot without as much as saying good-bye and I never saw him again.

By midday on 1 July the whole Italian force had withdrawn to their side of the valley. This enabled a working party to refill our water-tanks and me to get out with a truck to meet reinforcements which were coming to us up the escarpment. My job was to let them know if the coast was clear. Neither I nor the reinforcements knew for certain whether there were any Italians between us, but I reckoned the greatest danger to me would be from the eager-to-shoot escort to the convoy composed of the East African Recce Regiment. So, when I reach the top of the escarpment I fixed a precautionary white flag on to my car and went slowly down the twisting road, sounding my horn anxiously at every corner. This paid off and we met peacefully.

The reinforcements consisted of a second company of my battalion, a troop of the 22nd Indian Mountain Battery – and the Brigadier himself. The company was to remain hidden at the top of the escarpment with the 'loose column' role we had practised in the bush around Wajir, but the guns were to go on to the fort. When we arrived there we heard that a party of our men had been trying to dig some defensive positions around the wells that day but had been driven back by the Italian guns. We were doubly glad, therefore, to have some artillery ourselves at last – to get our own back.

During the last few days and nights I had been able to plot the positions of some of the Italian guns. This I had done by taking compass-bearings on the gun flashes from each end of our six hundred yard front and then plotting them on paper. One could also check roughly on these positions from the line along which the dud shells landed and slid along the ground. So, when 'Bulgy' Leach, who commanded the battery, arrived with his 3.7 Hows., I was able to give him some useful information.

The reprisal shoot was good fun and splendid for morale, but it had one disadvantage; it invited counter-reprisal from every Italian gun that could still fire. Since we could not afford to risk the loss of any of the very few guns we had, 'Bulgy' was ordered, after this one beautiful blast, to withdraw his troop back to Advance Brigade Headquarters at the bottom of the escarpment.

In the late afternoon the Brigadier told me to go with him and have a look at the Italian lines from a little hill outside our defences. I mentioned to him that snipers were sometimes active there but this didn't worry him. So, having warned our own troops not to shoot if they saw a strange and very senior officer crawling about in front of them, we went out, taking several Askaris with us to keep watch in case any of the opposition happened to be creeping about on a similar errand. We spent about half an hour looking at every Italian position we knew and trying to spot others. On our return journey he told me that he wanted me as Brigade Intelligence Officer and that I should join him next day when he moved his headquarters up to the fort. He said that we should be attacking the Italian positions with two battalions. When we got back to the fort, however, we found that my C.O. had already sent Jackson back to Brigade Headquarters at the bottom of the escarpment with my baggage, so the Brigadier took me back there with him. It turned out that this was the last time I saw the little fort.

That night the Italians surrounded Moyale again and made a determined attack. Our counter-attack force, the loose column company, was neither able to make contact with the garrison in the turmoil of battle nor to find any cohesive body of the enemy to fight against in the dark and was withdrawn. The garrison drove off the attack and so won the second round but, by dawn, the Italians had taken up strong positions commanding the road up the escarpment and it soon became clear that any attempt to get back to the top by any forces that we had would be a bloody one and unlikely to succeed.

A week went by with no further attack on the fort. It looked as if the Italians had decided on a war of attrition and the reduction of the garrison by siege. Surprisingly, however, our patrols discovered a few days later that the Italian troops had been removed from the strong positions they had held on the road summit and so, on 9 July, the garrison company was relieved without difficulty, Captain Henderson taking over with his company from Captain Drummond. This exchange must have coincided with the Italians receiving reinforcements because they made a more determined attack than any before on the night of 10 July. They fired over a thousand shells into the fort that night but, even so, our casualties were fortunately light, 4 killed and 7 wounded, and the garrison stood firm.

After this attack, however, the Italians did not withdraw and held positions on all sides of the fort. On the 12th the garrison commander reported that he was unable to replenish the water-supply but that he had sufficient to last six days. Their position was becoming critical.

The only solution seemed to be to order the garrison to evacuate the fort. There was a reasonable chance that they could creep out at night and make their way down the escarpment. An order was sent to David Henderson to do so on the 13th but Signals could not make contact with the fort that day. He got the message next day, however, and they came out that evening.

I had suggested to them that the best route might be down a valley which ran quite close to the fort, and the best time just after the moon went down. They decided, however, that there would be less chance of their being spotted if they left during the time the Italians normally had an evening meal, and this they did – most successfully. At the appointed time they went out in single file with stocking feet, wearing dark jerseys and carrying only their arms. Sarel Du Toit, who had helped me to shoot the trespassing elephant at Isiolo, led the party, and David Henderson brought up the rear.

They had not, of course, been able to blow up the ammunition and other explosives before leaving as that would have given the show away, so they threw it down the deep-pit latrines. Three wounded Askaris had to be left with a letter to the Italians requesting medical attention for them. But they didn't like this and, shortly after the garrison departed, hobbled after them. Two of them were picked up by a patrol of the 'Recces' next day and the third was believed to have been taken prisoner.

At the time of this exodus we did not know for certain whether the garrison would come down the valley all the way or partly on the road. So a strong patrol was sent up the hill with the object of either meeting them and helping them with transport or causing a diversion, whichever might seem the more useful at the time. We soon ran into fire from Italians on top of the escarpment and, after what was possibly a useful diversionary exchange of shots for about half an hour, we withdrew.

As we were passing back through our battalion forward position on the roadside, I saw 'Bulldog' Drummond, the company commander with whom I had been in the fort, lying down and looking through his field-glasses. I lay down beside him to have a chat and, as I did so, he rolled over with a bullet through his forehead. A little farther on we saw 'Morny' who said, 'Look, I've got a spare platoon, can I be of any assistance?' Lord Mornington was following the Wellington tradition: when I saw him a few minutes later he was sitting on the cab of his truck firing his pistol at a Savoia bomber which was making a low-level machine-gun attack on our column. Everyone who had a Bren or a Lewis gun was firing too – and effectively. Its wreckage was found about two miles away a little later in the day.

At the time of this struggle for Moyale, we up in front knew nothing about future plans and strategy. We lived our strenuous lives from day to day or, perhaps more accurately, from hour to hour. So, when the Brigadier told me on 1 July that he intended to move his headquarters up to Moyale the next day and was going to launch a two-battalion attack on the Italian positions, I supposed this could be the start of a general advance into Abyssinia. The project seemed somewhat ambitious since our information was that the Italian garrison of three Colonial battalions and four groups of Irregulars had recently been reinforced by some two thousand Eritrean troops. This, together with their ancillaries, meant a total of about five thousand men. Our job, however, was to carry out such decisions and not to query them.

Nevertheless, a month or two later with the advantage of hindsight and a little more experience, I felt it was a very good thing that the Italians had forestalled our attack through Moyale and driven us back down the escarpment and on to the plains that were to play an important part in their eventual defeat.

Perhaps we could have mustered a strong enough force to drive the Italians back from Moyale; we had just heard of the arrival in Kenya of the Nigerian and Gold Coast Brigades and a brigade group from South Africa. But there was another factor, perhaps more potent than manpower, that the route through Moyale was not suitable for a major advance into Abyssinia.

First, the road up the escarpment which would, perforce, be part of the Line of Communication, was a vulnerable bottle-neck which could easily be blocked by ambush, shell-fire or bombing and, secondly, on top of the escarpment one soon got into high rainfall country in which convoys could become bogged down for weeks. Far better, surely, to let the Italian convoys get bogged down on their five hundred mile journey bringing supplies from Addis Ababa.

In the meanwhile we found ourselves moving backward instead of forward. The day after the evacuation of Moyale, Brigade Head-quarters was moved thirty miles south to Debel. The Italian tails were up and their patrols were soon annoying us. They were often led by an Italian for whom we had great respect. We didn't find out that he was Major Benardelli, the Residente of Lugh Ferrandi, until he surrendered with the remainder of General de Simone's force at Jimma about a year later, so we called him 'Twinkletoes' because he could always be recognized by his small footprints – his boots were child's size. Our patrols went after him time and time again but they never managed to catch him. He and his men used to creep up at night, fire a few shots into our camp and then skip off through the bush with greater speed than we could muster. The first reaction by our troops to his few shots in the night was to fire off every round they had into the bush in all directions. This had to be controlled at once or we should very soon have run out of ammunition.

We were now faced with the problem of maintaining a brigade group in these inhospitable plains in order to halt or, at least, slow down the Italian advance into Kenya. This hinged on one commodity, water. The whole brigade group consisting of three battalions, the mountain battery, a detachment of sappers, some 'Recces' with their unprotected patrol cars and a field ambulance was, therefore, moved thirty miles still farther south to Buna, as unattractive a piece of the unattractive N.F.D. as it is possible to find. It had only one redeeming feature, a water-supply of sorts.

Here we dug ourselves in, surrounded the area with defensive barbed wire, made a small landing-strip for light aircraft, and blocked the road running north and south. There were two features within our perimeter, a dry river-bed and a small hill. The trees along the currently dry river-course were larger and shadier than all the other trees so I chose this site for Brigade Headquarters. The hill was of no value to us since, even from the top, one could merely see a canopy of bush stretching like the sea for miles and miles. Unfortunately, however, the hill enabled the Italian bombers to find our camp, and the tall trees in it showed them where the Brigade Commander lived.

Our headquarters were particularly vulnerable at that time as we had just received a truck-load of spirits and other luxuries from NAAFI.

I thought I had protected these riches adequately by storing them in a trench. But when, one day, I saw two Capronis coming straight for us and dropping sticks of bombs, never had I been more apprehensive. I leapt to a Lewis gun mounted ready in a small pit nearby and started firing at them, but with no more effect than the several thousand other rounds that our troops had fired off. This type of *feu de joie*, too, had to be discouraged and controlled during subsequent visitations by Capronis.

Once again 'Bulgy' Leach's guns became good morale-boosters. His were undoubtedly the most versatile gunners in the army. Not only did they perform the normal job of Howitzers, lobbing little shells into the enemy lines, but also, on occasions, firing over open sights at enemy vehicles or, as now, with the guns dug into the ground to cock the barrels up in the air, using them in an anti-aircraft role. I cannot claim that they ever shot a Caproni or a Savoia down but I am quite sure they frightened or, at least, surprised a few of them. Fortunately the bombs the Italian aircraft dropped were not very lethal and our precious supplies survived. One bomb fell only five feet from my camp-bed, penetrated about two feet into the soft dusty earth and went off 'poof' rather than 'bang'. The result was merely a filthy mess to be cleared up.

The bugbear of Buna was boredom. This was relieved to some extent by the publication of a weekly paper called *The Buna Bullsheet*, the amusing highlight of which was the social column. Then there were two tragi-comic incidents. First, a load of piping, ordered from railhead at Nanyuki to improve our water-supply, was rushed up to us in a lorry without an escort. The Indian driver managed somehow to drive through our road barrier and arrived unwittingly at an Italian outpost. The result, one Indian prisoner of war and, probably, an improvement in the water-supply at Moyale!

Why anyone should think that we needed pocket money in Buna is difficult to imagine – but somebody did, and this caused the second incident. The reputation of the Army Pay Corps is high, based on promptness and accuracy. So, on the last day of the month, a field cashier set out from Nanyuki for Buna in a small car with a large bag of money. He had never been in the Northern Frontier District before, in fact he had hardly been out of his office since leaving his bank in Nairobi to join the army. Unfortunately he was ambushed by some Italian 'Dick Turpin' and his merry men and bang went our pay.

One major sortie was made from Buna. The Italians had occupied Korondil, a rocky promontory some twenty miles north up the road along which we had recently withdrawn from Moyale. Their object was, presumably, to establish a small base from which they could harass us and force a further withdrawal southward. This would have meant pulling right back to Wajir, the next place where water was obtainable, so they had to be dislodged.

It happened that the Brigadier was away at a conference in Nairobi at the time, but a plan was made and two motorized battalions moved north from Buna at night with lights dimmed to attack the hill at dawn. A Nigerian battalion stormed the cliff bravely under heavy rifle and automatic fire and a few of them managed to scramble to the top. Luckily for them, when they reached the summit, exhausted and dazed, an Italian officer stopped his men from firing and took them prisoner.

This abortive and costly foray, a miniSpion Kop, did nothing, of course, to boost the morale of our troops, for many of whom it was the first taste of battle. It would have been more effective, and far sounder tactics, to infiltrate round to the back of the hill and block the road, their only line of supply. For excess of zeal and dash such as this the old army tradition should bear most of the blame, the tradition that no officer, senior or junior, should ever say that he considered the force at his disposal insufficient to attack and capture the particular bit of the enemy allotted to him. It just wasn't done. He would have a go at it, make a gallant attempt and, as often as not, come away with a bloody nose and a lot of unnecessary casualties. The tradition is indefensible but the consequences of failing to observe it were dire. If an officer had said, 'Yes, sir, but I estimate that I shall need an additional company to do the job plus a call on some guns and air support,' he would doubtless have been stigmatized as 'lacking in moral fibre' and his next step up the promotional ladder would have been jeopardized. It took a man of 'Monty's' stature to change this. He made no bones about it; he just didn't attack until he was damned sure that he had superior force and, preferably, overwhelming strength.

The army has changed. It was refreshing to hear almost the first words addressed to us at the Staff College at Haifa in 1941 by the Commandant:

'One of our main objects is to debunk the army. We do not necessarily want to follow the book. If any of you can think of a better way of doing something than is laid down there, a method which will economize in men, time, paper or labour, we will adopt it.'

Many ideas were produced and, though very few of them had not been thought of before, nothing was too fantastic for discussion.

Towards the end of August it was decided that it would be advisable to withdraw still farther south. Wouldn't it be better to ambush Italian field cashiers and loads of piping rather than lose ours, to leave the unhealthy area of Buna where dysentery was beginning to spread among the troops, and to pursue the policy of luring the Italians farther and farther into the Northern Frontier District?

Accordingly the Brigade moved back to its old stamping-ground around Wajir with its headquarters at Habaswein.

Were we overdoing the policy of luring the Italians southwards? We were getting rather near to the last natural, though puny, line of defence, the Uaso Nyiro River – and the Italians were still coming on. And, as they had just forced us out of British Somaliland, they would have more troops and transport available to send to Kenya. The picture was not a rosy one.

4

British Somaliland

AUGUST 1940

The Protectorate of British Somaliland was always regarded by the British Government as an adopted orphan and by the British Commonwealth as a poor relation. It had neither glamour nor panache as had India, no wealth of any kind and no value as a market for British industry. But the 'poor relation' had seen better days. In Ptolemy's maps, made in the first century AD, the country was marked *Myrrhifera Regio*, the land where myrrh and frankincense were found to supply the needs of Arabia, Egypt and the Holy Land, and this must have been the reason why Arabs and Persians visited and then occupied the coastal belt of what was then known as 'The Land of Punt'. A Greek merchant, then living in Egypt, tells us in his *Periplus Maris Erythraei* that trading was taking place at six points along the north and east coast of the Horn of Africa – and that customs dues were being collected by someone for somebody! A sure sign of prosperity.

Thereafter, strangely enough, little was heard of the country for some fifteen hundred years after which it became part of the Turkish Empire in the seventeenth century. It was sold to the khedive of Egypt in 1860 but he withdrew in 1884 owing to political difficulties in the Sudan and, at that point, Britain came into the picture. The withdrawal by Egypt had created a vacuum dangerous to Britain and her stronghold at Aden. Therefore, rather than risk the country being claimed by Germany or France in the current 'scramble for Africa', she entered into a treaty with the local people and took over the administration of the area as a Protectorate.

Having, however, no motive for assuming control of the country other than that of the dog in the manger, Britain had no real interest in the people or the development of its economy. Inevitably, therefore, in the course of time, a national hero arose to lead a *jihad* to expel the infidel invaders. His name was Mohammed bin Abdullah, though he is better, but unjustly, known as 'The Mad Mullah'. He fought unrelentingly against the British for twenty years between 1899 and 1920 and thwarted all attempts by Imperial, Indian and East African troops – and the R.A.F. – to catch, subdue or kill him. In 1909 he even forced the British Administration to withdraw from the hinterland to the coastal area for several years, but he then increased his pressure and the war continued, year after year, until Mohammed Abdullah died a natural death in 1920.

After the war of 1914-18 Britain had no money to spare for making roads, harbours and developing an economy for this sad, neglected little country which remained almost as it had been when the Treaties were made thirty years before, stagnant and inert: Ptolemy would have had no difficulty in recognizing the countryside if he had landed at Berbera in 1920 – or 1940.

Nowadays, along the coast of Somaliland which extends some four hundred miles on the south side of the Gulf of Aden, there are two small towns, Berbera and Zeila, and a number of smaller settlements. The temperature and humidity there are invariably very high but inland, after about twenty miles of dusty, dry desolation, there is an escarpment running parallel to the sea and the climate improves rapidly as one climbs to the higher country. Southward towards the capital, Hargeisa, which is eighty miles inland and four thousand feet above sea level, the rise is gradual but the farther east one goes towards the Horn of Africa, the steeper is the escarpment and the greater its height.

The country can scarcely be said to have an economy – now that myrrh and frankincense are a drug on the market – but I suppose camels, goats and sheep take pride of place, if it can so be described. With every justification little thought had been given to the defence of British Somaliland against external aggression until 1939. The possibility then arose of Italy, who had occupied neighbouring Abyssinia in 1936, joining in, so the prospects were discussed with our French allies in the contiguous French Somaliland. Their country had strategic value whereas ours had none. With a good port at Jibuti and a railway line from there to Addis Ababa it could be a useful springboard for the invasion of Italian Abyssinia. British Somaliland on the other hand was topographically more vulnerable and had neither a good port nor all-weather roads.

In view of this a joint plan was made in December 1939 by which Jibuti and Berbera would be defended initially if attacked but, if pressure became too great, the British forces would withdraw into French territory to reinforce the defence of Jibuti.

When General Wavell assumed command of the Middle East theatre of war in August 1939 he became responsible for planning the defence of British Somaliland (as well as of Egypt, Palestine, Trans-Jordan, the Sudan, Cyprus, Iraq, East Africa and the shores of the Persian Gulf). This, however, was an invidious task as, at the time, he had no control over the forces there. He was not given operational command until 13 January 1940 and the Colonial Office retained administrative control of the troops until 1 June 1940, ten days before Italy entered the war.

The position was even more difficult for Lieut.-Colonel (later Brigadier) Chater, D.S.O., O.B.E. of the Royal Marines, the commander of the troops in British Somaliland. When he applied through the Governor to the Colonial Office early in July 1939 for permission to construct defences on the two main approaches to Berbera, he was granted the sum of £900. By careful expenditure of this niggardly amount and the assistance of the Public Works Department, he managed to construct a few concrete 'pill-boxes' and reserve water-tanks. Then, in mid-September, a further request was made, this time to increase his strength by enlisting fifty more men into the Camel Corps. This too was granted – but not until the spring of 1940.

On 15 January 1940 – two days after he had assumed operational command of troops in Somaliland – General Wavell requested permission from the Colonial Office to mechanize two companies of the Camel Corps. But the bureaucratic Ministerial and Departmental mills ground no more quickly for him than for the Governor, and his application was not approved until 19 May. In January he had also asked for an extra battalion to be brought from Kenya to strengthen Colonel Chater's force. This was promptly agreed in principle but authority was not given for the move until 9 March. There was then delay in getting shipping space and the battalion arrived at Berbera on 15 May. Such parsimony, indecision and executive incompetence is only believable when it is known that, at that time, the War Office was, and rightly, endeavouring to wrest control of the armed forces from the Colonial Office, and the Foreign Office was vetoing any action which might antagonize Italy and influence her to enter the war against us.

In consequence of this good old British-type muddle and unpreparedness, it would have been quite easy for the Italians to have walked in from Abyssinia when they declared war on 10 June 1940 and taken over British Somaliland since the garrison consisted of only one battalion of the King's African Rifles, the Somaliland Camel Corps and a few Irregulars. In the event they decided not to do so, which gave Britain time to assess the position, make a plan and take steps to enable it to be carried out.

There appeared to be three alternatives; to reinforce the garrison so that it could withstand a full-scale invasion, to leave the country without fighting, or to resist an attack as long as possible with the limited force available whilst inflicting maximum losses on the enemy and then withdraw. It was not possible at that time to reinforce the garrison either from Kenya or Britain to the extent necessary to repel a strong Italian attack; to leave without resistance would boost Italian morale and do nothing to ease pressure on the Kenya front; so the third alternative chose itself.

Just as this decision was made and reinforcements were on their way from Kenya to Berbera, there came a stunning blow. After the French had capitulated in Europe in June, General Legentilhomme, the Military Governor of French Somaliland and a staunch ally, had assured us that he and his troops would continue to fight. On 23 July, however, he was removed and replaced by the Vichy French General Germain. Our right flank was wide open and our strength halved in one fell swoop. This meant that the whole of the Italian Eastern Army, about twenty-five thousand strong, was available for operations against us alone. It comprised some twenty Colonial battalions, four Blackshirt battalions, four groups of pack artillery, about thirty tanks, two sections of armoured cars and eleven groups of African Irregulars.

In view of this reversal General Wavell had to decide whether to change his plan and evacuate British Somaliland at once or stick to his original idea despite the loss of French support. Brigadier Chater had just received some additions to his small force, a Punjabi battalion from Aden and a further K.A.R. battalion as well as a light battery from Kenya so, when asked for his view of the situation, he replied by signal that there was a good prospect of holding his defensive positions if he could have two more battalions. The Commander in Chief, therefore, ordered another Punjabi battalion and the 2nd Battalion The Black Watch to cross to Berbera from Aden. His force then consisted of the Somaliland Camel Corps, the 1st Northern Rhodesia Regiment, the 2nd Battalion K.A.R., the 3/15 and 1/2 Punjabi Regiments, the 2nd Battalion The Black Watch and 1(EA)

1 'The Brigadier', Major-General C. C. Fowkes, C.B.E., D.S.O., M.C.

2 (*Below:*) The Northern Frontier District seen from Lolokwi

3 Tracks through the N.F.D. over which all supplies were carried

4 Wajir Fort

5 Approaching Mount Marsabit

6 On the track between Mount Marsabit and Lake Rudolf

7 Fishermen on Lake Rudolf

8 Baggage camels on the shore of Lake Rudolf

9 The fort at Mega

10 (*Opposite:*) Field Marshal Smuts with Major-General Godwin-Austen and Brigadier Pienaar

11 (*Below left:*) Two motorized South African brigades cross the frontier into Abyssinia

12 (*Below right:*) Major-General Brink inspecting defences at Marsabit

13 (*Opposite:*) A pontoon bridge replaced the old ferry across the Tana river at Garissa

14 (*Below left:*) General Wavell

15 (*Below right:*) Mogadishu. The Italian triumphal arch

16 The King's African Rifles enter Kismayu

17 The pontoon bridge, brought up from Nairobi by road, in position across the Juba river at Ionte

18 Cases of petrol being floated ashore from a British freighter at Kismayu

19 The Strada Imperiale. Tarmac surfaces from Mogadishu to the Abyssinian frontier

Light Battery with four 3.7 Hows. His total strength was something under six thousand men.

The principal road from Abyssinia to Berbera ran straight through Hargeisa. There was, however, another though longer route going east from Hargeisa to Burao and thence through the Sheikh Pass down to the port. There were two, and only two, good defensive positions, one on each of these two approach roads. The Sheikh Pass was a narrow defile comparatively easy to defend and block by demolition but the other, at the Tug Argan gap on the direct road from Hargeisa to Berbera, was four miles wide and by far the more vulnerable. But, since the French had failed him, he had a third approach to defend, through two passes leading to the coast at Zeila.

The Tug Argan, a sandy, dry river-bed one hundred and fifty yards wide, was about half-way between Hargeisa and Berbera. Behind it, on the Berbera side, were four hills on which Brigadier Chater's defences were sited and, in front, lay an open plain with only sparse scrub growing on it. These forward positions were manned by the 1st N.R.R. (less one company), the 2nd K.A.R., the 3/15 Punjabi Regiment and the machine-gun company of the Camel Corps. The Black Watch were in reserve just behind these positions at Laferug. The 1/2 Punjabi Regiment was holding the Sheikh Pass and the two approaches to Zeila. Detachments of the Camel Corps were patrolling in front of the Zeila passes, at Burao and at Hargeisa where there was also a company of the N.R.R.

If there had ever been any doubt in the minds of the Italian General Staff whether to attack British Somaliland or leave it alone, this was now dispelled. The raids made on their border posts by the Camel Corps and Somali Irregulars ('Illalos') were a nuisance, but the reinforced British garrison constituted a threat to their flank which had to be eliminated. And, besides, they wanted a quick spectacular success to raise morale in Italy as well as in Somalia and Abyssinia. So, when the expected attack came at the beginning of August, it was with everything they had and three large columns of troops moved across the border and towards Hargeisa with support from bomber and fighter aircraft. The Italians were, of course, full of confidence. An interesting sidelight on this came from the diary of a man in their 1st Motor Cyclist Group which was picked up after the first skirmish near Hargeisa. His first entry, dated 2 August, read:

We commence the first stage of our march. During our halt we are reviewed by Divisional General de Simone who spoke to us as only a valorous soldier can speak and said among other things 'Your task is to be the Advance Guard of the column, an arduous and difficult work which I know you will carry out to the uttermost. Our end is to reach Berbera and reach it we will.'

On 4 August the motor company of the Camel Corps encountered the forward elements of the Italian force near Hargeisa. They engaged them and inflicted considerable losses, setting one armoured car on fire and damaging two others with their Boyes anti-tank rifles. The Italian motorcyclist recorded this brisk little action as follows:

August 4th, 1940. Our exploration patrols have encountered British patrols about four kilometres from our camp ... Violent automatic and rifle fire arrests our march. In a second we are in fighting order. Fortunately the first violent enemy volley is lost in the air. We reply with our Tommy guns whilst our armoured cars take up their positions and attack the enemy with cannon and machine-gun. In a short while that spot, a short time ago so quiet and silent, has become the centre of a raging battle. The fighting becomes more furious. The armoured cars go in front of us to turn the enemy. One of them, the first, traitorously hit by an anti-tank gun, remains with all its crew out of action. The second, in attempting to pass the first in order to protect it, is hit in the petrol tank and catches fire. The fire assumes huge proportions and the flames shoot up towards the sky, lighting up the first shadows of approaching night. ... At 15 hours we enter Hargeisa. The enemy, stunned by our audacity and the rapidity of our movements, prefers once again to take to flight. The success of victory appears on every face. No word of rest.

Clearly the first blood went to the Camel Corps.

Next day the Italian force reached our covering positions at Hargeisa and, after a bombardment by artillery, mortars and machine-guns lasting three hours, attacked with twelve light tanks, overran our positions and forced a withdrawal. During 6 and 7 August the Italians made no further move and appeared to be consolidating their troops at Hargeisa. They resumed their advance on the 8th and encountered the forward delaying company of the N.R.R. and the machine-gun section of the Camel Corps on the 9th. They again overran our defences using three tanks of a larger type than before against which we had no effective weapon. (Captain Howden of H.M.A.S. *Hobart* sent a 3-pounder naval gun with three ratings to deal with these and it was used at Tug Argan. On 13 August two Bofors guns also arrived at the front.)

The large Italian main body took four days to move from Hargeisa

to within sight of the British defences at Tug Argan. Each night more
and more fires could be seen twinkling in their bivouac areas on the
hills around. The attack eventually came on 11 August, the day on
which Major-General Godwin-Austen arrived from England to take
over command. The War Office had decreed that the force was then
too large for a brigadier. (It's all right, I suppose, to change horses in
mid-stream provided both horses are good – but it's a bit difficult for
the horses.)

Early that morning a low-level air attack was made on the Black
Watch at Laferug. The battalion had no casualties but brought down
one of the Italian bombers by Bren gun fire. Shortly after this the
enemy started to shell the four main Tug Argan positions on four hills,
Black Hill, Knobbly Hill, Mill Hill and Observation Hill. Two of the
guns of the East African Light Battery were on Knobbly and two on
Mill. The naval 3-pounder was on Observation as were the two Bofors
guns.

Then the enemy infantry began their attack. Their first assault was
quickly thrown back by our guns. The Italian tactics were on the lines
of the Light Brigade charging the Russian guns at Balaclava – or
infantry attacking in the Battle of the Somme. They attacked one
defended hill after another, day after day for five days and four nights
in an endeavour to break through the gap and get their mechanized
column through to Berbera. *C'était magnifique mais ce n'était pas la
guerre.* The following account of the fighting was made shortly after it
by one of the officers of the Northern Rhodesia Regiment:

It seems incredible when I think of it now that in spite of the number of
things that were shot at us and dropped on us, our casualties were
extremely light, and certainly negligible in comparison with the number of
Italian casualties. We must have killed thousands. The African soldier was
fighting during these five days and five nights under the most unfavourable
conditions possible for him. He is in his natural element when fighting out
in the bush; but here he was given a position to hold and, however much
stuff the 'Itis' showered on him, he had no opportunity of using his bush
tactics. He just had to stay put and take it: and he certainly did this well.

The following is his comment on the performance of the E.A. Light
Battery after they had fired a thousand rounds in eighteen hours – and
they had never been in action before:

The shooting of our few light guns was simply amazing. On one occasion,
after an attack by 2,000 Italians had been repulsed on Knobbly Hill by

one of our companies, the bewildered enemy made some attempt to reform their broken columns and the Italian General, who incidentally wore a black jacket, white riding breeches and black top boots, and was riding a fine white horse, selected for the purpose a temporary landing-ground for aircraft which had been constructed about 2,000 yards from Knobbly Hill position. The officer commanding Knobbly saw what was happening through his glasses and advised our gunners to fire immediately. Without ranging they obtained direct hits which completely obliterated the Italian General, his staff and all those who were on the landing-ground.

As a further example of the gunners' skill, that same afternoon eight Italian tanks emerged from a village about two miles away. Our guns put every one of them out of action before they could do any harm.

On 12 August the assault developed in full strength and each of our four positions on the hills was attacked by large forces of infantry supported by artillery barrages. Mill Hill, which was the weakest of the four since its defences had not been completed, fell in the afternoon. Its two guns were lost but both were spiked before they were captured. That night the 2nd K.A.R. were driven back from the Mirgo Pass on the left flank. Italian possession of this would have threatened the road through to Berbera, but the position was partially recovered.

On 13 August enemy action was less aggressive. An attack on Knobbly Hill was broken up, two pack guns were captured and further attacks on Black Hill and Castle Hill, a mile behind it, were repulsed. During the night a convoy taking water and ammunition to Knobbly and Castle Hills was ambushed. Four of the vehicles had to be abandoned but the rest got through when the Black Watch escort drove the enemy off. Castle and Observation Hills were shelled all day on the 14th and, at four in the afternoon, infantry attacked the latter. This was thrown back but the garrison reported that parts of the defences had been destroyed by gunfire. During the day the 2nd K.A.R. made a further attempt to regain complete control of the Mirgo Pass. It was at first successful but they were driven back in the evening.

Observation Hill, which was vital to the defence of the whole position, was then under fire from enemy guns at very short range and their defences were severely damaged. A heavy bombardment lasting two hours in the afternoon of the 15th was followed by a fierce infantry attack under which the garrison at last fell, overwhelmed by sheer weight of numbers and near exhaustion after four days and nights of fighting. The officer commanding the Camel Corps machine-gun posts on this hill, Captain E.C.T. Wilson of the East Surrey Regiment, was awarded the V.C. Though seriously wounded on the first day of the battle, he kept his guns in action for four days, repairing them when they were blown off their stands and inflicting heavy casualties on the enemy. On the last day, two of his guns were blown to pieces but he, then suffering from malaria as well as untended wounds, kept his post firing until it was overrun. The award was made posthumously but he was later found to be a prisoner of war. There were many deeds of gallantry during that week. A number of decorations were won and many more were certainly earned by actions that were unobserved.

By the time Observation Hill was lost it was clear that the Italians with their great superiority in numbers of guns and men, could destroy each of our positions in turn, and the situation was seen to be even more critical when it was learnt that an Italian motorized column was advancing towards Berbera along the coast road. This had been halted, temporarily at least, by the R.A.F. and the Navy. It was at this juncture, therefore, that General Godwin-Austen decided to withdraw his force and evacuate it from the port. His decision, which was confirmed by Headquarters Middle East, prevented the inevitable eventual loss of the whole force.

The withdrawal from the Tug Argan positions was carried out during the night of the 15th. It was covered by the Black Watch and two companies of the 2nd K.A.R. at Barkasan, thirty-five miles from Berbera. The Italians had lost two of their aircraft when they raided Berbera on the 15th and, in consequence, the movement to the port continued without interference and embarkation began on the night of the 16th.

The Italians brought up a strong force of fresh troops, estimated at at least a brigade with artillery and tanks, to attack our rearguard. At one point, after repeated attacks, the situation became desperate and our force was in danger of being surrounded, but the position was restored by an awe-inspiring bayonet charge by the Black Watch. The rearguard then started a withdrawal in good order with the Black Watch holding their posts until night fell.

The withdrawal and embarkation was a remarkably well-organized operation and, despite the lack of facilities at the port, the whole force with the exception of a few hundred men holding the outskirts of Berbera had been embarked by the morning of the 18th. The Somali police and other civil servants had been paid off and had disappeared homeward and the majority of the Camel Corps had elected to do the same. The small white civil population, hundreds of Abyssinians, Somalis, Arabs, Indians and most of the troops embarked on the night of 17 August and left in convoy on the 18th. Most of the vehicles and stores had to be abandoned due to the lack of port equipment and lighters and the necessity for all loading and embarkation being done by night. These were destroyed before the remainder of the force left in H.M.A.S. *Hobart* which, as a parting salute, shelled the government buildings before steaming away on 19 August. On that day the Italian motorcyclist wrote in his diary:

> The wind is so violent that we have to get off our motorbikes which threaten to be overturned. The mad flight of the British is evident every-where. No sign of the enemy.

No, they had gone. But they could have left a message pinned to the District Commissioner's door – 'BACK IN SEVEN MONTHS.'

Another bitter-sweet, sad but glorious page of British history had been written. There had been mistakes yet almost unbelievable achievements, losses but appreciable gains. Our casualties were far less than might have been expected in the week's fierce fighting. The total of all ranks and races together was 260 of which 38 were killed, 102 wounded and 120 missing – though a high proportion of the missing must have been killed. The Italians admitted having 1,800 casualties.

It has been said that British Somaliland was lost due to Britain having run the Protectorate on the cheap. This is an overstatement. Whilst the British government had been irresponsibly negligent of the needs of the country and miserly and dilatory in its administration, Italy's military strength in Abyssinia was far greater than anything Britain and France could have assembled there to oppose it at that time. One must remember that the British government had been culpably negligent, miserly and dilatory about the defence of Britain, at that time, and very nearly went under, as did France, for those reasons. While General Godwin-Austen urgently needed more anti-aircraft and anti-tank guns and more air support, so did Britain.

Berbera could and should have had more effective defences and certainly an efficient small harbour – if action had been taken on a strong recommendation made in 1936. But, even had these improve-ments been carried out and even had Britain and France been able to send a sufficiently large expeditionary force to deal with the situation on the spot, it would have been neither sound nor practicable policy to do so. General Wavell's strategy was correct. It was better to fight the battles for Africa where he did. We had the Protectorate back in seven months. It would, perhaps, have been better to leave the Italians there a little longer – until they had made us some good roads and a harbour!

While the military problem in Abyssinia and Somaliland in 1869 was not comparable in magnitude with that in 1941, it is interesting to see how that magnificent man and soldier, General Sir Robert Napier (later Lord Napier of Magdala) dealt with it. The Emperor Theodore of Abyssinia had seized some British citizens and thrown them into gaol at his fortress home at Magdala, near Dessie. General Napier was instructed to take an expeditionary force from India to rescue them. He made careful plans and then took everything he needed by sea to the port of Zeila. On arrival, he first constructed two piers each three hundred yards long and then twelve miles of railway line which necessitated the construction of eight bridges. He was then able to off-load all his stores, equipment and transport (elephants!) at his base before marching four hundred and twenty miles inland to fight a battle and achieve his object. But that was in the good old days.

Some months after we had retaken British Somaliland and whilst I was stationed at Hargeisa, I was able to take a close look at the country, its people and its problems. Could it prosper or was its apparent poverty inevitable – and to what extent did it need 'protection'? The days of myrrh as a commercial crop were probably over but there must be agricultural or stock-raising possibilities of some kind. At the end of the nineteenth century Lord Delamere had seen vast areas of lush grazing there and found the big-game hunting so good that he had visited the country five times and had considered settling there. Captain Walsh, the British Resident at Zeila at that time, wrote: 'I suggested that he might there prospect for gold, select a suitable area for the cultivation of long-stapled cotton and collect aloes.' Was Somaliland a potential paradise? However, my main task was to examine the roads, water and food supplies, the human and livestock populations and any other points which should be included in army intelligence reports.

When I had arrived at Hargeisa I asked a resident where they got water: all the river-beds were bone dry. 'Yes,' he said, 'something must be done about that. You see it comes down in flood on occasions, sometimes as much as six feet deep, and roars away to the sea. But the wells are good. Our food, of course, is imported.' I pondered over these problems that night, but not for long. The night was still, the air cool and I slept well until the call of the faithful to prayer woke me at dawn.

I set off that morning for Berbera in a truck accompanied by a young sapper officer, Sergeant Rockett, and Jackson. They were in holiday mood expecting a bathe in the sea and a glimpse of Somali girls. But the country depressed me. It became more arid and dusty with every mile and the only animals we saw were camels and goats. Several times we came to belts of tall thorn-trees showing where a river lay but, as usual, they were all dry. The nearer we got to the sea the hotter it got. About half way we encountered a rather dejected and frustrated detachment of the K.A.R. sweltering in the heat and feeling they were serving no useful purpose. The young Kenya officer in charge did nothing to cheer us up by saying,

> You'll find it twice as hot in Berbera, sir. It's not too bad up here in the hills.

He was absolutely right: during the next few days we spent at the coast the temperature was never less than 115° in the day and 110° at night. As we drove into Berbera we saw that its appearance had not been improved by the recent bombardment but, even before that, it had obviously not been worth putting on a picture postcard. The sea was some way from the town and looked like a burnished copper sheet. I did not go for a swim. If one escaped getting heat stroke on the way to the water one only got an unpleasantly hot bath in it.

I found several friends in the garrison and all of them were, to my unexpressed surprise, cheerful and well. It is amazing how the British animal can acclimatize itself to almost anything. This is due, I suppose, to the breeding of generations of sahibs, bwanas and Polar explorers. Three days were enough for me. After investigating the inadequacy of the port, I left — without regret. If the Russians are really using this abominable place now for storing their rockets, I hope they enjoy it as little as I did then.

I was told that the Governor, in pre-war days, spent part of his time in Berbera but went as often as possible to a lodge up in the hills at Sheikh. So, feeling that we needed a change, we drove some thirty miles up the winding road, through the pass where Brigadier Chater had built a few defensive posts and arrived at the health resort. On the way Rockett, who had been unusually deep in thought for some miles said,

'You know, sir, if Robinson Crusoe 'ad landed 'ere instead of on that island in the Specific Ocean, I don't suppose he'd 'ave lasted for long, do you?'

This was rather a difficult question to answer off-hand so I stalled:

'He certainly wouldn't unless he had found a very good "Man Friday".' But all the Somalis we had seen so far looked fit and well on something. We must find out how they do it.

The Governor, we decided, had found himself a very pleasant hide-out. Sheikh is just over six thousand feet above sea level and, being on the edge of an escarpment, catches any breeze that is lazing around. The change from the climate of Berbera in such a short distance was startling and so welcome that we stayed a night there, sleeping peacefully instead of tossing about on a sweat-soaked undersheet.

Next morning we drove on to Burao through the now familiar and ubiquitous thorn-bush. The Camel Corps had its headquarters and depot there and I was hoping to find two friends. I also wanted to borrow an English-speaking Somali. The British officers were, to a man, dedicated Somalophils. The Somalis were smart, intelligent and brave soldiers, proud and pervidly Muslim. It followed, therefore, that however much they respected their officers, their officers were to them basically and immutably infidels. This factor, I feel, cannot be dissociated from the causes of the mutiny which followed some time later. I had a nasty feeling that alcoholic liquor might not be served in their Mess in the interests of Mohammedan-Christian solidarity. But I needn't have worried, the evening was a very cheerful one. In any case the Somalis could scarcely frown upon our liquor since they chewed a drug called *khat* which is said to induce 'light-hearted gaiety'. Splendid, but we just preferred Scotch.

We moved off next morning with the addition of Hamid, our guide and interpreter. He and Smithy, the sapper, got on like wild-fire and chattered away, so I was able to concentrate my attention on the country we were passing through. This became more and more desolate and arid as we went along and most of the few trees were leaning over. Could this be due to the wind? The light sandy soil, too, was being blown into drifts and dunes.

'What has happened to the country, Hamid? The trees are dying.'

'Yes,' he replied, 'for many years the rain has been getting less and less and the land dryer and dryer.'

We stopped to have a closer look. The trees were falling over because the soil had been washed or blown away from the roots. This was the first stage in desert formation due, if Hamid was right, to a change of climate. But I had my doubts about this. We had crossed several small river-beds, or *tugs*, now dry but which had shown signs of water having rushed down in torrents from time to time. We went on again. Smithy was busy with his compass and making notes of the mileage, the road surface and the number of *tugs* we crossed; Hamid was doing his best to get Jackson to talk to him, but with little success. My orderly was frankly bored with the whole proceeding and was trying to sleep in the back of the truck.

The only settlement of consequence in that part of the Horn of Africa was Erigavo, 150 miles from Burao, which we reached at midday. The District Commissioner and the police officer were away on safari but neither could have welcomed us more warmly nor been more helpful than the D.C.'s Somali clerk. Our unexpected arrival was an amusing diversion for the village and everyone turned out to inspect us and ask Hamid all about us. The clerk showed us some spotlessly clean huts to sleep in, had water and firewood brought for us and made us feel quite at home. When we had settled in he said,

'Will you please visit the hospital, sir? If you will do this the sub-assistant surgeon will try harder.'

I went there. The little Indian doctor was obviously glad that someone was taking an interest in his work. Business appeared not to be very brisk and he apologized for having only two patients, a girl who had been stabbed in the stomach and a man with malaria. Taking me over to the girl's bed, he told me,

'The intestines were exposed, sir, but I returned them all and sewed up.'

I felt some comment was required so I asked, 'Bowels open? 'No sir, but matter is in hand,' was the comforting reply. He was, I think, quite impressed by my question and my stock rose even higher when I asked him if he had adequate supplies of drugs. He certainly had, masses and masses of captured Italian stuff of every colour and kind. I could only hope he knew how to use it.

When I walked over to the administrative office I found two Somali children meddling with the wireless transmitter. On further enquiry, however, I was told they were the operators. They looked about twelve years old but must have been more. They knew their job. When I asked one of them the time he tapped a message to Hargeisa and, in a matter of seconds, said, 'One fourteen p.m., sir.' That sounded like lunch-time to me so I thanked them and walked back to see what Jackson had cooked up for us.

Hamid said he would take us to Dalo in the afternoon, a point from which we should be able to see the sea. We might be able to have a swim. I knew we had been climbing gradually on our way up to Erigavo but I didn't realize how much until Hamid took us through a strip of juniper forest.

'Whatever height are we at, Smithy?' I asked. Smithy took out his altometer and his spectacles, gazed at the oracle, then shook it, tapped it and finally said, 'It says sea level, sir, but I think it may have been damaged.' I was damned sure it had; we had just come out of the forest and were on the edge of a steep escarpment. The sea glistened in the sun – thousands of feet below us.

The only way down to the shore was by a camel track which wound down the cliff to the little port of Mait. It would be quite easy to go down to the sea – if one had a day or two to spare, but the prospect of the return climb daunted me and we walked back to Erigavo.

Since juniper cedar grew here I reckoned we must be at least five to six thousand feet above sea level. I could check on this at the D.C.'s office. They might also have rainfall figures which could throw some light on the mystery of the *tugs*. The clerk had everything at his fingertips:

'Yes, sir, we are at 7,900 feet above the sea and the rainfall is recorded in this book since many years.'

Hamid had been wrong, the rainfall was not less now than it had been in the past. It was now clear that the grass had been consistently overgrazed for years and now there was nothing to hold the rain water on the ground until it could be absorbed into the soil. So it rushed down the *tugs* into the sea – taking the soil with it. I had noticed this process of destruction soon after we had left Burao. It must be taking place over most of the country. How could it be stopped? In ignorance of the major tragedy taking place before their eyes, the people of Erigavo were happy; it was the next generation that would suffer, the children who followed us about laughing gaily and enjoying the fun.

The evening was cool at this height and we were glad to sit near the camp-fire Jackson had made while we were exploring. Then he brought dinner; soup and a delicious stew made from a young goat he had bought in the village for a few annas.

The next day we drove on twenty-five miles to Medishe. We were sorry to be leaving this highland paradise and going down again to the dry plains, so we were amazed when we reached a valley which was rather like the Garden of Eden of my imagination. Peaches, grapes, oranges were all growing in profusion as well as cauliflowers, peas and beans of several kinds. They were grown under irrigation from springs. Rockett had to eat his words. Robinson Crusoe would have thrived in that valley − provided he had a good supply of quinine to combat malaria.

One of the market gardeners gave us tea, very sweet and just as I like it. He apologized for not having coffee; he had run out, so I gave him some of ours. 'Stay the night,' he said, 'and I will kill a sheep.' I thanked him and explained that, much as we should enjoy his hospitality, we were already overdue at Hargeisa and must return that evening. I knew the local custom. If we stayed and ate his sheep the next gift must be from us − and I had noticed him looking enviously at our truck.

As we drove back through the night the country's problems revolved in my mind, looming, of course, larger than life in the dark. This was a British Protectorate and should, therefore, be protected − in more ways than one. There is no point in protecting a country against external aggression if its internal economy is allowed to run to ruin. Something must be done. The answer was and, of course, had to be 'Yes, after the war.' Soil erosion must be arrested by contour banks and grazing control and water must be conserved by a succession of dams on each *tug*. Such work is not difficult with mechanical diggers and bulldozers. The cost? Not one millionth of what it is costing to test the soil on Mars.

5

The Military Situation

JULY TO DECEMBER 1940

The main reason for defending Kenya was to prevent the port of Mombasa, an important link in our Line of Communication between South Africa and the Middle East, from falling into enemy hands. General Smuts had emphasized this when he agreed to send troops, aircraft, guns and equipment of every kind from South Africa to reinforce the defences of Kenya. The South African Ministry of Defence went even further and stipulated that no South African troops were to be used north of the Equator — not realizing, it seems, that the main training area on Mount Kenya was a few miles over this line!

There was a great difference of opinion, however, as to how Mombasa should be protected. By defence or by attack? Should only a small force be retained in Kenya for its defence or should a large force be built up capable of taking the offensive? The protagonists over this question were Mr Churchill, General Smuts and General Wavell under whose Middle East Command East Africa had been placed in February 1940. In July Mr Churchill started pressing wholeheartedly — he never pressed in any other way — for the transfer of a large number of the troops then in Kenya to the Middle East. He considered that Kenya could and should be defended by a much smaller force than it then had, some twenty thousand men after the recent arrival of three brigades from West and South Africa, and that the K.A.R. and the 'Settlers', reinforced from Britain by sea if necessary, should be able to do this.

He formulated his claim in the following minute dated 10 August 1940 to the C.I.G.S. for General Wavell:

We have yet to discuss the position in Kenya and Abyssinia. I mentioned the very large forces which you have in Kenya, namely, the Union Brigade of 6,000 white South Africans, probably as fine material as exists for warfare in spacious countries; the East African settlers, who should certainly amount to 2,000 men, thoroughly used to the country; two West African Brigades, brought at much inconvenience from the West coast, numbering 6,000; at least two Brigades of King's African Rifles (K.A.R.); the whole at least 20,000 men – there may be more. Why should these all stand idle in Kenya waiting for an Italian invasion to make its way across the very difficult distances from Abyssinia to the South, or preparing themselves for a similar difficult inroad into Abyssinia, which must again entail long delays, while all the time the fate of the Middle East, and much else, may be decided at Alexandria or on the Canal?

Without, of course, knowing the exact conditions locally, I should suppose that a reasonable disposition would be to hold Kenya with the settlers and the K.A.R. and delay any advance southwards, it being so much easier to bring troops round by sea than for the Italians to make their way overland. Thus we can always reinforce them unexpectedly and swiftly. This would allow the Union Brigade and the two West African Brigades to come round at once into the Delta, giving you a most valuable reinforcement in the decisive theatre at the decisive moment. What is the use of having command of the sea if it is not to pass troops to and fro with great rapidity from one theatre to another? I am sure I could persuade General Smuts to allow this movement of the Union Brigade. Perhaps you will let me have your views on this by tomorrow night, as time is so short.

Two weak points stand out in this assessment of the Kenya situation. First, far from 'waiting for an Italian invasion', we were then being hard pressed to stem one. If our recently acquired reinforcements had been taken away, it would have been a great stimulus to the invaders. That was, surely, not a suitable moment to reduce our strength: the Italians were almost in sight of Mount Kenya.

Secondly, we did not have 'command of the sea' at that time. The journey up the east coast of Africa was becoming increasingly hazardous: German submarines and surface raiders were taking a heavy toll of our shipping. (When we captured Merca, a small coastal town just South of Mogadishu, in February 1941, we found and released 179 British, 13 French, and 36 Jugoslavian prisoners of war from the Merchant Navy taken from seven ships sunk by a German raider which spent five months marauding off that coast.)

In view of these errors of judgement it is surprising to find that Sir Winston reiterated these views later on in his *History of the Second World War* in which he wrote:

Khartoum and the Blue Nile certainly required strengthening against the Italian-Abyssinian border, but what was the sense of keeping twenty-five thousand men, including the Union Brigade of South Africa and two Brigades of excellent West African Troops, idle in Kenya? I had ridden over some of this country, north of the Tana River, at the end of 1907. It is a very fine looking country, but without much to eat. The idea of an Italian expedition of fifteen or twenty thousand men, with artillery and modern gear, travelling the four or five hundred miles before they could reach Nairobi seemed ridiculous.

No, it really wasn't ridiculous. They nearly got there; and had our reinforcements been taken away they might well have succeeded. General Cunningham proved this point − in reverse. Four months after he took over the East Africa Command in October 1940, his forces moved nearly two thousand miles through Somalia and Abyssinia in ten weeks, capturing Kismayu, Mogadishu and Addis Ababa.

Preoccupied as he was with the war problems of Britain, our allies, Egypt, the Dominions and Asia, how could Mr Churchill arrange the detail of a campaign in Kenya? He had been there and he had fought in the Sudan, albeit many years ago, and he thought, therefore, that he knew these countries better than the younger men around him. He could not bring himself to delegate responsibility for the planning of this campaign to the Commander in Chief.

This was Mr Churchill's weakness: his strength we all knew. Thank God we had his dynamic personality and unflagging vigilance throughout the war; but thank God also we had, in General Wavell, a commander of exceptional intelligence and moral and physical courage who would always stick to his guns − if he believed them to be the right ones − ignoring any risk to his personal position.

His assessment of the military situation was that the large Italian army in Abyssinia, consisting of more than a quarter of a million men, was a threat not only to Kenya and Tanganyika but also to British and French Somaliland,* the Sudan and so, possibly, Egypt. Its strength lay not only in numbers. Mr J. Connell in his biography of Lord Wavell describes it as 'a huge well-trained, well-equipped army containing some of the most resolute, skilled and valorous troops encountered by the Allies anywhere in the world throughout the war'.

In 1940 they were in a position to send a force twice the size of ours into Kenya whilst still being able to safeguard their western and northern borders. It follows, therefore, that, if General Wavell had depleted his force in Kenya by giving up three brigades when Mr

* British forced to withdraw in August 1940.

Churchill pressed him to do so, it is well within the bounds of possibility that an Italian invasion would have succeeded.

The reinforcements from Britain, suggested by Mr Churchill, could not have arrived in time to prevent this, even had all gone well. But there was the possibility that they might not have reached Kenya at all as the submarine menace was increasing month by month. German submarines were being harboured by the Italians in their East African ports, Kismayu, Merca, Mogadishu and Massawa in the Red Sea and were playing havoc with our shipping from South Africa and the East.

General Wavell knew that, while the Italians held Somaliland, Abyssinia and Eritrea, he would have a Sword of Damocles hanging over his head while fighting his battles in North Africa. So, with characteristic thoroughness, patience and determination, he made his plans to deal with this threat.

It required a Titan among men to co-ordinate the many implications of these with his other great responsibilities throughout Africa, Greece, and Iraq since his objective in East Africa could not be achieved by the movement of a brigade here and another there; only a wide, comprehensive, complex and multi-prong attack could succeed. In the meantime he resisted all attempts to wrest from him the tools he would need.

Comment on the views held by Mr Churchill at this time regarding the campaign in East Africa would not be complete without reference to his misconception about the part being played in it by the Kenya 'Settlers'.

On 12 August 1940 he wrote the following minute for the attention of General Wavell:

> Let me have a return of the white settlers of military age in Kenya. Are we to believe they have not formed any local units for the defence of their own province? If not, the sooner they are made to realize their position the better. No troops ought to be in Kenya at the present time other than the settlers and the K.A.R.

There is nothing wrong in this: Mr Churchill was uncertain whether the settlers were pulling their weight or not and asked for information. His minute, however, is baldly recorded in his *History of the Second World War* some years later, without comment, clarification or correction and is, therefore, by implication, a slur on the British people in East Africa. His doubts should have been withdrawn as publicly as they were uttered since they were unfounded.

The situation was that, at the outset of the war in September 1939, there were six battalions of the King's African Rifles; two of these were formed in Kenya, two in Nyasaland, one in Tanganyika and one in Uganda. Each had seven or eight British officers and a warrant officer from the Regular Army. This British element was then increased to eighty per battalion by drawing on settlers who were in the K.A.R. Reserve of Officers, the Kenya Regiment and the Kenya Defence Force – the Territorials of East Africa. The six original battalions were expanded to fifty and only when the supply of local British was exhausted was Britain asked to send 'Imperials' from England to fill the gaps.

In addition to the K.A.R., settlers with special qualifications formed the E.A. Reconnaissance Regiment; the Kenya Independent Squadron; the E.A. Artillery, Engineers, Signals, Electrical and Mechanical Engineers (E.M.E.), Ordnance Corps, Supply and Transport, Pioneer Battalions and Medical Units. Others, with even more special qualifications, led guerrilla bands behind the enemy lines. Those who could not find a niche in any of these active units – and being in one's fifties was no bar to that – joined garrison battalions.

The force which General Dickinson had under his command in 1939 numbered under seven thousand. Thereafter it grew with remarkable speed so that, in addition to its major role in the Abyssinian campaign, a brigade group went to assist in taking Madagascar from the Vichy French, a complete division plus two brigade groups went to Burma and some thirty thousand men in Pioneer battalions to the Middle East. By V.E. Day the East African forces were just under 250,000 strong. East Africans, black and white, had not failed to respond to the call.

1940 was drawing to a close. Lieut.-General Alan Cunningham had arrived at the end of October to command the East African Force which was disposed at key points along the northern frontier between the Sudan and the Indian Ocean. The Italians were cock-a-hoop after pushing us out of British Somaliland in August. They were making a second road down the Abyssinian escarpment into Kenya north of Marsabit and our brigade was being sent to reinforce the small garrison there. The general line of defence was getting uncomfortably close to the Kenya Highlands.

But the situation was changing rapidly. Two brigades of the West African Frontier Force and a strong brigade group from South Africa had arrived in Kenya bringing our total strength up to 75,000 (33,000 East Africans, 9,000 West Africans, 6,000 British and 27,000 South Africans). With this reinforcement we should be able to turn the tide – but it was not the time to send any of these troops to another front.

6

Mount Marsabit

OCTOBER TO NOVEMBER 1940

In October 1940 our brigade was ordered to move westward from the Wajir area to go to Marsabit which was to be held 'to the last man and last round'. The importance of Marsabit lay in its water-supply. This delightful little mountain possessed many springs and little streams, the only ones for scores of miles on all sides. It would be necessary, therefore, for the Italians to capture this area if they were to advance southward on any line between Lake Rudolf and Wajir, either because they needed the water or because they could not leave us threatening their lines of communication.*

The force on the mountain was an odd medley of men. Our Brigade Group with its three K.A.R. battalions and ancillaries was shortly to be joined by part of the 1st South African Division. The Kenya Independent Squadron, known as Drought's Horse, was a volunteer cavalry unit mounted on polo ponies and mules. Then there were several groups of Irregulars commanded by intrepid gentlemen with suitably irregular names such as Carl Nurk, Kametz, Idot, Koch and, more regular but only in name, Jack Bonham.

When we arrived the place was a hive of industry. The sappers were constructing pill-boxes around the main-water supply and on each side of the two roads running to the mountain from the north. The Italians would have to use one or both of these if they decided to move south.

Our cavalry patrolled daily round the mountain on a belt of grass-

---

* An Italian colonel, captured at Soddu on 23 May 1941, who had commanded the force which took Moyale in 1940, said that he had been ordered thereafter to go on to Marsabit but that he had been unable to do so as he lacked the necessary supplies — and the roads were too bad. If he had had more supplies, and possibly more courage, it would have been easy for him to take Marsabit at that time as the garrison was minimal.

land below the forest from which they could see far and wide over the
lava-strewn plains below; the Irregulars came in periodically with hair-
raising stories about their forays and explorations over the border into
Abyssinia; and we were given the more humdrum task of making
grass huts for ourselves. These were to house the four thousand men
in our Brigade Group and a big and interesting job it was. Our
Askaris were, of course, experts at building in such materials and
competed with each other in design and quality. Some of the cottages
had porches and verandahs, some grass windows which really did
open and shut, and others neat stone and mud fireplaces and
chimneys.

I spent my evenings roaming about in the forest looking at the herds
of buffalo drinking at the several small crater lakes, and trying to spot
the elusive greater kudu with its long, gracefully curling horns.

Life was pleasant and peaceful and one almost forgot that there was
a war. One evening, however, the Brigadier upset the comfortable,
even tenor of our way by saying,

'We're off to Lake Rudolf tomorrow. I want to see what the
country is like along the shore. It could be possible for the "Itos" to
come down that way and we'd look awful fools if one of their columns
by-passed us and reached Nairobi.'

I glanced unenthusiastically through the window of our cosy grass
Mess Room at the parched, unfriendly desert. The lake was about a
hundred miles to the west of us — as the crow flies. There were two
long and circuitous routes we could take, each by a road of sorts. But
each would be a good deal more than two hundred miles and I just
knew the Brigadier had neither of these in mind: he would go across
country. I went to get the map and we studied it.

'We can't go straight there, damn it, because of that cliff,' said the
Brigadier. 'We shall have to go quite a long way south first to get
round it.'

The cliff ran round the west and south sides of the mountain and
about ten miles from it. It was a useful protective barrier as no vehicle
could scale it; but it was a nuisance to us just then.

From a point about fifty miles away on our main road south the
map showed a thin red line running north-west, just about the
direction we should need. The map explained that this sort of red line
indicated 'roads, other' whereas a dotted line would mean a 'track
(motorable in some cases)'. Surely then ours would be 'motorable in
all cases' so I said,

'Shall we try this way, sir? It will probably only be a track, but some vehicle must have gone along it at some time.'

He settled for that: there was really no alternative.*

I went off to tell the men who were to come with us; Sam, the Brigadier's orderly officer, Sergeant Rockett who was in charge of our transport, two orderlies, three African drivers and three Askaris. Jackson was disappointed. His roving eye had detected possibilities of the *dolce vita* in Marsabit village: he would be safer with us.

The others were excited at the prospect of a change and a bit of adventure.

'A week's sailing, swimming, and sunning at the seaside,' said Sam. 'What could be better?'

We left early next morning with one small and two large trucks. The Brigadier and I went ahead with his orderly and a driver to find the thin red line we were going to follow. When we had done forty-five miles I asked the Brigadier to slow down. He was driving, as usual, as if he were in a rally and the dust made it impossible to see the road-side. I was scanning every bush and rock for signs of the wretched track but without any luck. So, when the speedometer showed fifty-five miles, I asked him to stop.

'We must have overshot the mark, sir. I think we had better go back five miles.'

As far as I remember his reply was 'Humph'; but he turned back and we met the other trucks at about the place where I had expected, or rather, hoped to find the track going off to the west. I knew we couldn't expect a signboard but I thought we should, at least, see some old tracks. If there ever had been any they were now indiscernible and overgrown.

There was only one thing to do. 'I suggest we cut off here, sir, and strike north. Then, after a while, if we haven't found it, we can come back on the other tack. We should hit it somewhere.'

He replied to the effect that we were soldiers and not bloody sailors; but he agreed and off we set.

The bush was sparse and didn't worry us, but we could only move at walking speed in low gear because the volcanic soil was very soft and the wheels sank into it. After about an hour, and on our third tack, we found it, skirting round a small rocky hill. We then swung

* I found out some years later that the line we took from Marsabit to Lake Rudolf was, as exactly as one can determine from sketch maps, that taken by Lord Delamere in 1897. He was then on the last lap of his historic journey from British Somaliland to Kenya travelling with a train of camels, a form of transport superior to ours for crossing sandy river-beds.

along gaily at a good ten miles an hour – but only for half an hour. The dry, sandy river-bed in front of us did not appear to be any great obstacle and the Brigadier, driving like Jehu, put the truck into it at speed. Half way across, however, it shuddered and stopped, the wheels sunk deep in the soft sand.

The Brigadier had a wide reputation for being hot, quick, and even bad-tempered. My friends used to tell me they were jolly glad they weren't in my shoes at Brigade Headquarters. Being a 'new boy' I was suitably awed – and waited for it. When we came to a sickening halt in the sand, therefore, I fully expected a vituperative flow of barrack-room rhetoric and was more than surprised when he quietly said:

'How extraordinary. I've crossed dozens of these things before without a hitch. I can't have been going fast enough.'

With considerable relief at this calm acceptance of the calamity, the. driver and I got out the chains and, after laboriously digging and jacking up the back wheels, put them on. We then filled in the deep ruts we had made in our attempt and reported that all was ready for another go. Not a hope. The chains merely enabled the wheels to throw out more sand and dig in more quickly. We were now down on our axles. The Brigadier was obviously a bit worried but still not unduly perturbed.

As the chains alone were clearly useless, I decided to try to improvise a drift by cutting bush and laying it across the river bed. But, at that moment, Sergeant Rockett arrived with his big truck. Not only did he save my bacon but he literally saved the whole trip from failure. Taking in the situation at a glance, he said,

'Don't you worry sir, I'll 'ave you out in a jiffy.'

He produced a steel hawser, hooked it to the back axle of our truck and on to the front of his, and then, reversing gently, he pulled us on to *terra firma*. Next, he and his driver took half a dozen stout wooden planks out of his truck.

'Thought these 'ere might come in useful. We 'ave a lot of them ruddy sand rivers where I come from in Tanganyika. Now you lot,' he said to the Askaris in his own Cockney-Swahili, '*weka hi hivi*' (put them like this).

In no time two rows of planks were laid over the sand and our truck moved gently on to them. When it could go no further we took up the rear planks, laid them in front, and repeated the process. Slow but sure. Later in the war we became more efficient at this sort of thing and carried rolls of army track or metal channelling. This time I quietly blessed Sergeant Rockett.

It was dusk by the time we were all safely across. I reminded Sam to get the Brigadier's camp-chair out and take him a whisky — just in case. In the meanwhile we organized a good log fire and the camp-beds. We had a good night but, for some time before I got to sleep, I pondered over the unexpected self-control of the Brigadier in the river bed.

This was my first experience of a very admirable trait in his character; one which enables a man to become a leader of men. Whenever anything went wrong, and I was to be with him on more than a few occasions during the next three years when things did go wrong, he was calm, clear-headed and constructive. But, of course, just as what goes up must come down, there was another side to his character. When a battle was over or any other important task accomplished, there had to be an explosive release of pent-up tension. Then was the time, I found, to attend some urgent call elsewhere and disappear.

Another thing about him, you always knew where he was. When life was operationally quiet he would be in his office, embarrassing his staff by his detailed knowledge of each of their jobs. But if there was a scrap, however big or small, he would be there, and in the forefront of it. Just as he had to creep around in front of the fort at Moyale to see for himself, so, when we took Kismayu, he was the first man in.

He never changed. Two years later in Burma when he, as a major-general, was commanding a division in the Kabaw Valley, I only just managed to get far enough forward to find him. To do so I started in a jeep, left this stuck in the mud, rode a horse, crossed a river on an elephant and, finally walked and walked to locate him eventually with the foremost company of the front battalion, the retreating Japs just in front of them.

Next morning the Brigadier said to me,

'Come along, we'll walk on ahead and have a look at the country while they load up.'

I put on my equipment with pistol, water-bottle, field-glasses, and compass, seized a map, and off we went. The track was easy to follow, the sun warmed our backs, little dik-dik skipped across our path and some startled francolin ran away into the bush. In spite of all the junk I was carrying, I could just have managed a shot-gun as well: we could have done with a bird or two for the pot.

We left the track and climbed to the top of a small rocky knoll. We could see for miles and miles across the Kaisut Desert.

'Well, if I were an "Ito" I wouldn't come across this sort of country,' said the Brigadier. Then he quickly added, 'But, by God, they have. Get down!'

I crouched down and looked through my glasses in the direction he had pointed. Sure enough, two men in strange uniforms and helmets were scanning the country just as we had been doing. We waited and watched for a minute or two. There were only two of them.

'Come on, let's get 'em,' said the Brigadier.

Crouching down and darting from bush to bush, we gradually closed in on them. At twenty yards we stood up, levelled our pistols at them, and the Brigadier challenged them in a mixture of Italian and Swahili:

'*Vieni qui. Mano juu.*'

Startled, the two men complied. Then one of them said,

'Christ man, what the bleddy hell are you doing?'

We had heard South African spoken before: no Italian, however cosmopolitan, could use the English language quite like that. We all laughed. The Brigadier said,

'Well, it's good to see you. You've come up with General Brink, I presume. Why didn't someone let me know that you'd arrived and might be prowling around my bit of country? Anyway, come and have some breakfast.'

As we all walked back they apologized and explained that they hadn't been to Marsabit yet but were sappers on their way there – and having a look around like us. Later, having arranged to meet again after our return to Marsabit, we set off in our different directions.

All that day we plodded on. We encountered five more dry river-beds, but our technique had improved. Having got the first big truck across on the boards, we used it to tow the others over. This saved a great deal of time. After leaving our pseudo-Italians we never saw another soul. Considering the sort of country we were in, this was not surprising. But, as we gradually approached Mount Nyiru, a great rock of a mountain with cool green forest on top, the country changed and the bush became thicker and even lush.

Just as we appreciated the change of scene and better country, so did the elephant. The whole place simply teemed with them. There was plenty of water for them from the springs on the mountainside and plenty to eat there too. Furthermore, the area was sufficiently inaccessible to deter most hunters: they had found a veritable elephant paradise.

Suddenly we reached the road we had been expecting, running

north and south. This was clearly being used regularly: we were back in civilization. By that time we felt we had earned a rest and stopped for the night.

During supper the Brigadier said to me,

'There's no need for all of us to go down to the lake tomorrow. You and I will go in the small truck and leave the others to do some cleaning and maintenance.'

I saw poor Sam's face drop: he had been looking forward to a trip to the seaside. So, later that night, I suggested to the Brigadier that Sam would probably be more useful to him next day than his orderly. Sam came with us, but it was a disappointing day for him. There were no girls, no band on the end of the pier – in fact no pier at all!

As we bumped our way down towards the lake next morning with Mount Nyiru on our left, we could see Mount Kulal straight in front of us. The gap between these two mountains formed a funnel through which an eighty or ninety mile an hour wind often blew. This was caused by the warring influences of the lake and the desert.

When the lake came into view, Teleki's volcano stood out on the southern shore in a setting as stark and desolate as the moon.

'Count Teleki must have been a tough chap to have got here on foot,' said the Brigadier. 'He didn't know where his next drink of water was coming from or whether he'd ever get back home. I'm afraid I must give him best: I'd rather be in this truck with some food, water, and whisky.'*

We reached the lake shore at a point opposite South Island. It was an awe-inspiring sight, not unlike the English Channel on a rough day. The wind was getting up and whipping the white horses into action. I was glad we didn't have a boat or the Brigadier would have insisted on trying to catch one of the big two hundred pound Nile perch.

We drove a few miles farther north. The track along the lakeside

---

* When Count Teleki discovered Lake Rudolf in 1888 he was accompanied by von Hohnel who kept a record of the journey. His description of the lake which follows is more vivid and dramatic than mine.

'Into what a desert had we been betrayed? A few scattered tufts of fine stiff grass rising up in a melancholy fashion near the shore were the only signs of life of any kind. Here and there, some partly in the water, some on the beach, rose up isolated skeleton trees, stretching their bare sun-bleached branches to the pitiless sky. No living creature shared the gloomy solitude with us. To all this was added the scorching heat and the ceaseless buffeting of the sand-laden wind, against which we were powerless to protect ourselves on the beach which offered not a scrap of shelter.'

was certainly passable for motor transport in the dry weather and there was plenty of fresh water from springs in the slopes of Mount Kulal. The conclusion we reached, therefore, was that, whilst it would be possible for the Italians to use this route, it was not likely they would attempt it. This opinion was reinforced as we moved southward during the next two days over the abominable road up to Baragoi and through Barsaloi to Isiolo. If they did decide to try it they would have to send one of their field companies ahead to carry out the repairs that our Public Works Department, luckily in this case, had failed to do.

The traffic slowed us down next day – the elephant traffic. I remembered an old elephant hunter saying to me years ago that he had once been bicycling along a road when he met an elephant.

'What would you have done, young man?' he asked.

I probably replied that I should have turned the bicycle round pretty smartly and made off. But he said,

'Nonsense, just ring your bell and the elephant will get out of your way.' We should have had to do this very often on the way back, but we deemed it more prudent to wait politely each time they crossed in front of us and give them right of way.

During one of these traffic jams the Brigadier said, 'Get out, I'm going to take a photo of them.' Screened by a bush, we crept up to a big one. He got his picture and signalled to me that we should now move back. As we did so we glanced up and saw two more elephants browsing peaceably towards us. Not having a bicycle bell handy, we dodged and got back to the truck.

When we reached our old stamping-ground at Isiolo, I said to the Brigadier, 'We're quite near to Nanyuki, sir. Don't you think we should just run up there and see if there are any problems about our Lines of Communication?'

It was only fifty miles farther on and I should have liked to have popped into the sports club for a beer and a chat. Also I knew the Brigadier's wife was living there. Unfortunately his reply was,

'A disgracefully pleasant idea – but no. We must get back to work.'

On our way north we stopped at Archer's Post to have a word with the South African Air Force there. They had a good air-strip surrounded by huge acacia thorn-trees under which they could hide their Fairey 'Battles' and Fighters. We knew they were doing reconnaissance flights up to and along the Abyssinian border and the Brigadier wanted to ask them to keep a watch on the Lake Rudolf shore road.

I must say we looked pretty scruffy when we drove up there. We were covered with dust from head to foot and our bush shirts and shorts were crumpled and filthy. When I saw the very smart South African guard at the gate I said,

'We'd better go round to the tradesmen's entrance hadn't we, sir?'

The guard commander looked at us with justifiable hesitancy but, when he noticed the Brigadier's still slightly blue pennant on the truck, he saluted and allowed us to pass.

The Commanding Officer gave us a warm welcome and, after telling his adjutant to give orders for a close observation to be kept on the lake shore, he pointed out on the map to us a place where the Italians were making a road, or repairing the old one, down the escarpment South of Mega. He then took us over to his Mess for a wash and brush-up.

Over a long, cool drink I noticed him looking at the Brigadier with curiosity. I felt certain he was asking himself, 'Is this the conventional, traditional, professional British officer? Do British brigadiers, and pretty old ones at that, go bumping around the country in trucks looking for Italians?' But he was obviously relieved to see that they did that sort of thing rather than just sit at their headquarters wearing scarlet uniform and sipping madeira. They got on like wildfire. The Brigadier told them where they could find the best sand grouse shooting in the world – at Shaffa Dikha nearby; we gave them the names of our friends in Nanyuki on whom they should call; and we told them the name of the Australian whisky they should not accept from NAAFI at any price.

Just as we were about to leave, the Air Force C.O. said to me,

'Why not stay with us for a few days? We'll fly you all over the part of the country you're interested in. We are taking photos every day of the road the "Itos" are making. They're working fast and it looks as though they'll be able to use it in about a week.'

The Brigadier thanked them and agreed. Jackson offloaded my bed-roll and took it over to a comfortable tent they gave me under the trees. Then best of all – I had a bath.

We flew north early next morning. Before we left the pilot said,

'There's only one bad thing about these Fairey "Battles", they have a blind spot. If one of the Fiat CR42s creeps up behind and just below our tail, none of us can see it. So when we get near the frontier, I want you to lie on your stomach and look through that glass plate on the floor and tell me if any Fiats get up from the deck at Mega.'

I said, 'O.K.' In a few minutes he signalled to me, and I got down on my stomach. I could see the road below us twisting and turning about. This made it impossible to get the whole picture we wanted in one run so the pilot had to twist and turn as well, and then go on another line of flight. In consequence it was not long before I realized I was going to be sick. But into what? I had an idea and made a sort of soufflé dish out of my map. This served its purpose well and I was about to dispose of it through the sliding-glass panel when I realized that the map was marked SECRET. With praiseworthy attention to security I placed the dish on the floor and resumed my vigil. It was only a matter of seconds before I saw two CR42s taking off. I told the pilot and he, with a final regurgitating lurch round and downward, beat it for home leaving the Fiats far behind.

Afterwards I was told how rewarding my security precaution had been. Had I opened the glass panel, the contents of my dish would have been hurled into my face!

After breakfast I went over to see the Adjutant in his office. When I saw he was obviously having a serious talk with several of the pilots, I apologized and made to leave. But he called me in and said,

'I'd rather you get the true story about this from me before you hear the garbled report that will be round town tomorrow. It's this business about the "Oubaas". We nearly shot him down yesterday.'

I almost, quite involuntarily, said 'Christ man!' But quickly realizing that, if I did use their favourite national expletive, they would think I was being facetious, I changed it to 'Good Lord' and sat down to hear what had happened.

General Smuts had flown up from South Africa to assess the military situation and discuss possible future developments, first in Khartoum with General Wavell, Mr Anthony Eden and the G.O.C. in the Sudan, Sir William Platt and, later, with the newly appointed G.O.C. in East Africa, General Cunningham in Nairobi. His conclusions from these talks together with his own personal observations would be the basis for the recommendations Mr Churchill had asked him to make.

After these high-level talks General Smuts wanted to see as much as possible of the situation on the long northern frontier of Kenya and, of course, his own men. This was a formidable task because the Union, by that time, had three Infantry brigades in Kenya, a strong element of the Air Force, Artillery, Engineers and ancillary units of every conceivable type.

In order that the General's visit should be kept secret, he was referred to in all signals as 'Mr Smith'. This was a futile piece of red tape. No 'Mr Smith' would look like General Smuts with his little beard, nor would he talk to his troops in Afrikaans so, within a few hours of his arrival, 'Mr Smith' became a myth — and the 'Oubaas' (old boss) a reality.

One particular security precaution was necessary, however. He had flown up from South Africa in a Lockheed 'Lodestar', an aircraft that was virtually unknown in East Africa at that time. So, lest this might be mistaken for a new type of Italian bomber, the General used one of the South African Junkers planes we knew to take him around Kenya.

In spite of this precaution, however, when one day he changed his itinerary in mid-flight and told the pilot to fly over Archer's Post, his unannounced plane was mistaken for an Italian bomber returning from a raid on Nanyuki or Nairobi. Two keen fighter pilots scrambled into the air and one of them put a burst of machine-gun fire into the Junkers before he realized his mistake. Happily this did no serious damage and the old gentleman emerged later unscathed, justifiably angry, but perfectly capable of continuing his tour of Kenya in order to make his report to Mr Churchill.

After a few happy days with the South Africans I reluctantly returned to Marsabit. I told the Brigadier that the Italians were moving pretty quickly with their work on the road down the escarpment from Mega, and that it could, possibly, be in use in a week.

'Right. I'll send a motorized patrol up as far as the frontier tomorrow,' he said. 'I want to know if the "Itis" are holding those two hills astride the road at Furroli.'

The patrol consisting of one company left at dawn. The distance to the frontier was about one hundred miles. They were to signal progress reports to us at half-hour intervals so that we could send an aircraft from the Marsabit airfield to fly over them as they reached the frontier, on towards the Italian road work, and then back to let the patrol know what he had seen by dropping a message on them.

At that time we had three Hartebeeste aircraft, two-seater biplanes with the gunner facing backwards. One of them was ready to fly off at a moment's notice but the airfield was thickly blanketed with fog and, hidden by the fog, where scores of camels and goats grazing. The pilot cheerfully said,

'I'm ready to go off any minute on a compass-bearing if only you can clear the ruddy animals off the field.'

I got the Askaris from the platoon guarding the airfield to hold hands and move slowly in a line across the runway in the direction of the take-off, driving the animals before them. We then gave the all-clear signal and the plane sped away with the rear gunner waving to us as they disappeared into the fog.

We expected the Hartebeeste back in about an hour and a quarter. We were not worried when they failed to arrive within that time, however, because they wouldn't know that the fog had cleared at Marsabit and would probably have landed on a small air-strip down on the plains at Turbi. We were completely puzzled, however, when the patrol signalled that they had neither seen nor heard any aircraft.

Some three hours later a car came back from the patrol and I asked the driver if he had seen the plane. 'Yes,' he said, 'there it is', and he pointed to a low hill only half a mile away. We could see it clearly. The pilot must have swung to his left almost as soon as he was airborne, had not gained sufficient height to clear the hill, hit the crest with his wheels and turned somersault. The fog had completely blanketed the sound of the crash.

Although we had not gained any information about the enemy through this expedition, shreds of news kept coming in indicating that the Mega area was being reinforced. Such reports were brought in from time to time by Jack Bonham and his Irregulars, a band of 'brigands' who were in contact with Italian-paid 'brigands', loosely termed Shifta. In peacetime these tough, freelance soldiers of fortune made a good living by raiding Kenya tribes such as the Gabra, Rendille and Boran who eked out a living from their camels and goats. In wartime, however, raiding of this sort was not on so they became informers, telling us, for a consideration, what they, or the Italians, wanted us to know and vice versa. The problem always was to sort out the grain from the chaff; to decide which report was reliable and which dubious.

One day, shortly after our abortive expedition to the border, Jack Bonham signalled to us that he had just received information from the Shifta that Italian troops were concentrating at Gardulla, a small town about one hundred miles north of the border. This could, perhaps, tie up with the road work on the escarpment. Jack was waiting with the Shifta at North Horr so the Brigadier said, 'You had better fly up there and check up on this report.'

I had always hated travelling by train with my back to the engine; I preferred to see where I was going. It was even worse being towed backwards in a Hartebeeste. To add to this discomfort the Chalbi Desert, over which we had to fly, was flooded as far as the eye could see; we might have been crossing the Atlantic. Luckily the air-strip at

North Horr was on slightly higher ground than this vast temporary lake and we landed safely.

Jack met me and took me to his camp. Nearby a number of dirty, bearded, wild-looking men were sitting together under a tree. They seemed to be quarrelling and all were talking at once.

'Who the hell are these men, Jack?' I asked. 'Have you been taking some prisoners?'

'Good Lord no; half of them are in my army and the others are the Shifta who have brought us the report about Gardulla,' he said. 'They are just having a friendly "get-together".'

Before interrogating our visitors, I told Jack I should like to have a word with his interpreter. But when he said, 'All right, I'll fetch him, he's with those chaps under the tree,' I changed my mind. If the interpreter was such a close buddy of the Shifta, he would back their story, right or wrong. So I went with Jack over to the small hut which served as a police station and asked to borrow an interpreter from them – and in informal civilian dress, normally a blanket. I told him to come unobtrusively to the meeting, not to say a word, but to listen to everything that was said, and tell me afterwards who said what.

When the proceedings started the Shifta leader, through the interpreter he knew, repeated the original story and made a strong recommendation that three specified targets at Gardulla should be bombed – that is, he said, if we really wanted to beat the Italians. I listened, put a few questions to him, and came to the conclusion that there must be Italian troops there and that a surprise bombing of their barracks or camp would be a deterrent to their advancing down the new road. He had described exactly where the camp was, as also the other two proposed targets, buildings which were being used for military stores. If they were depots for ammunition or petrol, they too should have our attention.

I thanked the Chief, assured him that they would be rewarded at once for their valuable help, and left the meeting.

At the police station the other interpreter gave me his story.

'Yes, *bwana*, I am sure he is right when he says there are many Italian Askaris at Gardulla and he says he will light a big fire near the camp on the day of the bombing so that the aeroplane can see it easily. Lakhini (but) – they did not say properly what is in the other two buildings. When they were talking among themselves, they only said dangerous people lived in those houses.' One, he thought, was probably an enemy of the chief and, from a chance remark about the other, 'That will fix her,' or words to that effect, she must be an unpopular female relation, possibly his mother-in-law!

The police interpreter was, shortly afterwards, promoted; the camp at Gardulla was duly bombed; but the other two target personalities are, so far as I know, still living.

20 Light tanks, guns and lorries which were captured when the
British took Agordat

21 The Italian envoy is taken back to Harar in an East African
armoured car to demand the immediate surrender of the town

22 The bridge over the Awash, blown up by the retreating Italians but replaced within a few hours by British engineers

23 Prisoners cross the Awash – a precarious scramble across the twisted debris of the mined bridge

24 South Africans march into Addis Ababa

25 The aerodrome at Addis Ababa was bombed repeatedly by the S.A.A.F.

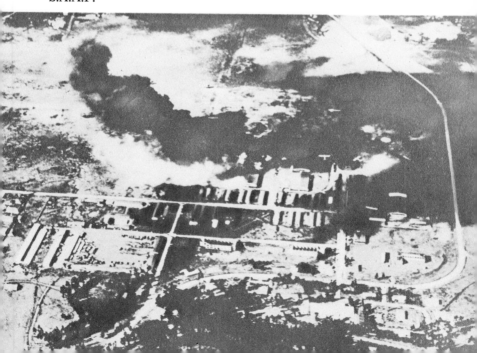

26 Burnt-out and damaged Italian planes on the aero-drome at Addis Ababa

27 Lieutenant-General Sir Alan Cunningham and Major-General Wetherall after the signing of the armistice at Addis Ababa

28 The Sudan Defence Force patrol their 1200-mile long frontier with Abyssinia

29 The Abyssinian frontier – approaches to Keren

30 British troops starting to move towards Keren

31 Manhandling motor transport through one of the demolition areas

32 Bombs falling on Keren

33 A cableway for taking light loads between Massawa and Asmara

34 (*Below:*) Demolitions along the road from Keren to Asmara

7

General Wavell's Strategy

We had settled down to a quiet country gentleman's life at Marsabit when we were ordered to leave our comfortable grass cottages in the forest and go to Garissa, the unpleasant, hot and unhealthy place on the Tana River. Though we did not know it at the time, General Wavell's complex plan was unfolding and our brigade was to take part in a major attack on Italian Somaliland to capture Kismayu.

Whilst we in Kenya, with our small but rapidly increasing resources, had been staving off and delaying the tentative advance of the Italians, General Wavell's preparations for a three-pronged drive into Abyssinia had been going ahead and he was almost ready to start. General Platt was threatening the Italians in the north from the Sudan, the Abyssinian Patriots were worrying them in the west and we in Kenya were gaining strength and beginning to change over from a defensive to an offensive role.

The essence of the Commander in Chief's plan was to divide and contain the large Italian forces at as many points as possible on these three fronts. To achieve this he had to make feint attacks in several places where he had no intention of pushing them very far, concentrate his main force where he intended to make his major drive — without, if possible, disclosing this to the enemy — and hide any weaknesses.

There was no question of General Platt being able to disguise the direction in which he would launch an attack on Abyssinia from the Sudan. There was only one way he could get there with the large force necessary and that was through a seemingly impregnable gorge flanked by mountains. The Patriots had no wish for disguise. Like a swarm of bees they were stinging here, there and everywhere and keeping an increasing number of Italian troops engaged in internal security measures. But General Cunningham could, and did, keep the

Italians guessing, even after his main drive had gone in towards Kismayu.

In January 1941 he had three divisions under his command; the 1st South African commanded by General Brink, and the 11th and 12th African Divisions commanded by Generals Wetherall and Godwin-Austen respectively. General Brink was given the task of advancing into Abyssinia in the west so he ordered his 25th East African Brigade to push northward on the west side of Lake Rudolf and his other two brigades, the 2nd and 5th South African, to move northward from Marsabit into southern Abyssinia with Mega, Moyale and Yavello as their main objectives.

It was not intended that this should develop into a major invasion of Abyssinia as the rains were due to start shortly and the roads in the high country would then become impassable. This feint attack with a strong force was very valuable, however, as it caused the Italians to reinforce this western front with troops from other areas and ruled out any question of their sending reinforcements to their Juba army.

It was possible, too, that some success in pushing the Italians out of southern Abyssinia would stimulate a rising in the Galla-Sidamo Province, but this did not materialize as there was little support for the Emperor in that area.

There were two roads from Marsabit into Abyssinia, one north-east to Moyale and another due north through Dukana. The former climbed a steep and easily defended escarpment so General Brink elected to take the other though longer route. After descending the lava slopes of Mount Marsabit it crossed the sandy and sometimes flooded Chalbi Desert and then virtually disappeared in rough bush country. However, thereafter it was an easy climb into the highlands — up the road I had seen the Italians making or repairing for their own use when I flew over it with the South Africans in a Fairey Battle.

The two brigades moved north in the last week of January 1941. They cleared two small Italian outposts inside Kenya and then crossed the boundary and camped the night of 30 January on Abyssinian soil between two mountains with the memorable names of Dibandibba and Murdur. Next day one brigade turned westward towards El Gumu and Hobok and the other eastward to Gorai. Gorai was a small, well-sited and defended fort but by skilful tactics and the use of artillery and armoured cars to support the infantry, it quickly fell. The Italians made little or no resistance at El Gumu and Hobok and the brigades moved on towards Mega.

This was a different proposition altogether. The fort and the surrounding hills were heavily defended, on one side there was a 3,000-foot escarpment, reconnaissance was difficult due to continuous rain, night temperature on the heights was near freezing and supplies were short due to Italian bombardment of their transport from the air. Nevertheless, by clever tactics, blocking the road from Yavello down which the Italians attempted to send reinforcements, manhandling guns through mud and up hills and, above all, by sheer perseverance and determination, they stormed and captured the fort on 18 February after three days hard fighting.

In the meanwhile a patrol of Abyssinian Irregulars attached to the brigades had found that Moyale had been evacuated, so General Brink was in control of the southern part of Abyssinia – but bogged down in the mud. So also were the Italian forces confronting them, the 21st and 24th Divisions with a further division, the 22nd, west of Lake Rudolf. In this way three enemy divisions plus one thousand six hundred Banda Irregulars with European officers and N.C.O.s were contained in the west and prevented from reinforcing their Juba River army.

General Cunningham's main attack was to be through Italian Somaliland to the Juba River and so, in preparation for this, he had moved his other two divisions, the 11th and 12th, down to Bura and Garissa on the Tana River leaving only one brigade in the centre of his wide front – at Wajir.

But this too, the 1st South African Brigade, was shortly to move towards the Juba to join in the main drive and, when it did, there would be a gap of some three hundred miles – between Moyale and Afmadu – in which there would virtually be no fighting troops at all. Had the Italians known this they could have driven straight through to Nairobi.

There were no spare troops to fill this gap so a 4th (Australian) Division was invented with its headquarters at Wajir. One battalion and a large Signals unit did the job. Dummy tanks were moved from place to place by night on trucks and were then camouflaged – with careful inadequacy so that they would be distinguishable in the photos taken by Italian reconnaissance aircraft – and realistic track marks were made around them. Seven Signals vans were kept fully occupied transmitting and receiving hundreds of previously prepared messages for the enemy interceptor sets to pick up. The Italian commander at Bardera was alerted and told by his higher command to make preparations to counter this threatened attack in the centre. The bluff succeeded.

It was 'touch and go' whether the advance into Italian Somaliland could be made in time. Unless a start were made in early February the whole plan would have to be postponed for several months because the big rains, due to start in March, would turn the roads into morasses. The unsolved problem was how to supply the troops with water. There was no reliable existing source between the Tana and Juba Rivers, a distance of some 200 miles, and General Cunningham could not guarantee to reach the Juba in any specific time as he would have battles to fight on the way. He could not say 'go' unless he could either transport water by road or find it along his line of advance.

While the whole situation in Kenya had been changed with the recent arrival from South Africa of an infantry division, guns, aircraft, armoured cars and light tanks, the most important items at that time were the trucks, road-making machinery and water-boring equipment which came with them. They were as manna from heaven. The South African sappers started to work at once and rough tracks through the bush soon became passable roads. General Cunningham then knew that he could, at a pinch, start his advance and carry water by road with the newly acquired motor transport. This would be risky: the position would only be really satisfactory if some of the boreholes now being sunk produced water. It was said at the time that when Mr Churchill asked General Wavell, 'When the hell is Cunningham going to get moving towards Kismayu?' the correct answer would have been, 'As soon as Sergeant Van der Merwe and his rig strike water at Hagadera.'

The Sergeant did – in the last days of January.

Behind the scenes there had been high drama over the water problem. Churchill had been saying for some months that Wavell should go into Abyssinia at once or send the South African and the two West African brigades to Egypt. Wavell, determined to keep them until he was ready to move, stalled saying that the South Africans required further training, acclimatization, and experience with malaria precautions etc.! At the beginning of January, however, when the South Africans had been in Kenya for five months, Smuts entered the fray. He too wanted to see some action so he signalled to Churchill recommending an early offensive. Churchill was, of course, delighted at this support for his own view and he told the C.I.G.S. to get on to Wavell who got on to Cunningham. Cunningham said firmly that he was as eager as anyone to move but could not do so until he had solved the water problem. Wavell supported this contention, so generating considerable Churchillian heat which was expressed in a personal signal to him on 26 January – almost the exact day when water was found at Hagadera. Cunningham replied that he was off to Kismayu and everybody cooled off.

When orders were given for the main advance into Italian Somaliland to start, the 1st (South African) Brigade moved eastward from Wajir and crossed the frontier, at the small post of Dif. They encountered little opposition on the ground mainly because a month earlier they had carried out a strong and successful attack on the frontier post of El Wak and, as a result of this, nearly all Italian troops other than Banda had been withdrawn from the border towards Afmadu and the Juba River. But they were severely harassed by enemy aircraft until, on 2 and 3 February, the Hurricanes of 3 Squadron S.A.A.F. shot down or destroyed on the ground at least twelve and possibly fourteen Italian planes. The highest scorers were Captain Jack Frost and Captain van Breda Theron, each of whom won the D.F.C. After that the *Regia Aeronautica* was seldom in evidence during the advance to Mogadishu.

In the meanwhile the two other brigades in the 12th Division, our 22nd and the Gold Coast Brigade, moved forward from Garissa into Somaliland. So did the 11th Division which consisted of the Nigerian Brigade and the Northern Rhodesian Rifles from their starting-point, Bura on the Tana River.

The overall situation at that time was summed up as follows by Mr John Connell in his biography of General Wavell: 'By the end of the first week in February an immensely complicated delicate series of major operations, spread over a huge area, inhibited by every kind of administrative, communications, transport and climatic difficulty, was well in train.'

The master plan had started to unfold and the three-pronged attack to develop.

The three prongs were different in character and had different roles to play. General Platt's force, which was to attack the Italians from the Sudan, consisted of the 4th and 5th British Indian Divisions (the former with recent successes against General Rommel in the Western Desert to their credit) supported by six squadrons of aircraft and plenty of guns and armour. His was an experienced, well-equipped professional army backed by years of tradition.

The 'Patriots' were the Resistance Movement in Abyssinia which had carried on guerrilla warfare against the Italians ever since the invasion of their country in 1936. Some of them had been forced to take refuge in Kenya, British Somaliland or the Sudan to save their families from the mass punitive measures taken against them by the Italian army, but the movement had continued sporadically in the mountainous areas in north-west Abyssinia under the stimulus of several stalwart leaders.

To evaluate the Patriots as a military force they must be put into two categories, the freelance medieval-type mercenaries who, at the behest of their feudal chieftain, rallied round him bringing their own arms and food; and then those who enlisted as Irregular soldiers and were paid and equipped. The latter were mainly recruited from those who had sought refuge outside Abyssinia.

The strength of the freelance movement was incalculable in ordinary military terms just as its harassment of the Italians was of inestimable value – when its potential and limitations were recognized. Their enthusiasm ebbed and flowed with the fortunes of war: at times it was ebullient and at others near moribund, whilst their numbers could vary from thousands to dozens in a matter of days. They were courageous but rash, at times co-operative but always unorganized, and the modicum of discipline they had was due only to feudal custom. Most, but by no means all of them, had a burning desire to drive the Italian invaders from their country. Their tactics were to ravage the enemy like wolves then slip away like foxes, slip away to live and fight another day. They obtained arms and ammunition by ambushing Italian army vehicles and raiding depots. The country was never tamed and the Italians had to maintain garrisons throughout the land and, at times, stage punitive operations using armour and air-craft as well as infantry. The maintenance of internal security was a drain on their military strength – but it provided good training for their troops. It was to foster, nourish, encourage and organize these rather intangible and nebulous allies that Brigadier Sandford and his band of helpers entered Abyssinia from the Sudan in August 1940 to establish a secret base in the forest and prepare the ground for the return of the Emperor.

Some of the Abyssinians who were being enlisted and trained as Irregulars had been in Kenya since 1937, others had just arrived at Mombasa after being evacuated from British Somaliland, whilst a number had just walked across the border into Kenya and volunteered their services. They were being trained as scouts and general fighters by some splendidly irregular white officers.

Lastly we, the third prong, consisting of the South and East Africans, were 90 per cent enthusiastic amateurs with a leavening of 10 per cent professionals. We were good material but, at first, completely inexperienced in warfare. However, with the material resources of South Africa and good leadership, we could develop into a useful force.

8

The Advance into Italian Somaliland

DECEMBER 1940 TO FEBRUARY 1941

Our move from Marsabit to Garissa meant a journey of about five hundred miles as we had to go back to within thirty miles of Nairobi and then turn east.

Passing through the farms and coffee plantations near Thika made one long to get back to see how one's own crops were faring and how the men were doing. Had they pruned the coffee trees too lightly this year? They hated cutting off any branches with berries on them thinking this wasteful. But a tree could only ripen so much and if one left too big a crop on it the branches would die back. That meant no crop the year after.

I was travelling with Sam at the time. It was particularly tough for him because his father's coffee plantation was almost in sight when we swept off eastwards towards Garissa. However, he had had some leave recently and was telling me about it:

'My old man looks ten years younger since he has been back in the Navy. The Kenya Navy only has two or three launches, of course, but he dashes about in one of these as if he were in command of a destroyer again!'

'Good for him,' I said, 'but what about the coffee?'

'It's super, better than ever before. Mum's running the place jolly well. She's got more patience with the Africans than Dad – and they like that.'

We were in the middle of the dry season and its problems. I hoped they were not irrigating the coffee on my plantation. I was always being urged to do so at this time of year, but that would bring it into flower at the wrong season and the blossom would then dry off with the hot sun.

By the time I had stopped worrying about this we had left the last of the farms and plantations behind and were speeding along the dusty, uninteresting, featureless road which led to the Tana River some two hundred miles away. There were no hills to look at, the land was flat. Nor were there any fields or glades because the country was entirely covered with thorn-bush. Camels and goats seemed to exist on it – but it was no good to God or man. We knew it was pretty well the same as far as the Juba River and, for all we knew, it could be the same as far as the Horn of Africa.

But Sam took my mind off the bush and kept me interested by telling me about the different crops he wanted to try after the war.

'I'm sure we shouldn't have all our eggs in one basket,' he said. 'My old man nearly went bust ten years ago when the bottom fell out of the coffee market. When I get back I'm going to plant acres of pawpaw trees and produce papain. Then, if I can get hold of a bit of land up Limuru way, I shall grow Pyrethrum.'

We argued the 'pros' and 'cons' of these prospective money-spinners for some time and then I turned to Jackson, who was sitting behind us. He was a farmer at heart and I asked him what crops he grew.

'Only maize, potatoes, and bananas, *bwana*. Then I have all I want to eat and plenty of banana beer to drink.'

'Well,' said Sam, 'you won't starve or die of thirst, but you won't get rich.'

'But I am rich, *bwana*. I have two wives, two cows, and some children. I have all I want.'

I replied with the Swahili word *kweli* which means 'really?', 'how true', '*n'est ce pas*', or 'of course', according to the intonation. A good language, a rich one too.

Time passed quickly. Suddenly we saw an Askari standing in the middle of the road and waving a flag at us. We had arrived at the camp-site. We got out, stretched our stiff limbs and got to work. The Askaris were soon busy with their pangas cutting firewood and the poles to make our customary little grass huts.

When the sun went down the night air was pleasantly cool. Sitting out in the bright starlight, gazing at the glow of camp-fires and listening to the laughter of the Askaris, one forgot the desolation of the countryside and thought of better and more important things.

Only in conditions such as these did one make so many friends and enjoy to the full the simple pleasures of life. At that moment my soliloquy was interrupted by Jackson bringing one of those simple pleasures, a mug of tea laced to the exact strength he knew I liked it.

Next morning I went to see the river which was two miles farther along the road. To camp nearer to it meant malaria for a certainty. I was surprised to find there was no bridge across it; everything and everybody had to be ferried over. How were we to wage a war with an antediluvian piece of nonsense like this? But I needn't have worried: within a week the sappers had provided us with a pontoon bridge that would carry any vehicle we had, even an armoured car.

The river was infested not only by malarial mosquitoes and crocodile but, at certain seasons, by elephant. It was, therefore, a favourite hunting area but, as there was no hunting in wartime, the elephant population and its depredation of crops increased until it was necessary for someone to shoot a few and drive them away from the cultivated areas. One old elephant had the impertinence to make regular raids on the District Commissioner's garden in Garissa where the vegetables were particularly succulent. The Commissioner, being a man of some dignity, was outraged. This was *lèse majesté*. So, when he heard that Jack Bonham, who before the war had been carrying out elephant control for the Game Department, had arrived with us, he saw, or thought he saw the answer to his problem.

The note he sent to Jack was the sort of thing some senior civil servants write to their juniors, it was somewhat peremptory. But Irregulars, even more than most of us, dislike peremptoriness so Jack came and discussed the matter with me. We made a plan which hinged entirely on Jack being sent off on a longish patrol in a day or so. This was quite easy to arrange because we wanted him to contact John Llewellin who was scouting about somewhere on the frontier with his Irregulars.

Jack sent a polite reply to the District Commissioner promising to help him. He caught the elephant that very night in *flagrante delicto* and shot it – in the D.C.'s garden. Next morning he left Garissa for the border.

Now the moving of four or five tons of elephant is quite a job, particularly when it has been lying around for a bit. After a couple of days there was an unpleasant smell in and about the house and this grew worse day by day. The health officer respectfully told the D.C. that the offensive and rapidly decomposing body should be removed at once, and the Public Works Department, with equal respect, said the job was not within their terms of reference. I believe the angry and defeated D.C. then went on safari, probably to get a breath of fresh air. How the carcase was eventually disposed of, I know not. This was partly because I went with Jack to see John Llewellin. He was commanding the Kenya Somali Irregulars patrolling the border with

Italian Somaliland where they had had several brushes with their Italian counterparts, the Banda. Here was a perfect example of a round peg in a round hole. John had spent some eight years of his service in the Colonial Administration in various parts of the Northern Frontier District, spoke fluent Somali, knew every bit of that vast area and also the history and clan structure of the people. He had never been a keen office wallah so, when General Dickinson accepted his offer to join the Irregulars, he was as happy as a sandboy, striding around his domain or doing a 'recce' along the frontier strip in a Land Rover. Perhaps 'sandboy' is not the correct word as he must have been near the fifty mark – but that wasn't a subject any wise man broached with him. When Jack and I found him on the boundary near Liboi, 'Long Llew' eyed us through his monocle and said, 'Have you brought my gin from NAAFI? Can't drink the filthy water here without gin you know.' We apologized for not having anticipated this need, produced a fair substitute, and, when I set off back leaving Jack with him, I promised to send supplies up to him – together with the necessary angostura bitters.

In the middle of January the Brigadier received orders to occupy Liboi as part of a general move forward by the two divisions to the Italian Somaliland border. It so happened that the Brigade Major was then on leave and the Staff Captain had rushed back to Nairobi to inspect his newly born baby. So I, once again, was left holding the metaphorical baby, just as I had been on the declaration of war on Germany, and my heart sank when the Brigadier said: 'Get out an operation order at once.'

Grimly I got out my text book and put down all the headings; Information, Intention, Method and Administration. Then I gradually filled it in. Later, with some apprehension, I took the draft to the Brigadier. He grunted, corrected my mistakes and omissions and then said, 'Have it typed – and get the distribution right.'

Only much later did I realize how lengthy and long-winded these text book orders were compared with those issued subsequently in the war which were brief, succinct and often just verbal.

It was quite a tricky business moving a Brigade Group into country held, albeit lightly, by the enemy. With thick bush on each side of the road it would be only too easy for the Banda to ambush us. The Brigadier decided to move in three columns. The first, a reconnaissance group, was to consist of some armoured cars, a detachment of sappers and two companies of infantry. The second, the main striking force with two battalions and Advanced Brigade

Headquarters, was to follow an hour later. The commanding officers of the two battalions were to be with Brigade Headquarters so that orders could be given to them immediately in case of need. The third column, to follow several hours later, contained all the administrative odds and ends including a water-carrying transport company plus infantry to protect it.

We left the Tana River on 23 January, moved some hundred miles towards the border, closed the whole force into a Boer War type camp, or *laager*, protected its perimeter by a thorn fence, and bivouacked for the night. At dawn next day the recce column went forward again and the leading armoured cars came under fire two miles before reaching the border.

The enemy Irregulars had prepared an ambush for the armoured cars as we had anticipated. They had dug a ditch across the track and nearly succeeded in setting fire to the leading car with Breda bombs and bottles of petrol. They withdrew when the other cars and the infantry fired on them killing several, but there were three further similar attacks before we reached the border where we stayed for two nights.

This was our first experience of being short of water: we had to manage on a gallon each per day for everything; drinking, washing, cooking, shaving and brushing one's teeth. It was remarkable, though, how well one could do on this – if one had a good sponge. We were better at it than the Askaris who only learnt through uncomfortable experience that they could not have the good daily splash they liked under a shower, a tap, or in a river or pool.

Every drop of water we used was being brought up to us in old petrol tins on lorries from the Tana River, now over one hundred miles behind us. The South African Engineers had been drilling for water at Hagadera, about half way between us and the river and, as soon as we could clear the Banda from the Liboi area, they would start another rig there.

Liboi was not the thriving little country town one might imagine from looking at the map. It was merely the point where our track from Garissa met the boundary cut and, so far as we could see, ended. There was a corrugated-iron hut there which had seen better days, but there was no indication what purpose it had served.

Our major objective was the garrison town of Afmadu, one hundred miles East of Liboi – as the crow flies. This probably meant about one hundred and fifty miles for us, winding through the bush. The map showed that there was a track of sorts to it and several 'water-holes, seasonal' on the way there at places named Dobli, Hawina, Del Hola, and Beles Gugani.

The first thing to do was to reconnoitre into Somaliland to find out what the track ahead was like, if there was one, and where the Banda now were. The only information we had was from two of the ambushers we had captured. They told us that their *sotto gruppo*, or small detachment, was based on Hawina, thirty-five miles farther on, with their Group Headquarters at Beles Gugani. But the tactics of the Banda, we knew, were not to defend any base but to maintain a mobile screen in front of us and to delay and harass us by ambush and sniping.

When, therefore, the Brigadier said to me next day, 'Take two of the armoured cars and have a look at the country ahead,' I said 'Yes, sir,' and went over to have a talk with the officer commanding the section of the Rhodesian Armoured Cars.

'We don't know what the country ahead is like,' I told him, 'but there must be a track of sorts through the bush in which the visibility looks to be about thirty yards. We must expect to be sniped and, possibly, ambushed, so I propose to ask the Brigadier for a section of infantry to follow about a hundred yards behind us in a truck. Then, if we are ambushed or get stuck in a drift, they could cover us while we get ourselves out. That would prevent the Banda from doing any funny stuff with petrol bombs.'

He agreed and I went back to the Brigadier to put the proposal to him.

I expected he would consider me 'lacking moral fibre' for asking for more men but, as I was advocating the use of his own favourite ploy, the loose column exercise we had practised so assiduously at Wajir, I was on a fairly good wicket and got what I asked for.

It was difficult going and we had to twist and turn through the bush. Before long some shots were fired at us and we heard some grenades exploding away in front. This, we found out later, was a means of letting their friends farther back know how many vehicles were coming.

After about three miles the bush became less thick and a track clearly visible. The going was then quite good. We never saw a soul but I had the uncanny feeling that they could see us. Just as we had thought, they were withdrawing as we went forward and would return when we did. With these slender pieces of information we returned to Advance Brigade Headquarters – this consisted of the Brigadier sitting under a tree.

Next day a South African reconnaissance aircraft flew over us photographing the track and the country ahead. These pictures were turned into maps and dropped on us the day after. They showed that the track had not been maintained for some time and appeared impassable in places on account of gullies made by the last heavy rains. Nevertheless two companies of K.A.R. with some armoured cars managed to reach Hawina on 27 January. They met with some resistance but soon overcame it and took possession of the small water-hole there and a camp nearby in the bush where the Banda kept their supplies and reserves of ammunition. The main advantage we had gained by this advance was that the road machinery could work right up to this point — and in two days it was doing so.

We wanted to get the bulldozers working as soon as possible on the next stage after Hawina because the aerial photographs had shown that the track beyond that was almost non-existent. The Brigadier decided, therefore, to move straight on and take Beles Gugani. This was expected to be a tougher proposition as it was garrisoned by regular troops as well as Banda.

The task of taking it was given to the 1st K.A.R. supported by a platoon of armoured cars and a troop of the 22nd Mountain Battery. This force moved to within about two miles of the village of Beles Gugani on 3 February and attacked at daylight on the 4th. Contact was soon made with the enemy forward positions but, when they saw our Askaris coming for them with fixed bayonets, they took to their heels. Our men followed up, yelling wildly, overran the front positions, and pressed forward to the main defences. This was too much for the Italian garrison who then fled in disorder leaving machine-guns, rifles, and large quantities of ammunition. There was neither opportunity nor need to bring our guns into action.

The most important item captured was the well. Although the new bore-holes were producing some water, the Transport Company was at full stretch and this would bring them a little relief. The well water was not very good but this was not surprising when, two days later, we found the body of a dead Banda in it.

The success of this exemplary, set-piece, text book attack was, of course, exhilarating and morale-boosting — but it had another side. I had been anxious over the outcome because my brother had been leading the attack in one sector. When I followed them up, however, I was assured that not one of our men had been killed and only six wounded — two officers and four Askaris. Since the Italians had been defending prepared positions with machine-gun as well as rifle fire, this was almost incredible and showed that they had fired hastily and high in their anxiety to be out of it and away.

That evening I went over to the 1st K.A.R. bivouac area, found my brother, and said.

'Well done, old chap. A very stout show.'

'I suppose it was – in a way,' he replied. 'I know it's no use fighting a war with gloves on, it's got to be all or nothing. But, do you know, I had to stop two of our Askaris pulling some of the Banda down from a tree where they had hidden so that they could bayonet them. They said "But you told us to kill them, *bwana*." It was no good my saying, "Yes, but not when they are in trees, not in cold blood", because, to them, that would be a distinction without a difference! God knows what the future repercussions of our "civilizing influence" will be.'

He was right of course – and, perhaps had a psychic glimpse into the future ... Mau Mau? Vietnam?

Unfortunately our 'civilization' has no absolute meaning. We are evolving from barbarism, but have a long way to go before we reach the stage at which logic and reason replace force. Mussolini declared war on us, not we on him, and now nothing on earth would stop him – except force. Perhaps God has not performed the duty of universal headmaster as we had hoped He would. So, in the meanwhile, down with Savoia and *Avanti Britannia*!

That night we were just settling down comfortably, the Askaris, justifiably pleased with themselves, chattering and laughing, when all hell was let loose. Bullets whined overhead from two sides and exploding, but fairly innocuous, 'letter-box' grenades added to the inferno. It must have been an Italian patrol which had left Beles Gugani before the battle and returned somewhat late to find the place in other hands. Luckily for us all the shots were high and did no damage. We returned their fire and, shortly afterwards, they disappeared into the night.

Jackson and I set off back to Brigade Headquarters early next morning. We must have been only half awake because we forgot to take my camp-bed. This led to my indiscretion about which I learnt later from my Italian farmer friend, Davico di Quittengo. I sent a signal in clear from Brigade to 1 K.A.R. which read: 'Please send my camp-bed left Beles Gugani.' I added my name.

Davico who, at that time, had a Signals van equipped to intercept our messages, picked this up and, knowing that I was with, or associated with the 1st K.A.R., was assisted in compiling our Order of Battle by my carelessness. In the event this piece of information didn't help them very much: it is even possible that they panicked after finding out that the 1st K.A.R. were on their tails again!

Our Brigade was ready to move forward to capture the small garrison town of Afmadu. When we had done this the other two Brigades in the 12th Division, the 1st South African and the Gold Coast Brigades, would pass through us and move to two points on the west bank of the Juba River.

This movement of our three Brigade Groups, now almost four hundred miles from base in Nairobi and comprising some fifteen thousand men, was a complex business which depended for its successful achievement on accurate timing. Our task was to take Afmadu on the morning of 11 February, not sooner and not later.

We knew from aerial photographs that the defences were very similar to those around our fort at Moyale. It was strongly protected on all sides by wire and was held by regular troops, the 94th Colonial Infantry Battalion, supported by artillery, machine-guns, and mortars. There could also be a large number of Banda in the fort if they had withdrawn there after being pushed back from Hawina and Beles Gugani. We had a further report that a larger force than that in the fort was camped in the bush nearby to reinforce them or counter-attack – our old friend the loose column again.

The Brigadier moved his three battalions, the guns and his own headquarters to different points around Afmadu on 7 February. We were all well hidden under tall shady trees and as the Italians did not send out any patrols, an uncanny, unreal euphoria set in. This was brief, however, because someone carelessly set fire to the tinder-dry grass. It blazed furiously and swept quickly along in an unstemmable tide – but luckily only on the other side of the road from our bivouac areas and the road made a good fire-break.

We were luckier than we then realized. The grass fire burnt itself out in about half an hour leaving a black waste, but the bush had caught fire too and the stumps were still burning when night fell. Apparently the Italians thought these were our camp-fires and signalled for Savoia bombers to come and blast the area. This they did thoroughly and, I am glad to say, accurately. Not a single bomb fell on our side of the road.

In the meanwhile our patrols had been busy: it was necessary to find out as much as possible about the ground defences and to observe the firing of our guns which were registering. I found that by climbing one of the trees at Brigade Headquarters I could see the buildings quite clearly. But this was not good enough for the gunners, we were about a thousand yards away. Even our forward positions, about five hundred yards from the enemy wire, were not good enough for them owing to some thick bush, so two of them crept nearer still and established an observation post on the edge of the Italian landing-ground, two hundred yards from their defences.

At midday on 10 February the Brigadier gave out his orders. Two battalions were to move to the north of the township and take up positions for an attack at dawn next morning. During this move, and at dawn, the third battalion was to demonstrate on the west side. The guns and machine-guns were sited to support both the feint and the real attack. That afternoon the fort was bombed by our Junkers and Fairey 'Battles' and shelled by the Mountain Battery.

This was too much for the garrison. They all slipped away in the night and, when the attack went in at 5.30 next morning, the cupboard was bare – or almost. One Italian, who had somehow been left behind, said to me sadly,

'You have only to make a noise like an armoured car and you will be in Mogadishu in a fortnight.'

He was right – to the day!

We found that Afmadu, far from being a township, would hardly rate as a village: there was only one decent building in it. Thinking this would do as our headquarters, I went in. But Michael Biggs, the Brigade Major, had beaten me to it and had already found himself a desk and a chair.

'We've just heard that part of that Colonial battalion has made off towards the Juba,' he said. 'The Brigadier has sent the 5th K.A.R. to follow them up. I don't expect they'll have any luck, though; it will be like looking for a needle in a haystack in the bush. They won't use the roads because the armoured cars are patrolling them.'

'What about asking for an aircraft to look for them?' I suggested.

He had, of course, already done so. It's not often that one can catch a brigade major out. They are chosen from the exceptional few who are both hard-working and intelligent and are the material from which future generals are selected. The German army had a subtle formula for grading their officers which went something like this:

Staff Officers must be both intelligent and industrious;
Commanders need only be intelligent;
Work can always be found for those who are lazy and unintelligent,
But never for those who are unintelligent but industrious.

Michael was in the first category, but even he had his problems. I have already said, and it was an understatement, that the Brigadier was never at his best after winning a battle. He had just won one, so Michael said, 'Let's get out of here before the old man comes. We ought to have a look around the place.'

First we went to the side of the perimeter we had intended to attack. The battalion on that front had planted and exploded several Bangalore torpedoes under the barbed wire defences to make gaps for the attacking troops to pass through. The result was far from satisfactory.

'Make a note of that,' said Michael. 'We must put in some practice with these torpedoes. If the "Itos" hadn't run for it, we should have had some heavy casualties here.'

By the landing-ground we found two abandoned Bofors anti-aircraft guns.

'I didn't know they had any of these. But the odd thing is that they don't appear to have been fired. That was lucky for our bombers. Make a note of this for Div.' I did.

When we got back to our newly acquired office I had a good look around the building. It had obviously been the residence of the Italian district commissioner. He had left no papers of any value but something far more important at that time, a sunken marble bath. Now was the time to use it, before Divisional Headquarters took it over. But, just as I was getting undressed, the Brigadier sent for me. Dirty and disappointed, I went to find him. He was sitting in his car. He said he didn't like the look of the office we had found for him – but I don't think he liked the look of anything or anybody that morning.

'They've run into some Italians in the bush on the east side of the village,' he said. 'Get after them and find out what is happening.'

I went over to our transport lines, collected a small truck, Jackson, two other Askaris, and a Bren gun. Sergeant Rockett was, as usual, worrying about his trucks and fussing around them like a hen with chicks.

'Yer won't knock it abaht will yer, sir. Yer remember that other time ...' I thanked him and drove off.

We cruised slowly along the road towards Kismayu. The surface was soft and dusty and, before we had gone very far, we saw unmistakable tracks where a large number of men had crossed over and gone into the bush. I turned off the road and tried to follow the tracks but decided to give this up: the noise we made would be heard a mile away and, also, Sergeant Rockett wouldn't like us to go barging through this sort of stuff.

We went on on foot for about half an hour when, suddenly, we came across the dead bodies of several of our Askaris. They must have run into an ambush. We fired a burst from the Bren into the bush ahead and, getting no reply, went on.

About twenty yards ahead there was a small clearing which, until a matter of minutes ago, had been the sleeping quarters of about fifty Italian officers. They must have fled into the bush in confusion at a moment's notice when flushed by one of our patrols. I stood there knowing just how Aladdin had felt when he discovered his cave. There were luxurious sprung camp-beds mounted on sledges, tables, chairs, half-packed suitcases with silk pyjamas, bottles of eau de cologne and hairbrushes lying about abandoned in their haste. An eerie silence reigned. I slipped an attractive cake of soap into my pocket. I think Jackson noticed this but, as I couldn't think of the Swahili for 'Cleanliness is next to Godliness', I went on.

'Shall I go back and fetch the truck, *bwana*? We could do with a lot of these things.'

How I wished I hadn't brought Jackson. I remembered distinctly telling him that, later, there would be spoils of war, booty, and loot. Here it was – for the taking. Luckily our attention was distracted at the moment by a rustling noise. I signalled to Jackson to be quiet and we crept forward. It was some camels grazing peacefully around a pile of sacks of some kind of food. It was they, presumably, who had pulled the sledge-type beds through the bush. A little further on we came to the kitchen area – with a meal still cooking. This was all that remained of the 94th Colonial Infantry Battalion.

We returned to Afmadu and arranged for Transport to collect the booty. There was a lot: I know they had to make two trips.

9

Kismayu

14 FEBRUARY 1941

An official account of the operations of the 22nd East African Brigade records that, on the day of the capture of Afmadu, 'The Gold Coast Infantry Brigade and the 1st South African Infantry Brigade had passed through Afmadu towards their respective objectives and by nightfall it was possible to withdraw the majority of the 22nd East African Infantry Brigade into reserve for a well-needed night's rest.'

We had three good nights' rest – and I got my bath – but, on 14 February, we were told by Division to go hot-foot to Kismayu. The brigade which had been moving on a line parallel to ours from Bura on the Tana River had been held up and had not reached Kismayu as had been expected. The Italians had mined their track and the Banda were being particularly offensive to them.

My indefatigable Brigadier, with the scent of battle still in his nostrils, snorted, 'Get a couple of trucks and a small escort; we'll go and see what the devil is happening down there.' It took me half an hour to organize the party. I shouted to Sam, 'Bring your spade and bucket, we're really going to the seaside this time.' Then, after I had been to face Sergeant Rockett again, I told Jackson to pack up and arranged the escort with rations, water and ammunition. Meanwhile the Brigadier had been working out plans for the Brigade with Michael: he wanted two battalions to follow him and one to remain at Afmadu.

It was of vital importance that Kismayu should be captured – and quickly. The success or failure of the Cunningham drive depended on this. We were carrying supplies and water to last until 21 February so, if further supplies could not be shipped into Kismayu harbour during the next few days or, failing this, dumped on the shore for us near Gobwen, a general withdrawal back to Kenya would be necessary.

The sandy road running south-east to the coast was fairly good and, as the old man drove like Jehu, we soon left the escort far behind. Had the Italians evacuated Kismayu or should we meet with a warm reception? What had happened to the other brigade? We had to find out. I reckoned it was about seventy miles to Kismayu but the map we were using was not very reliable. When we had covered thirty miles we found the Rear Headquarters of the South African Brigade: their main body had struck off across country eastward to the Juba River.

The Divisional Commander, General Godwin-Austen, was there so the Brigadier took the opportunity of borrowing a few armoured cars and a battery of 18-pounder guns – just in case we ran into any difficulty at Kismayu. This seemed just as easy as popping across the road to borrow a bit of tea from one's neighbour. But I heard the Divisional Commander say, 'Don't you keep them a minute longer than necessary, we shall need them tomorrow by the river.'

Whilst this high-powered negotiation had been going on, the C.O. of our front battalion caught us up.

'What's the situation?' he asked me.

This was a difficult question to answer. I felt like saying that all I knew for certain was that it was a lovely day but I realized in time that this would not be a suitable answer to give to a senior officer and one who was obviously uneasy about the numerous current uncertainties. So I refrained from being facetious and told him all I knew – which was little indeed.

'We must assume,' he said, 'that Kismayu is still occupied until we are certain that it is not. Furthermore, there must, undoubtedly, be another enemy force somewhere on our right and in contact with the 21st Brigade coming from Bura.'

A more worrying point, however, was that his speedometer, when compared with his map, showed that we should now be well into the Indian Ocean. The Brigadier, unperturbed even by this discovery, pressed on. Shortly we passed through the South African Brigade outposts whose anti-tank rifles were pointing ominously in the direction we were going.

After a further twenty miles I said,

'I think we must be somewhere near the cross-roads where the Bura road comes in, sir. Do you think we should go a bit slower?'

'Nonsense,' said he, and put his foot even harder down on the accelerator. But, just as he said that, we shot across the other road. We then stopped, looked and listened. We should also have offered up a prayer of thanksgiving. The sappers following us found that the Italians had recently removed mines from the middle of the road, presumably to use it themselves, but had left them embedded on each side.

We could now smell the sea, or so we thought. A mile or two in front of us rose the red sand-dunes, some two hundred feet high, which run all along the coast both north and south of the Juba. We scanned these with our field-glasses and were able to pick out some of the Italian positions on the lower slopes.

'We'll now go on and try to draw their fire,' said the Brigadier. He was in no mood to be told that this was scarcely the job of the Brigade Commander, so on we went, slowly this time, until we saw a wired barrier across the road. By then our escort, the borrowed armoured cars and the forward company of our leading battalion, had caught us up. The armoured cars fired some bursts at the road barrier and then at the positions on the dunes. There was no reply so we towed the barrier away — using a good long cable in case it was booby trapped — and motored on, over the dunes and into Kismayu. The Italians had gone.

The change of scenery was sheer delight: coconut palms instead of bush, a clean, white beach instead of grey dust and, above all, water; miles and miles of it, millions of gallons of the beautiful blue stuff.

The town was *en fête*, uproariously and drunkenly so. It might have been the Relief of Mafeking or the end of World War I. The entire population must have been in the streets to welcome us and several hundred of them, in a long line, were dancing the Conga, dragging looted cinema film behind them and chanting wildly. Had Gerald Durrell got the Fon of Bafut to coach them, they couldn't have done it better.

It is said that *veritas* is in *vino*. But I wondered whether, had they been sober, they would have welcomed us so warmly. After all we had abandoned them when we ceded Jubaland to Italy after the 1914-18 War.

I couldn't let this thought worry me for long: we had other things to do. We set up our headquarters in a splendid building and ran up the Union Jack. We had proper office chairs and desks — and even a telephone.

'Put me through to the Duca d'Aosta, I want to give him some advice,' said the Brigadier laughing. But the line was dead.

Just then the escort commander came in. 'Are there any Italians left here?' asked the Brigadier. 'Yes, sir. One. He's at the post office. He destroyed the equipment and then got as drunk as a coot so we're leaving him there for the time being.'

In the meanwhile our two battalions had arrived and hundreds of Askaris were having what was probably their first ever bathe in the sea and were revelling in it.

Our Signals were, by then, in contact with Command Headquarters in Nairobi. They told us that the G.O.C. was on his way up to us in his De Havilland 'Rapide'. They also told us to find out whether the Italian coast batteries on the two islands at the entrance to Kismayu harbour, Dei Serpenti and Mlango wa Papa, were still manned. If so the sooner we unmanned them the sooner would the navy be able to send us a ship from Mombasa which was ready to leave and laden with supplies of all kinds — including some bottles from NAAFI. Command Headquarters really was on the ball.

I went down to the harbour to beg, borrow or steal a couple of boats with crews. Never have we had so many willing but incapable helpers. They could scarcely stand, never mind row or swim. But I got some volunteers from the Nyasaland Askaris in the 1st K.A.R. who were expert sailors on their own lake. Then a young Kenya subaltern came up and said, 'I do a bit of sailing at Mombasa, sir. Can I go with them?' So I put him in charge of the expedition. He took one local man with him who, after an involuntary ducking, had sobered up a bit. They rowed in good style over to Dei Serpenti and were back in two hours after finding the island abandoned and the guns spiked.

The 5th K.A.R., not to be outdone nautically, took a small dhow across the harbour next morning and occupied Mlango wa Papa. We were then able to assure Nairobi that the port was safe but that a pilot would be needed to take the ship into harbour as a vessel of some kind had been sunk there a few days ago.

When General Cunningham arrived he held a conference in our luxurious but, sadly only temporary, headquarters. I had not met him before nor, I think, had I ever known such a dynamic man. Our original objective, he said, had been achieved. This had been to capture Kismayu and drive the Italians across the Juba River and out of Jubaland. It was now clear that the Italians could be pushed farther back and out of Mogadishu and it was administratively possible for us to do this now that supplies could be shipped from Mombasa into Kismayu harbour. He concluded by saying that what he wanted now was movement and more movement, forward and farther forward, and NOW. We felt we had been trying pretty hard — but we began to have doubts. To the Divisional Commander he said,

'Your men must stop fluttering about like a lot of old hens and get across that river.'

Fine, but since the men in question had been very busy capturing the two airfields near Gobwen at the mouth of the river, they had certainly had no time to 'flutter'. But this, of course, was an army *façon de parler* in order to *encourager les autres*.

The next point — where was the 21st Brigade? No one really knew so the answer seemed to be to send someone to find out, and that was me. It was not for me, as a very junior captain, to enquire what had gone wrong with the Brigade Signals and why couldn't he find out the position through normal channels. Nor could I suggest that, if the Brigade was held up, there could be some enemy force down there between them and us and, if so a stronger body of men than Jackson and me would probably be needed to deal with it. So I took a small truck with Jackson, another Askari and a Bren gun and off we set.

It was almost dark by the time we got back to the mined cross-roads and turned left — into *terra incognita*. Or was it 'terror incognita'? I laughed at the feeble joke: Jackson wouldn't understand it so I didn't try to explain it to him.

The track, which had obviously been used regularly and recently, turned and twisted through the bush and around trees. My main difficulty was that I had no idea whether the lost brigade was a mile or a hundred miles away. Never mind, *Que sera sera*, as the Italians would say.

No dammit, that wasn't Italian, it must be Spanish.

I started humming the toreador song from Carmen. A silly song; I don't believe there are such things as toreadors now. They have matadors. My mind rambled on; it kept me awake.

'Mirador, Parador, Humidor, Cuspidor — I couldn't think of any more. But I'd rather be in a Mirador or a Parador than a Cuspidor or a Humidor!'

I had made up my mind what to do if some Banda did suddenly appear in front of us. I should just dash past them and not fire a shot: they would expect anyone coming from the north to be friend not foe.

By then the moon was up. This made driving more difficult. I nodded once or twice, then woke with a start:

'*Angalia miti, bwana. Polepole,*' said Jackson several times. 'Look out for the trees and go slowly.'

The moonlight together with the headlights made the trees appear to move when we swung round a bend. They were only shadows — but they looked disquietingly like Banda. If they were trees, they must be the Birnam Woods on their way to Dunsinane!

We had been travelling for nearly three hours but had only done some sixty miles. We were all pretty tired by then and the two Askaris were drowsing peacefully when a rifle shot cracked through the night and alerted us all. I slowed down a bit, listening intently, and then, about a hundred yards ahead, there was a barrier across the road. I slowed down still further to give the impression I was going to stop, then changed gear ready to make a dash round it when we got nearer.

But Jackson saw them before I did:

'They're our Askaris, *bwana*. Stop.'

We stopped, got out, and walked towards them so that they could see we were not Italians. For a moment I thought they were going to go through the old text book procedure:

'Halt! Who goes there? Take five steps forward and give the countersign.'

That would have stumped us: we hadn't a clue what the password was. But we were all right, out came the old familiar:

'*Nani wewe?*' (Who are you?)

'*Sisi tu.*' (Only us.)

'*Mzuri, pitani.*' (All right, come along.)

He took down the barrier and we drove through. I said I wanted to see the Brigade Commander so he told me to drive on about a mile when I would see his board up on the left.

It was midnight: hardly the time for a social call. Nevertheless the Brigadier was glad to get some news, surprised that the entire enemy force in front of him had disappeared, and relieved that the track ahead was not mined – we were the living witnesses to this!

In half an hour we set off in convoy with him on the return journey and arrived back in Kismayu at dawn. I found that my Brigadier had returned to Afmadu and so followed him there.

10

The Juba River

FEBRUARY TO MARCH 1941

After the Italian withdrawal from Afmadu and Kismayu, General de Simone regrouped his whole force along a new line of defence on the east bank of the Juba River. This comprised six brigades of regular troops from the 101st and 102nd Divisions with artillery and armoured cars and also six groups of Irregulars. His main concentrations were at and around the small towns of Jelib and Jumbo where there were bridges, but he had a mobile reserve which could be moved quickly up or down the road running along the east bank to defend any point where a crossing might be attempted. He only retained two small footholds on the western bank, one at Gobwen near the mouth of the river where he had two airfields, and another at Bulo Erillo opposite Jelib.

This plan was undoubtedly the soundest he could adopt. There would have been no advantage in clinging on to Afmadu, isolated as it was, and he could not have held Kismayu for long against bombardment from air, sea and land. It should not be thought, therefore, that this further withdrawal indicated that the Italians were demoralized and on the run. This was far from being the case, at that time, as was shown by their stubborn and courageous defence of the Juba River line for over a week and which only collapsed due to the great advantage the attack has over the defence in modern mobile warfare. If an attacking force can get even a small column through or round the enemy positions, it can exert a stranglehold on supplies and communications – and on the windpipe of morale – which is difficult to counter.

The Juba River meanders over hundreds of miles from its source in the Abyssinian highlands and reaches the Indian Ocean at a point just north of Kismayu. Along each bank there is a strip of lush green forest and bush varying in width from a few hundred yards to several miles.

At Gobwen, where it was thought possible that a crossing could be made, the river is almost two hundred yards broad and far too deep to ford so, on its lower reaches, it presents a formidable military obstacle.

The opening of the harbour at Kismayu had made it possible for General Cunningham to continue his operation, but he still had a number of problems. His strength was less than that of the Italians but his four brigades were fully motorized so his numerical inferiority did not worry him. His greatest difficulty was how to cross the river without a bridge or a ferry. The Italians had burnt their bridge at Jelib, the one at Jumbo had been destroyed by our bombers to prevent the escape of the Kismayu garrison, and a ferry had been put out of action either with the same object, or by the enemy to prevent our using it. A pontoon bridge was being brought up by road from Kenya on sixty trucks but this convoy could not move as quickly as we had done.

In making his plan to cross the river the Divisional Commander knew that direct attacks on the enemy's two strongest points, Jelib and Jumbo, even if successful, would be very costly. But he had to test the defences at each of these places: it was just possible that a quick surprise crossing could be made. But, even if it were not, he wanted to give the impression that he might try again after building up greater strength. His first task, however, was to drive the Italians from the two positions they still held on the west bank.

The Gold Coast Brigade started the offensive when their 2nd Battalion captured Bulo Erillo on 13 February. It was a very tough proposition. The Italian rifle and machine-gun posts had been wired and mined and lanes had been cut in the dense bush so that their armoured cars could go into action. Despite the fact that the officers and B/N.C.O.s had blacked their hands and faces, nearly all of them were either killed or wounded in the attack. Nevertheless, the Italians were driven out and a battery of 65-mm guns and five armoured cars were captured. In the meanwhile the 1st South African Brigade had been moving towards Gobwen and its two airfields which they secured against little opposition. When they reached the river, however, they came under intense artillery and mortar fire. It was then clear that no quick crossing could be made either at Jumbo or Jelib. So, leaving one South African battalion opposite the former to worry and hold the garrison there, and a similar force from the Gold Coast Brigade to give the appearance of threatening Jelib, he withdrew the remainder of the two brigades whilst seeking more propitious sites to put, or build, bridges.

The search was on. Brigadier Pienaar, the commander of the South African Brigade, flew up and down the river looking for a suitable place for the pontoon bridge – when it arrived. He selected a position at Ionte, a few miles upstream from Jumbo, and set about establishing a bridgehead there, although it was obvious that the Italians were in considerable strength on the opposite bank and they launched attack after attack against the few South Africans who managed to cross the river in collapsible canvas boats. These, however, were countered by machine-gun fire from the armoured cars on the west bank. The Italian casualties at this one place alone testify to their courage and determination: fifty-six were killed and over two hundred wounded.

The bridge from Kenya arrived opportunely just as the bridgehead, one thought, was secured. The sappers had it in place by the next morning but the Italians had still not given up and, just as the final work was being done on the decking and General Godwin-Austen had walked on to it to perform the christening ceremony, shells started bursting all around and a heavy ground attack was put in against the one company on the east bank. Brigadier Pienaar at once ordered his armoured cars over the bridge. It held their weight – all was well. They rumbled across and then charged over an open grass glade and routed a strong Italian force supported by field and machine-guns. The bridgehead was finally secured and the South Africans started crossing in strength for their next task, to capture Jelib.

While the hectic battle for the bridgehead was being fought at Ionte the Gold Coast Brigade, less a similar 'prodding' force to keep the pressure on the Jelib garrison, were hunting northward for another site for a crossing. They found one near a village called Mabungo. As this was about thirty miles north of Jelib, it was hoped that any work being done there would escape observation by the Italians. The flow of the river at this point was considerably less than at Gobwen and, as the water was only about eighteen inches deep, it was decided that a ford could be made to serve our very temporary need. This was made by filling sandbags and laying them on the river-bed.

The plan was for the 22nd Brigade, supported by a squadron of armoured cars, a company of light tanks and a section of the 22nd Mountain Battery, to cross the river by the ford and make its way somehow round behind the main enemy defences at Jelib. This composite body, to be known as Fowcol, then moved across country from Afmadu to Mabungo on 19 February.

When we arrived at the riverside, the scene was like Brighton beach. The river was alive with bathing Gold Coast Askaris getting rid of the dirt and dust of Somaliland and the banks were crowded with sight-seers watching the sappers at work on the crossing. East Africans from the 5th and 6th K.A.R. and Nyasalanders from the 1st Battalion were laughing and chatting with the Gold Coasters.

'*Jambo, habari ya siku mengi?*' ('Hello, how are you? Long time no see.') said the East Africans.

'*Moni moni, muli bwino?*' ('Good morning, are you are all right?') replied the Nyasas.

But the Gold Coasters taunted them both: 'Ha, you done come, eh?' They wanted everyone to know that it was they who had pushed the Italians across the river and were holding the bridgehead for us.

About a hundred Gold Coast Askaris were filling, carrying and laying sandbags on the river-bed and, in a few hours, a good-looking causeway had been built up and covered with army track. It looked neat and substantial but I wondered if it was really strong enough to take all our vehicles – particularly the heavy armoured cars, the tanks carried on trucks, and the guns. But it did. Next morning more than 150 vehicles crossed over without mishap. A great achievement by the sappers.

That evening there was sporadic firing. A small group of Banda patrolling the road up the east bank had seen that something was happening and they would report this to Jelib. But, with any luck, our column would have disappeared by the time any sizeable force could come up the road to attack us. In any case it was more likely they would expect us to come down the road towards Jelib – but we had other plans.

Our task was to cross the river and the road, dive into the bush and find our way through it to the road running from Jelib to Mogadishu. What the Banda had probably seen that evening was a bulldozer. The riverine forest and bush on the east bank was very thick indeed as far as the road, a distance of about two miles, so the sappers cleared a track for us through it. The information we had indicated that the bush east of the road was light and the map showed a camel track about seven miles in from the river running south-east. This could be just what we wanted.

There were no further shots that night and we slept peacefully. At four o'clock next morning, 20 February, the long column crossed the river and moved slowly forward through the bush. From the road we set a north-easterly course in order to join the camel track at the point nearest to us and, with an armoured car in front to knock the bush down, we pushed ahead. An occasional glade raised hopes that the bush was getting thinner but instead it became worse. The armoured car had to be changed frequently as the water in the radiator soon boiled with this unorthodox work. At times it was necessary for Askaris, working in shifts, to cut and clear the bush the armoured car had crushed. We were scarcely moving at all.

I was in an enviable position. Normally I should have been responsible for seeing that the column kept moving in the right direction and for plotting our position. But, on this special occasion, we had a sapper officer allotted to us who, in civilian life, was a surveyor and navigator, so my role was merely that of, I hoped, a friendly and constructive critic. When we had passed the seven mile mark and found no track, I told him about my experience in the bush between Wajir and Garissa.

'Of course one can't spot these camel tracks on the ground you know,' I said. 'The lines on the map merely show the general direction along which camels filter through the bush at certain seasons.'

This didn't cheer him up. I fear it wasn't meant to. I felt I knew this sort of country better than he did. However, I was wrong. When we had done thirteen miles we came upon a track of sorts. Although its general direction appeared to be due south, which was towards Jelib and not what we really wanted, it was decided to use it for a time and then correct our course later by striking east. After this we moved along merrily at a good two miles an hour and, by dusk, had covered twenty miles. There we camped.

We had with us a *soi disant* guide. Somebody had produced him and said he might be useful so we took him along with us for luck. I had a talk with him that evening to find out if he was likely to be of any help to us.

'Do you know the Uebi Scebeli River?' I asked.

'Yes, well,' he replied.

'Good. When shall we get there, then?'

'We shan't get there at all with those things,' he said disconsolately, pointing at the armoured cars.

That wasn't encouraging; I wished we hadn't brought him. But, when I asked if he knew Jelib, he had better news.

'Yes, I was there two days ago, *bwana*, and I'll tell you a funny thing. The only Italian *bwanas* left there are ones with one star on their shoulders; the others have all gone off somewhere in their cars.'

Could there really be no senior officers left there? This must be an exaggeration – but, possibly, there was something in it.

There wasn't much sleep for us that night; we were over-anxious,

wondering whether we should be able to reach the main road in time
to put the Jelib garrison in the bag. At the present rate of progress we
should be too late.

We were off again at dawn. Michael, as Brigade Major, was the
man who bore more of the brunt and stress of this odd journey than
anyone else. Time and time again he was sent by the Brigadier to the
head of the column to urge the sweating and striving Askaris and
drivers to greater efforts just when all our tempers were becoming a
little frayed at the edges. I simply don't know how he managed to
restrain the Brigadier from getting out of his car and joining in the
bush-cutting himself − because I kept as well out of the way as
possible during that exasperating and infuriating day.

Occasionally we came out into a glade and our hopes rose, only to
be dashed again when we had to resort to pushing and slashing our
way through more thick stuff at a snail's pace. The attack on Jelib was
due to begin next morning at dawn. How could we get there in time to
help when moving at this rate?

We then tried tacking eastward and found a dry water-hole which,
the guide said, was Reidab Dere. But one of our reconnaissance
planes flew over during the morning and dropped a message saying
that he reckoned we were about six miles west of that. But we were not
interested in the ruddy water-hole. All we had to do was to push on as
fast as possible and as near to south-east as we could manage. It
didn't matter so much where we hit the main road as when.

Another aircraft came over in the afternoon. We were still too far to
the east. Yes, we knew that and didn't give a damn. We pushed on.
The map we were working from was suspect and, in any case, to plot
our position by dead reckoning from the speedometer and compass
was quite impossible, turning and twisting as, perforce, we had to do.
So, being a perfectionist, our navigator said he would take an astrafix.

By then tempers were no longer just frayed, they were in tatters. I
said I thought this was a waste of time and that we should push on
south-eastward. I was unpopular and we waited for the astrafix. This
confirmed the aircraft's report and, as it was by then dusk, we camped
down for the night at, we believed, Ballei Ier. But it turned out to be
Duddum Gudud! Diddum matter?

On the third morning we were off again at 5.30 and for six hours
pushed, bashed, and tore our way through some of the worst country
we had encountered. By then we could hear firing from the direction of
Jelib. Were we going to be too late to do our job? A small party of
Banda fired at us at one point but we drove them off. Then at 1 p.m.

35 Asmara

36 (*Opposite:*) Italian
ships lie scuttled in
Massawa harbour

37 Looking across the Omo river gorge to Abalti which lies beside the gigantic, thimble-like rock in the distance

38 The Blue Nile flowing through a gorge at a point about 100 miles north-west of Addis Ababa

39 South Africans up in the mountains at 11,000 feet above sea
level, just before the fall of Dessie

40 The Asmara-Dessie road

41 Amba Alagi

42 Ras Seyoum and his men and the Sudan Defence Force closed in on Amba Alagi in the west

43 (*Below:*) Fort Toselli, the main outer fortress at Amba Alagi, falls to General Mayne

44 The Italian garrison surrenders and marches out of the 'impregnable' fort

45 Last came the Duke of Aosta himself

46 The Crown Prince leads a column of Patriots whilst his father takes the salute

47 Camels carrying stores and ammunition from the Sudan up into the Abyssinian highlands

48 An Italian machine-gunner's view of the Wolchefit escarpment

49 The King's African Rifles enter Gondar

we reached what turned out to be the dry bed of the Uebi Scebeli River. The guide was surprised and said, '*Kweli, bwana.*' I didn't tell him that I was just as surprised as he was.

After crossing the river-bed we found a broad track running southward and the Brigadier ordered the armoured cars and tanks and a company of the 1st K.A.R. to push along down this as fast as possible. I got a lift in the front car and, as we sped along, we felt we were at Brooklands or Brand's Hatch after our snail's pace through the bush. After about a mile we came out into open country and, almost immediately, we were fired on from a ridge in front of us. We just ran right through them, some surrendering and others making for the bush.

A little farther on we came across a field hospital. The Brigadier, who had caught us up by then, leant out of his car to give orders for a small party to guard it and we all then raced for the main road.

We hit it just as a large Italian convoy was passing – *en route* for Mogadishu. Some of our armoured cars swung left and others right, roared along the convoy, established a road block at each end and soon had a battery of guns and all the enemy vehicles with their surprised occupants tucked away in car parks in the bush. Meanwhile the Askaris were making compounds out of thorn-tree branches for the prisoners. Many of these were officers. It seemed that our guide and informer could have been right: none of them had more than one star on his shoulder.

At the moment when we debouched from the bush on to the main road to Mogadishu, the 1st South African Brigade, having fought its way north from Ionte and occupied Jelib, was hot on our tail. Elements of the Gold Coast Brigade had reached Jelib very shortly after them, some having struggled through the bush on the west bank against strong opposition whilst others had used the road running south from the Mabungo crossing down the east bank. All this we did not know at the time, so our armoured cars and tanks set off back along the main road towards Jelib to join in the battle. After a very short distance, however, they met the Transvaal Scottish (somehow without firing at each other!) who told them that the town had surrendered. After brief greetings and congratulations our A.F.V.s turned, picked up the Brigadier and me and went off northward in pursuit of the retreating Italians.

It was a Mad Hatter's Tea Party of a drive. We kept passing Italian cars and trucks going south to Jelib. They all thought we were friends, not foes, and waved happily to us as they went by – and we waved back. They would soon be in the bag we had prepared for them. We were running short of petrol but were able to go far enough to make sure there were no enemy troops south of Modun, the base for their Juba army, and then returned at dusk to Brigade Headquarters on the roadside.

Had our expedition through the bush been worthwhile? The answer is yes — with qualifications. Had we been able to reach the main road twenty-four hours sooner, we should have captured more of the enemy transport than we did. We should probably not have taken more prisoners because most of the fleeing troops were making their way north along the seashore on foot and, by doing so, saved us a lot of trouble. A few days later they walked into the prisoner of war camps we then had made for them up the coast at Brava and Merca. Our main contributions to the battle were hypothetical ones. Had the Italians held out longer in Jelib we should have been able to attack them in the rear. Also the fact of our cutting their supply line contributed to the disintegration of their force. However, with the inestimable benefit of hindsight I have often wondered why, after the first day's experience of crashing our way at snail's pace through the bush, we didn't send for the bulldozer which helped us on the river bank. It is strange, too, that we were not as usual provided with aerial photos of the route. These would have shown the width of the belt of bush we were plunging through — and even, perhaps, some camel tracks!

Divisional Headquarters gave us the all-clear to go forward next day so the Brigadier sent a spearhead force off at daylight consisting of the A.F.V.s and two companies of the 1st K.A.R. They came under fire from Italian guns at Modun, ninety-nine miles from the Juba River, but they dashed straight ahead and overran the enemy positions. The garrison at Modun had been shelled the day before by H.M.S. *Shropshire* and was in no mood for more. Our force took possession of the installations and stores and handed them over next day to Division.

At that point the Nigerian Brigade took over the lead from our 22nd Brigade and swept on to Mogadishu, a mere one hundred miles farther up the coast, occupying it on 25 February. The 22nd Brigade went on to the seaside towns of Brava and Merca where it was to stay for a while as Divisional Reserve.

The success of the Juba operation was due to a number of different factors. The drive of General Cunningham, the tactics of General Godwin-Austen in holding the enemy at his strong points whilst penetrating his defences at the weaker ones, the mobility and speed of our forces which bewildered the Italians, the fighting qualities of our inexperienced soldiers and the neutralization of the Italian Air Force by the S.A.A.F. Then there were Italian failures and weaknesses. They had a mobile brigade in reserve but no real defence in depth. Once they knew, therefore, that our armour was round the back of them, a large number of their African troops fled and melted away into the bush leaving the white officers and N.C.O.s to fight on – as many did.

I have only mentioned factors in the field: the Staff work and the supply system behind us by sea and land can only be described as titanic.

Mr Carel Birkby, the war correspondent of the South African Press Association, summed up the achievement of General Cunningham and Major-General Godwin-Austen at this stage as follows:

The whole operation will go down in military history as a classic. Ahead of the troops was the naturally strong defensive line of a river; behind them was the spectre of the impending rains. They were operating 600 miles from their headquarters. General Cunningham had had to face the worrying strategical problem of maintaining three fronts, in Turkana, Abyssinia and Somalia each 600 miles from Nairobi and with no lateral communications between them. [People in England] will appreciate the position if they imagine his base at [Cherbourg] and his three fronts at [Marseille, Madrid and Milan]. All of them were reached by roads which army engineers hewed out of the bush as they went.

This picture of the operational scene gives an indication of the magnitude of the task of the Command Headquarters Staff in Nairobi. This was in the able hands of Brigadier (later Major-General) Edwards who consisted of about six and a half feet of calm efficiency. They had to administer and maintain law and order in the area the army had taken over which was the size of France, Belgium and Holland put together; protect a rapidly lengthening line of communication; supply a widely dispersed army of some seventy-five thousand men with everything they needed to move, fight and live; and also feed about twenty thousand prisoners of war and, in some areas, a civilian population as well.

In Mogadishu the occupation went smoothly. The five thousand remaining civilians – an estimated two thousand had fled – accepted their defeat philosophically, and even with pleasant surprise when they read in General Cunningham's Proclamation (dated with characteristic confidence 1 February) that their lives would be subjected to no more interference than was necessary. So, after some initial apprehension, the children went back to school, the women to the market and the men to their favourite cafés where they sat and chatted as usual, drinking coffee and gazing nostalgically over the white sandy beach to the sparkling beauty of the Indian Ocean.

The municipal engineers had been ordered to keep the essential services operating, the lord bishop sadly tolled the cathedral bells and the Italian police prevented looting and controlled the traffic, albeit with some difficulty since they had been told that, henceforth, vehicles would drive on the left-hand side. A number of things were, of course, in short supply; but with skill and ingenuity the Italians had managed to make locally many of their requirements which had been unavailable from Europe for many months. Two of these, though not in the category of necessities of life, were boosters of morale: lipstick and liquor. At that time we were only interested in the latter and this we purchased at Signor Gioffi's shop. Whether one wanted whisky, gin, brandy or rum, it all came out of the same enormous glass jar of spirit made from locally grown sugar cane. When bottled, however, it was flavoured with essence and coloured according to one's choice and a suitable label was then stuck on. The tartan one for whisky was particularly realistic. No; life was not too bad in Mogadishu; one could even get a meal – of sorts – at the Hotel Croce del Sud.

Outside the town, however, there were problems. Looting was rife in the countryside, several thousand discontented and hungry natives were living in a slum quarter on the sand-dunes nearby and the communities in at least two of the townships up-country were on the verge of starvation. The twenty thousand prisoners of war had to be taken by sea to Kenya as soon as possible where they could be fed and housed more easily, and there were 1,300 political detainees, Abyssinia and Somali irreconcilables including some women, who had been found living in appalling conditions in a prison on the coast south of Mogadishu. As they had been on a starvation diet, some for several years, they needed urgent medical attention.

The greatest need was for food, and army stocks were running low. Some supplies had already come by sea from Mombasa to Kismayu and more were on the way – direct to Mogadishu, we hoped. But there was a snag. We had laid magnetic mines by air outside the harbour to prevent enemy ships entering, and these had to be removed. An old wooden hulled ship, the *Lindi*, had been sent up from Kenya to do the job but this was expected to take at least ten days. Merca harbour could be used if it were possible to repair the damaged tugs and find men to operate them with the lighters. They were found – in Merca itself. Two hundred and twenty-eight merchant seamen taken from British and Allied ships sunk off the Somaliland coast had been held in a prisoner of war camp nearby and they all volunteered to help. The harbour was in operation in a few days.

In the meantime one of our bomber aircraft flew 350 miles to Rocca Littorio to evacuate invalids and women and children and then 700 miles up the coast to Dante on a similar mission – and to take some food. The inhabitants had grown tired of a diet of fish and dried beans! They said that supplies had not reached them by sea owing to our blockade nor by road, as there was no petrol. If ever there was a case of 'Water, water, everywhere nor any drop to drink' this was it – but for 'water' substitute 'petrol'. The Italian forces had abandoned 380,000 gallons of the stuff in Mogadishu alone, an appalling and unpardonable military mistake. Had it not been for this we should have been unable to continue the advance to Addis Ababa so promptly.

Arrangements had been made to take our own and enemy wounded back to Kenya by sea and a hospital ship lay off Merca to do this. Happily this task was much lighter than had been estimated and feared. Never before had there been so few casualties in a comparable campaign. The total of all ranks and races in General Cunningham's force in operations in Somalia and southern Abyssinia up to the capitulation of Mogadishu was 52 killed, 132 wounded and 13 missing.

The 22nd Brigade had fewer problems to cope with down the coast at Brava and Merca but their life was by no means all play and no work. A few miles inland ran the River Uebi Scebeli. Its water had been harnessed by a succession of weirs and locks to irrigate a large area of the flat and fertile land on either bank. When the British drive into Somaliland started the Italian farmers and their wives who operated the scheme were evacuated and it was of vital importance that they should return in order to produce foodcrops. This required some organization because they had fled to Mogadishu in some haste leaving all their farm tools and implements – and these had been thankfully taken by the local Somali people. However, the K.A.R. soon fixed this. A stern order was given that everything that had been taken was to be piled up outside each Somali village within twenty-four hours – or else. It only remained for army trucks (captured) to collect and distribute it all next day (using captured petrol).

A further task to ensure law and order was the sending of a

motorized patrol each day to make contact with the Gold Coast Regiment. They had been mopping up in the Juba River area with their base at Iscia Baidoa so their patrols met ours half-way, at Bur Acaba. Then there was the seemingly perpetual flow of Italian troops, white and African, asking to be made prisoners of war. They were the ones who, to escape the hazard of being involved in further warfare after they had withdrawn from the Juba River line, avoided the road and trekked on foot up the coast.

Despite these tasks and the perennial one of collecting arms, ammunition, equipment, stores and supplies that had been abandoned, there was time to enjoy life. There was excellent wild-fowl shooting along the Uebi Scebeli and everyone revelled in being able to bathe in the warm sea and be clean again. On the outskirts of Merca there were a few delightful villas on the sea front. The war seemed hardly to have touched the occupants: children played on the beach and bathed and paddled while their mothers watched over them. This led to a little mild fraternization.

The days passed pleasantly but, unfortunately, Jackson and I became estranged. It happened one morning when I was sitting in my office listing all the various items captured. There were guns galore, ammunition by the ton, trucks, petrol, stores of every description and thousands of prisoners — but all of them men.

'I know, Jackson, but all the eligible ones have fled up to Addis Ababa. You must be patient.' Once again I was postponing the day of reckoning. I might have got away with this if it had not been that, in some of the delightful villas on the sea front, there were some delightful Italian ladies who were obviously very pleased at our arrival. They gave us a warm welcome and this, of course, did not go unobserved by Jackson. Here at last, I thought, was the *dolce vita* I had read about, the fruits of victory ripe for the picking. But the fruit turned out to be bitter: the lovely ladies told us that we were wonderful because, now that we had won the war, their husbands would soon be back home!

11

The Battle of Keren

JANUARY TO MARCH 1941

The greatest and certainly one of the most important battles of the East African campaign was that fought at Keren in Eritrea. In terms of the large forces engaged, the stubborn fighting, the duration of the battle and the heavy casualties on both sides, it must rank as great so long as men continue to settle their differences in this primitive manner. It was important since, had not the pressure it exerted on the Italians drawn off half their forces in East Africa from their other fronts, General Cunningham's drive from the south could not have succeeded as it did. And, conversely, General Platt's success at Keren was in part due to the simultaneous attacks on the Italians by the Patriots in the west and the South and East Africans in southern Abyssinia and Somalia.

When Italy declared war in June 1940 the military situation in the Sudan was very similar to that in Kenya. The frontier with Abyssinia and Eritrea was long and vulnerable and the forces available to defend it few and ill-equipped for modern warfare. It was easy, therefore, for the Italians to seize the Sudan frontier towns of Kassala and Gallabat, which they did in July 1940. An attempt was made by a British force to retake Gallabat in November but it failed and, thereafter, our policy was to harass the enemy continually in the Kassala area until we were strong enough to drive them out. This was most effectively done by a small and very mobile body called Gazelle Force. Due to these tactics, the activity of the Patriots on his left flank and the gradual reinforcement of our troops in the Sudan, General Frusci, the commander of the Italian Northern Army, started to withdraw his troops back from the frontier towards the foothills of the Eritrean plateau in November. The British forces were then not sufficiently strong or mobile to follow but, by the middle of January, General Platt had two divisions, the 4th and 5th Indian Divisions, with artillery,

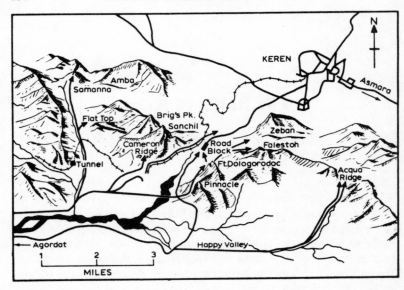

tanks and air support. He then made a rapid and brilliant advance into Eritrea through Kassala, culminating in the capture of the two strong Italian bases of Agordat and Barentu on 2 February with six thousand prisoners, eighty guns, twenty-six tanks and four hundred trucks.

The remainder of the enemy forces fled, those from Agordat direct to Keren while those from Barentu, being unable to get across to the direct road, had to make their way along mountain tracks to the main Adowa-Asmara road. The 4th Division and Gazelle Force pursued the retreating Italians but were checked by their blowing up a bridge and the fleeing enemy column, though frequently attacked by British planes, managed to reach Keren through the steep, narrow Dongolaas Gorge which they then blocked by three enormous demolitions.

Just before Agordat fell the Italian garrison at Keren consisted of only one Colonial brigade. This desperate situation was redressed by rushing up another Colonial brigade, the 11th Regiment Savoia Grenadiers and an Alpini battalion from their final strategic reserve in Addis Ababa. These reinforcements arrived on 1 February and the remainder of the Agordat garrison on the next day, whilst the refugees from Barentu were gradually filtering in across country. In addition, two other Colonial brigades were summoned from the north and one from the Gallabat area. In all, their troops who took part in the defence of Keren numbered some thirty thousand men. Artillery support was very strong with one hundred and forty-four guns sited to cover every approach. The demolition of the Mussolini Bridge on the road from Agordat and the blocking of the Dongolaas Gorge had saved time to reinforce and reorganize their defences.

Opposing them General Platt had around thirteen thousand men in six brigades with 6-inch and 3.7-inch Howitzers and 25-pounder guns.

The approach to Keren is across an open plain two miles broad which is dominated by a series of mountain peaks extending as far as the eye can see and rising steeply two thousand feet or more. There is only one pass through this wall of almost sheer rock, the gorge which had been blocked. There appeared to be another possible way through this mountain barrier, up the so called Happy Valley, but this was a delusion.

One thing was certain, the demolitions in the gorge could not be cleared until the enemy gun positions covering them had been captured or silenced by bombing or gun-fire. When the leading elements of the 4th Division and Gazelle Force arrived on the scene on 3 February it was decided, therefore, to make an immediate attack on the mountain known as Sanchil commanding the west side of the gorge. The 2nd Battalion The Cameron Highlanders reached and held a ridge half-way up and, next night, a Punjabi Regiment passed through them to continue the assault. They got to the very peak but were then driven back. We had failed, but 'Cameron Ridge' was reinforced and held as a springboard for a future attack.

When the main body of the British force arrived on the plain on 6 February an attack was launched by a fresh brigade, this time up Happy Valley. The leading battalion started at night and climbed steadily but the men were handicapped by having to carry their machine-guns, ammunition, signal equipment and rations and water for three days. (The British force had no pack-animal transport: two mule companies from Cyprus arrived too late for the battle.) Their task was to capture another ridge, known as Acqua, and thereafter 'exploit success' towards Keren itself. This, however, proved to be impossible owing to intense gun, machine-gun and mortar fire from near impregnable enemy positions.

On 10 February the Division tried again, this time with a battalion on each side of the gorge. They climbed and fought their way up to the peaks but only two platoons remained for the final assault on Sanchil; the rest were carrying up water, food and ammunition or taking wounded down. This, and a second attempt to capture the Acqua ridge, failed and, after five days of hard fighting and great gallantry on both sides, the attack was called off. But the 4th Division held grimly on to the ground they had won and retained a precarious foothold on the mountainside for three long weeks, resisting all attempts to oust them.

The nut was harder to crack than had been expected and General Platt decided to bring the 5th Division into the battle in addition to the 4th.

But first he had to build up supplies and ammunition from railhead one hundred and eighty miles away for this greater project. All available transport worked day and night at this task and, at the same time, the R.A.F. continued to attack enemy positions and the Divisional artillery to shell them. 'D' day was 15 March.

On the eve of the renewed offensive there was a good omen: R.A.F. bombers blew up an enemy train of forty trucks carrying thirty thousand shells. The plan was to capture Fort Dologorodoc and, on the morning of the 15th, troops of the 5th Division were waiting behind Cameron Ridge to attack. They could not hope to cross the gorge from there and survive, however, until enemy posts on Samanna and Sanchil were taken, as machine-guns from there were plastering the opposite slopes below the fort. Troops from the 4th Division had, that morning, made a successful assault on the former but had not been able to push the Italians from Sanchil. Nevertheless, that evening one battalion of the 5th Division managed to get a footing on the other side of the valley and capture an outpost below the fort. Then, before dawn on 16 March, the 9th Brigade of the 5th Division, led by the 2nd West Yorks, scrambled up the mountain in the moonlight and surprised and overwhelmed the fort taking four hundred Grenadier and Eritrean prisoners.

Next morning the 29th Brigade, also of the 5th Division, went through and occupied the forward slopes of Falestoh and Zeban. But this was not the end; it was the beginning of ten days of the fiercest fighting in the battle for Keren. The troops of the 5th Division, clinging to their mountainside positions, were under fire from Italian guns and mortars in three sides and were attacked time and time again by infantry and tanks. The R.A.F. kept them supplied with ammunition and food by air drop and they and the artillery broke up several of the Italian ground attacks almost before they had started by bombing and shelling the enemy's assembly areas. Despite this, eight separate attacks were made on them in their inadequate improvised defensive positions. The first of these was by a brigade newly arrived from the north, then by the Alpini Battalion, by the crack Tipo Battalion and by the most resolute of the Eritrean battalions. But they held fast and remained a firm wedge deep inside the enemy's lines.

In the meantime another attack had not succeeded in capturing Sanchil and we had suffered severe casualties there and on Flat Top. A new plan was needed and General Platt decided to silence the enemy fire from Sanchil by 'saturation' gun-fire and bombing instead of making any more infantry attacks and then force a way through the gorge. At dawn on the 25 March, therefore, the 10th Brigade, which was the third brigade in the 5th Division, attacked and captured some enemy positions along the railway from which fire was covering the road blocks. They then swept up the road, overran the Bersaglieri Battalion which was defending the first road block, and captured many prisoners including the commanding officer. That opened the way for the British 'I' tanks to move up laden with explosives with which the sappers cleared the demolitions.

While the 10th Brigade was fighting off several counter-attacks, the 9th Brigade came in from their positions on the slopes below Fort Dologorodoc they had held so long, and cleared the enemy force which was defending the next road block. By night time on the 26th the road was open and, at dawn next morning, our tanks rolled into Keren town. General Frusci had ordered a complete withdrawal during that night and there was no opposition. The siege which had lasted fifty-three days was over and white flags were flying from several of the peaks – including the hitherto indomitable Sanchil. Keren had fallen but, great achievement though it was, it was only part of the main objective, the elimination by capture or destruction of the enemy fighting forces.

There had been dreadful casualties. Our own were 536 killed and 3,229 wounded. The Italians, in one period of five days, lost 1,135 men killed and had 2,300 wounded and, as General Frusci departed, he announced that he was leaving 3,000 dead – 'who will guard Keren until we return'.

But, in spite of these losses, the thousands of prisoners and the hundreds of deserters, many got away and a substantial force consisting of elements of the 80th Colonial Brigade and the two Grenadier Battalions with sixty-seven guns was holding another formidable defensive position on the road to Asmara, the gorge at Ad Teclesan. There was little heart in the Italian defences, however, and when some of our infantry found they could get through the pass by way of a railway tunnel, and a ground attack by infantry with 'I' tanks was made before dawn on 31 March, resistance ended.

Some of the enemy headed down the two roads leading southward to join the Duke of Aosta at Amba Alagi, but a large number of them were caught at Adigrat by our pursuit force. Others trekked to General Nasi's stronghold at Gondar, some five thousand went on to Asmara and surrendered their arms there, whilst more than ten thousand were taken when Massawa capitulated a little later.

The epic story of Keren would not be complete without a tailpiece about the Italian navy. A certain Rear Admiral Bonnetti commanded the Red Sea Squadron and he had seven destroyers at Massawa. Towards the end of the débâcle on land he ordered them to sea. One of these was sunk by our navy close to Massawa, two out of four sent to attack the fuel tanks at Port Sudan were sunk by our Fleet Air Arm and two ran aground near Jedda on the other side of the Red Sea. The remaining two, under orders to attack Suez, just disappeared and were believed sunk.

Meanwhile the Admiral had been given an ultimatum from General Platt by telephone from Asmara to Massawa that, if he allowed the nineteen ships lying in the harbour to be scuttled or the port installations damaged, the General would not be responsible for feeding the forty thousand Italian civilians in Asmara.

Bonnetti referred the matter to Rome and was told to go ahead and destroy the port and sink the ships. British troops and tanks pushed their way through road blocks and hurried down from Asmara to the port. A white flag hung out of the Bonnetti window. Did he want to discuss terms for surrender or did he want to gain time for further destruction? Fires were raging in the dock area. Then the flag went down. He had again referred to Rome and been told not to capitulate. So a joint British and Free French attack went in on the port by the Highland Light Infantry and the Foreign Legion which breached the defences. Admiral Bonnetti was found sitting despondently beside the harbour. He had been trying to break his sword over his knee – but it would only bend, so he threw it into the water. It was recovered later and taken as a trophy to Headquarters in Khartoum.

The dockside cranes and equipment had been destroyed and all the ships had been scuttled – but not effectively. It was found possible to raise them all afterwards. With the fall of Massawa the Italian, German and Japanese raiders and submarines had lost their last base in the Red Sea and on the east coast of Africa. Ships from the U.S.A.

and from the Far East with supplies for the army in Egypt at once resumed the use of this route and, with the elimination of the Italian forces from Eritrea, aerial reinforcement from the States through West Africa and up the Nile Valley was safe from enemy interference.

12

The Long Haul to Addis Ababa

6 MARCH TO 6 APRIL 1941

Anyone who had thought there would be a prolonged seaside holiday at Mogadishu was very wrong. General Cunningham had been in a hurry to get there and he was in a hurry to be off on the next stage, the long thousand-mile haul to Addis Ababa. His policy was to maintain unrelenting pressure on the Italians and, also, it was of great importance to get as far as possible before the rains started and made movement over unmetalled roads difficult. He had set his sights high. It remained to be seen, however, whether the Italians would make a determined stand in the difficult mountainous country ahead.

After the battles on the Juba River the G.O.C. had regrouped his forces. General Wetherall, commanding the 11th Division, retained his 23rd (Nigerian) Brigade and took over the 1st (South African) and the 22nd (East African) Brigades whilst General Godwin-Austen kept his 24th (Gold Coast) Brigade and received in addition the 21st and 25th (East African) Brigades and the 1st Battalion Northern Rhodesia Regiment. Soon after the fall of Jelib the Gold Coast Brigade had been sent up the line of the Juba to Bardera and Lugh Ferrandi. This move was to give the Italians the impression that our main advance would be in that direction whereas its real object was only to clear remaining enemy troops from that area and then, weather permitting, join up with the 21st Brigade in the Neghelli/Yavello sector. After the capture of Mega by the 1st South African Division on 18 February, Divisional Headquarters and the two South African Brigades had been withdrawn, the 5th destined to move to the Middle East and the 2nd to assist in retaking British Somaliland. Rain in the south-west of Abyssinia was preventing any further advance and the 12th Division was given the unenviable task of sitting it out, holding the front and keeping the Italians guessing.

The Nigerian Brigade, which had taken over the lead to Mogadishu after the crossing of the Juba, started the main drive towards Addis Ababa by sending a mobile advance force northward from Mogadishu along the Strada Imperiale on 1 March and the remainder of the Brigade followed a few days later. This route was chosen in preference to the Strada Royale which, though a little shorter in miles to Addis Ababa, went north-west through Neghelli and the Lakes where heavy rainfall was expected. The road, metalled and macadamized as far as the Abyssinian border, about two hundred and fifty miles, passed at first across hot, scrub-covered coastal flats. The countryside changed dramatically to green fertility after about fifty miles due to a large government scheme under irrigation from the Uebi Scebeli River, but then relapsed into more semi-desert which extended with little variation as far as Jigigga, seven hundred and forty-four miles from the coast.

Along the whole of this distance there was no hill or pass which the Italians could hope to defend successfully. There were, of course, a few hillocks and wooded knolls but the terrain was such that those could easily be by-passed if necessary. The danger to our columns, however, was from the air. When an infantry division is moving by motor transport it occupies approximately ninety miles of road – and requires almost twelve hours to pass a given point. It is, therefore, very vulnerable – particularly where the cloud of dust created by this movement on unmetalled roads is visible from the air for, perhaps, eighty to one hundred miles and, after the tarmac ended, the whole road had been churned into dust by the transport of the retreating Italians.

In that open country, trucks could disperse quickly on each side of the road in the event of an air attack, but they would not be able to do so further north in the mountainous country. The success of the invading force depended greatly, therefore, on whether the Italians could be prevented from attacking the columns from the air. Before the days of radar the interception of aircraft was generally a matter of chance and the only effective way of disabling the enemy was to attack his air bases. The S.A.A.F. planned to do this, but Mogadishu was too far from them – they needed the use of airfields farther forward. Their opportunity came quickly. The leading troops reached and occupied Jigigga with its good airfield on 12 March and the South African Air Force was there next day.

We had been on top of the *Regia Aeronautica* since the arrival of the Hurricane fighters, but certainly not in complete command of the air. The Fiat CR 42s did not have the speed of the Hurricanes but they were very manoeuvrable, their pilots clever and enterprising and, when operating two or more together, warranted great respect. For example, in raids on our air strips at Dagabur and Jigigga they destroyed six of our aircraft. Their Savoia and Caproni bombers were slow and generally easy prey to our fighters, but the Italians continued to attack us resolutely with them despite heavy losses. They seemed to have an endless supply of them. We knew they had about two hundred aircraft of all types at the beginning of hostilities but, presumably, at least half of these were on the Eritrean front.

On 14 March the S.A.A.F. struck at the Italian air base at Diredawa with its two satellite airfields and, on that and the following day, put twenty enemy aircraft out of action. Six were shot down, nine destroyed on the ground and a further five damaged. Our losses were two Hurricanes. This major success gave our advancing troops a clear sky for some time.

When the Nigerians reached Jigigga they experienced a new and, to them, less friendly climate. They were up at six thousand feet above sea level and the nights were cold and the hills ahead green. The way through those hills was by the Marda Pass, the first and most formidable of the enemy defended positions along the road into the Abyssinian highlands. So a halt was called to reconnoitre the Italian defences and to await the arrival of the next brigade, the South Africans.

There was another reason for waiting a while. From Jigigga a road ran eastward through British Somaliland to its port, Berbera. It was in Italian hands but, if we could retake it and use the port, our supply line would be five hundred miles shorter than the current one from Mogadishu. It was known that there was a considerable Italian force in British Somaliland including their 70th Brigade. What we did not know, however, was that, as soon as they heard that our forward troops had blocked their line of communication at Jigigga, they had made off across country into Abyssinia. The only clue to their whereabouts was provided by their commander, General Bertello, who was identified riding a mule through Diredawa sometime during the following week. (He was to cause us some anxious moments a few weeks later down by the Lakes.) What they did not know was that a striking force from Aden was due to attack and capture Berbera on the night of 15 March. Brigadier Smallwood of the Nigerian Brigade, therefore, sent one of his battalions and a detachment of the 'Recces' to assist this force if necessary. In the event, however, there was little resistance. Two ships of the Royal Indian Navy escorting the striking force shelled the town, whereat the garrison dispersed into the hills whilst the troops from Aden were ferried ashore without opposition. They included Abyssinian Irregulars and one of the Punjabi battalions evacuated from Berbera seven months before. Two hundred Italian prisoners were captured, the rest fled and the 'Recces' and the Nigerians hurried back to Jigigga.

In the meantime South African armoured cars and artillery had arrived there and patrols had located many of the enemy defences on the hills each side of the Marda Pass. It appeared to be a stiff proposition with many fortified points along a four-mile front, and our patrols had been unable to find any way around them. General Wetherall decided to attack with two Nigerian battalions and have the South African Brigade in Reserve. The approach to the pass presented a problem since it had to be across an open plain several miles broad with no cover whatsoever and the Italian gunners could see every movement on it. Finally it was decided to have a motorized charge across it and defeat the gunners by speed.

At 8 a.m. on 20 March the infantry raced over the plain in trucks six abreast to within about a mile of the base of the hills. There they took to their feet and advanced in very open formation. The two battalions were astride the road, the one on the left to cause a diversion while the main attack was to go in on the right. The guns started firing from both sides and, when the infantry reached a line about five hundred yards from the slopes, rifle and automatic fire opened up as well. At one point, quite by chance, our shelling started a grass fire among the enemy positions. This produced a very useful smoke screen which the gunners then proceeded to feed with smoke shells. It is almost unbelievable that anyone could have survived the fusillade that ensued, but most of them did. Shooting from up in the air on the hillsides luckily induced the Italians to fire high.

By late afternoon two platoons of the Nigerians managed to reach the top of one of the hills but ran out of ammunition and were forced back. A little later, however, others reached another hilltop, drove the Italians from it and held fast. From that time on their enemy was the intense cold more than the Italians. When the sun went down a near freezing wind started and seven wounded Nigerians died of exposure that night. Thirty-two of the battalion were killed in the assault. Considering the hazardous nature of the attack it was fortunate that this figure was not very much higher.

The bombardment of the Italian defences together with the achievement of the Nigerians in reaching them on the hills caused the desertion of many of the enemy's African troops and the rest of their force withdrew during the night. Next morning our armoured cars were able to move through the pass after wire, mines and demolitions had been cleared. Judging by the number of the defensive positions and the quality of arms and equipment abandoned, including forty machine-guns, the enemy must have been at brigade strength.

After the Marda Pass the road climbed gradually through wooded hilly country where the advance was more difficult and liable to ambush – and the first came at the Babille Pass. Any devotee of 'Western' films would recognize this immediately and know that it was held by Red Indians. It was a narrow gorge with steep almost vertical sides of granite rock. However, a second gap was found through which an old disused road had passed and which had been blocked by demolition. Some of the Nigerians and South Africans managed to get through this and behind the enemy and then, once again, the Italians withdrew.

Next morning, 25 March, an Italian announcement was broadcast that Harar had been declared an open town. This old historic place was our next objective and the key to the capture of the more important town of Diredawa on the railway from Jibuti to Addis Ababa. However, despite this statement our forces met strong opposition at the Bisidimo River where an artillery duel took place. The Italians were using medium and field guns sited on high ground near Harar. Their gunners were accurate – and so they should have been. They had been able to register from each position to which they had planned to withdraw on to the ridge, road or valley they expected our troops to occupy. The South African gunners had no such advantage but their counter battery shooting was brilliant, courageous and aggressive. Two batteries of the 7th Field Brigade went into action from the only possible but uncomfortably vulnerable position. They were under intense fire themselves but eventually managed to silence the enemy and, when a section of 6-inch Hows. arrived and went into action, the Italians abandoned their guns and were off.

The South African gunners had been helped in an odd way. Since the ground was rain-sodden and soft, the enemy shells, fitted with delayed action fuses, dived deeply into the pudding-like earth which reduced the force of their explosion. This action is best described by one of the gunners who was there:

You can imagine what it feels like to have to take up a gun position when there are twelve guns firing at you. The less thinking you do the better.

You just get on with it so that you can fire back. It took us exactly eighty seconds to offload the guns and have them in line of fire and in about three minutes time we fired our first shots. I expected to get blotted out at any moment because, where we were, in an area of one hundred and twenty yards each way, there were well over two hundred practice craters which the Italians had made. Fortunately for us they used a slightly delayed-action fuse on their shells and the ground was wet as well. If it had been rocky we should have caught it properly. Even so, I can't understand why we weren't hit because they kept on making craters only four or five feet from our guns.

It was known that the Italians had put one of their crack brigades, the 13th Colonial Brigade, into the battle for Harar, but we had learnt from deserters that two regiments of infantry had mutinied and that some seven hundred deserters from that brigade had attacked and looted a government farm nearby. It was no surprise, therefore, when the advancing South Africans and Nigerians encountered no further resistance and confirmation of the announcement that Harar was out of the fight was received with a statement that an emissary was on his way to surrender the town.

March 26 was a cold, wet day. The Divisional Commander was at his advance headquarters. They were not very impressive and consisted of merely two or three small tents, some tarpaulins thrown over poles, a wooden table bearing a few enamel mugs and three or four camp-chairs. The General, standing by the Signals van, looked anxious. His main interest was in an African crouching over a small fire of sticks into which he was blowing gently to fan the feeble flames. There was reason for the General's anxiety; there seemed little prospect of the kettle boiling, and he wanted his tea.

At that moment his A.D.C. came to tell him that the Italian emissary had arrived. The General watched impassively as the Residente, wearing a good deal of gold braid and accompanied by a young officer as interpreter, approached. The African cook continued to blow hopefully at the flames and add a few sticks from time to time, heedless of the dignity of the situation, so the Residente produced a document which he proceeded to read and the young officer to translate. It proclaimed Harar to be an open city which would be surrendered at 7 a.m. the next morning. This was not good enough for the General who demanded its immediate capitulation — or else. He had no intention of giving the Italians until morning to withdraw their forces and move off towards Addis Ababa. The Residente protested, the General was adamant and the emissary was then whisked off back to Harar accompanied by armoured cars and a company of Nigerians with fixed bayonets. The Provincial Governor and the bishop then handed over the town and our armoured cars blocked the road to Diredawa.

All that night groups of Italian troops kept coming in to surrender, some on foot, others in trucks and some even hauling guns. They were all directed to a marshalling area and disarmed.

In the rush, excitement and hurly-burly that day no one could appreciate the beauty of the countryside around Harar with its fertile valleys, wooded hills and splendid climate. Then there were other amenities such as the new hotel − where there was still some champagne. But almost everyone was hoping to get quickly down to Diredawa in the valley where even the nights are warm. On the Cunningham principle of wasting no time, the Transvaal Scottish were already on their way there. But it was to prove difficult. The road down into the valley, several thousand feet below, twisted and turned round hair-pin bends and along precipitous cliff edges. It was an easy road to block − and the Italian sappers were good at blocking roads as well as making them.

General Wetherall's plan was for the Transvaal Scottish and the Royal Natal Carbineers to go down this road through the Hubeta Pass, cut the railway line at Diredawa and then proceed one hundred miles westward to Miesso. At the same time the third battalion of the South African Brigade, the Duke of Edinburgh's Own Regiment, was to move westward from Harar along the line of the Chercher Hills to capture Asba Littorio and then drop down into the valley to join the other battalions at Miesso.

The Transvaal Scottish were first stopped ten miles from Harar where a bridge had been blown up. A brickfield nearby, however, provided plenty of material for filling the gap and they were soon able to move on. Two miles farther along the road another bridge was down − and this was over a much deeper gully. But to the 'Jocks', many of whom were gold-miners in peacetime, this was no great problem and they soon built two stone retaining walls thirty feet high, filled the space between them with more stones and across went the troop carriers. A further demolition had to be dealt with and a deviation made over a stream and then they rushed on in a hurry to reach the top of the pass. It was expected that the Italians would be defending that point and they wanted to try and push then out of it before dark.

Their guess was correct. Reaching the top of the pass at 3 p.m., they found the Italians were entrenched in strongly defended positions in the hills each side of the road. Further demolitions could be seen and these were on a far larger scale than any before. In places the face of the mountainside into which the road had been hewn had been dynamited and blown away leaving nothing but a deep chasm. The road was under rifle, mortar and machine-gun fire so no repair work could be started until the enemy had been driven from the hills.

On the left the Transvaalers pushed the Italians from two ridges in succession. Then, faced by the setting sun and an open plain, they waited until dark before advancing farther. On the other side of the road the enemy had two very strong positions reinforced with stonework, one above the other and dominating the pass. Armoured cars and mortars were brought up to fire on them but it was not until anti-tank guns smashed the stone walls that the lower one was silenced. Infantry climbed a thousand feet up the mountainside to reach the higher position, then dashed along a narrow ridge to attack the Italians from above and behind. This was completely successful and, when the Transvaalers, after a night flanking movement on the left side of the valley, found the Italians had slipped away in the dark, the pass was theirs. This was a highly skilful and daring operation. Shells and mortar bombs had been hurled at them as well as very heavy small-arms fire. The last stronghold had been manned by fifty determined white Italian officers and N.C.O.s collected from units which had disintegrated, yet the Scottish lost only one man killed. Their booty included thirty trucks, three field guns, two mortars, a score of machine-guns and two hundred prisoners. Incidentally some of these prisoners, all the trucks and the field guns fell into their hands because the Italians, in a panic, had blown the last demolition before they had time to get away.

The South and East African Engineers and the Nigerian Pioneers then started the herculean task of remaking the road through the pass. It was estimated that this would take eight days. They bulldozed, filled, built, bridged and strove all day and night – and finished it in thirty-six hours. Diredawa then capitulated and our forces drove into the town on 29 March. The citizens were dismayed. They had been told that their army could hold the Marda Pass for a month whereas we had taken it in a day and a night. Now the Hubeta Pass had been forced in that same short time.

General Cunningham then moved his Advanced Force Head-quarters to Harar and had messages dropped by air on Adama, Awash and Addis Ababa demanding the surrender of the capital. A reply was required the next day by air, 2 April, to arrive at Diredawa at a specified time so that the aircraft would not be fired on. Right on time a Savoia flew over. No one knew for certain whether it had come to drop bombs or a message. Happily it was the latter. It read 'Back tomorrow same time' or words to that effect. So South African bombers flew off to attack enemy transport between Addis Ababa and Dessie and fighters to machine-gun targets between Miesso and Addis. The next day the Savoia returned, arriving exactly on time and bringing an emissary. He was taken up to Headquarters at Harar while the Springbok pilots entertained their Italian counterparts at the hotel in Diredawa. Each knew only a few words of the other's language but they managed to swop stories of the battles they had fought against each other in the air – and would perhaps fight again next day. 'Do come and see us when you get to Addis,' they said. 'Our wives would be delighted to meet you.'

Terms for the surrender were not agreed so the Italians flew back to their base – to return again next day with the emissary – and a case of wine for their hosts. (A funny thing, war, isn't it?) Once more, however, no agreement was reached and the Italians flew back to Addis. So did the South Africans – to bomb and machine-gun their aerodrome. They set fire to some of the buildings and, on that and the following day, destroyed nine Savoias, three Capronis and a Fiat CR42.

While these negotiations were taking place the war on the ground continued. It was the turn of the 22nd Brigade to take over the lead again and they passed through the South African Brigade at Miesso at 1 a.m. on 2 April – where they had run out of petrol. By 11 a.m. the advance guard, consisting of the 6th K.A.R. and armoured cars, had contacted the enemy near Arba, a few miles short of the Awash River, and had come under artillery and machine-gun fire. One company supported by a section of the 22nd Mountain Battery attacked on a flank and had dislodged them by 3 p.m. During this action some Italian medium tanks were seen but they were not used. Road blocks were then cleared and the advance continued.

It was known that the railway bridge over the Awash River had been destroyed but, at 5.30 p.m., a muffled roar indicated that the road bridge had also been blown up. It was clear that our crossing of the river was going to be opposed and, at dusk, the Brigade halted some five miles short of the gorge. The country each side of the river is flat so that in order to defend the line of the river the enemy would have to hold positions on the very edge of the gorge and, thereby, be an easy mark for our gunners. The cliff itself is some two hundred feet high at this point and the river about thirty yards wide but not too deep to wade across. It was known that there was a passable ford about a mile south of the road bridge which had been used for the old Abyssinian road.

At dawn next morning the 5th K.A.R. was ordered to send patrols forward on a wide front to test the enemy defences and locate any other practicable crossing-places while the guns were to prepare to give covering fire for an attack later in the day. Three companies were detailed for this operation. By the railway bridge on our right there was stiff opposition, so our guns were ordered to concentrate on that area to distract attention from our centre and left where platoon-strength patrols were crossing the river against less opposition and beginning to scale the west side of the gorge with covering fire from our machine-guns. They reached the summit, quelled any further resistance by bayonet charges and the battle of the Awash was over before it had fairly begun. Two M.C.s and two M.M.s were awarded for gallantry during these intrepid and highly successful attacks up the cliffside – to Lieutenants Langridge and Howard, Lance-Corporal Farah and Private Boiyo.

By that evening our small force had taken prisoner seventy officers and one hundred and three Italian other ranks from the 37/40 Anti-tank Battery and the 3rd Company of the Machine-gun Battalion of the 10th Regiment Savoy Grenadiers. Next morning the 5th K.A.R. went on to capture Awash village and two officers and one hundred and eighty-two ranks of 3 Company 504 Blackshirt Battalion and a further two hundred of the 210 Regiment of Fanteria d'Africa. The enemy had been of the cream of the Italian army.

In the meantime six of our armoured cars had been manhandled down into the gorge at the old ford, across the river and up the other side. At times this required as many as two hundred Askaris on the ropes at one time. Downstream the sappers, finding that the buttresses of the road bridge were almost intact, erected a box girder across them and, at 2 a.m. on 5 April, the Brigade Group started using this to cross the river. Their immediate role was to ensure that the retreating enemy forces, which were believed to be going south down two roads from Adama and Moggio towards the Lakes, did not turn back and threaten our flank on the road to Addis Ababa. So, leaving the 6th K.A.R. and two companies of the 5th K.A.R. to make sure of this, the remainder of the Brigade drove on. When the leading troops reached the Garibaldi Pass, they met an envoy in the person of Fausto

Fabritus, a major in the Italian army who had been sent by General Mambrini, the chief of police in Addis Ababa. He was escorted by an armoured car and thirty men of the 219 Blackshirt Battalion and brought a request to the British forces to occupy Addis Ababa as soon as possible in order to protect civilian life and property from the local Abyssinians. The Brigade pushed on with all speed while instructions were sought from higher authority regarding this strange request. Strange because there were found to be six thousand five hundred armed Italians in Addis the day after the fall.

Brigadier Fowkes had always said that he would reach Addis Ababa first with the 22nd Brigade. He was then well to the fore, leading the field and determined to win the race by hook or by crook. Some of the stories told of the measures he took to ensure this may be apocryphal but those who knew him will be certain that there was some substance in them. One thing I do know; his Brigade transport and his alone had sufficient petrol to get there. Whilst in the Mogadishu area he had told his transport officer, Budge Gethin, to acquire, 'liberate' or seize enough of the petrol abandoned by the Italians to take his Brigade Group a thousand miles. That efficient officer went into the petrol-running business enthusiastically and, during the 'rest' period at Merca, had dumped hundreds of drums at various hideouts along the Strada Imperiale.

All went well and according to plan. He was first over the Awash River and well placed with only one hundred and forty miles to go. But at this point the Divisional Commander intervened. He had orders from Force Headquarters that the South Africans should have the honour of being first into the capital, so he sent a personal signal to our Brigadier saying 'Halt and allow 1 SA Bde to pass through' – or words to that effect. Undaunted the Brigadier dealt swiftly with this. Following the Nelson tradition he turned a blind eye and replied that the signal had been mutilated in transmission and was not understood. All his vehicles had plenty of petrol so on they sped.

He had already envisaged the possibility of the General then sending another message to him by despatch rider so, in order to avoid any such catastrophe, he had instructed his rear party not to allow anyone to pass up the column – in, of course, the interests of security. But, as he bowled along, his blue pennant flying in the breeze and Addis Ababa almost in sight, the Divisional Commander played a trump card – he sent a plane to stop him. The pilot spotted the column without difficulty and then, flying so low that the drivers instinctively ducked their heads, dropped his message bag with ribbons fluttering almost on to the bonnet of the Brigadier's car. This was *force majeure* with a vengeance and he halted – ten miles from the capital.

In the event the honours were divided fairly. General Wetherall was accompanied by Brigadier Fowkes, Brigadier Pienaar of the 1st South African Brigade and Brigadier Smallwood of the Nigerian Brigade when they went to the Duke of Aosta's residence for the signing of the armistice.

13

Mopping Up around the Lakes

2 APRIL TO 22 MAY 1941

The two forces the Brigadier had left at Adama and Moggio to block the roads south soon found out that the boot was on the other foot: the prospective blockers had been blocked. The retreating Italians had already blown up both the bridges across the Awash River and were dug in on the south bank to oppose our crossing. However, since this showed clearly that they had no intention of attacking our Line of Communication with Addis Ababa and were only concerned with protecting their own withdrawal from the fray, we can halt a while in the story in order to review the overall situation.

There were known to be seven Italian divisions south of Addis Ababa at that time. Four of these were opposing General Godwin-Austen's 12th Division in southern Abyssinia, a strong force was defending Jimma and the line of the Omo River between there and Addis Ababa, and it was believed that there were two divisions in the area of the Lakes and Soddu. A division, particularly at that stage in the campaign, was a somewhat loose term and although unexpected reinforcements were arriving for them from Addis Ababa since it had been declared an open city and from the remnants of General de Simone's Juba army, none of them would have been up to strength. Nevertheless it is probable that they numbered somewhere around forty thousand men. This is borne out by the fact that, from the start of the mopping-up operation on 5 April to the fall of Jimma on 4 July, Brigadier Fowkes' 22nd Brigade alone took twenty-two thousand five hundred and thirty-eight prisoners — and several thousand more after that in the far west.

This Italian army in the south was in a large net. It had to be a large one because the distance from the Awash River where we were held up down to where the 12th Division was immobilized by the rain is two hundred miles, and the breadth of the operational area from Maji,

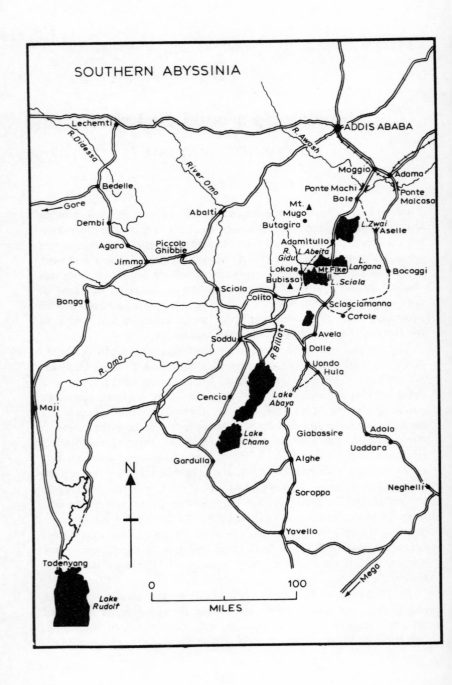

SOUTHERN ABYSSINIA

Lechemti

R Didessa

Gore

Bedelle

River Omo

Dembi

Abalti

Agaro

Piccola
Ghibbie

Jimma

Bonga

R. Omo

Sciola

Colito

Maji

Soddu

Cencia

Gardulla

Lake
Chamo

N

Todenyang

Lake
Rudolf

0   100

MILES

ADDIS ABABA

R Awash

Moggio

Adama

Ponte Machi
Bole

Ponte
Malcaso

Mt.
Mugo

Butagira

L. Zwai
Aselle

Adamitullo
R.   L. Abeita
Gidu

L.
Langana

Lokole
Bubissa

Mt Fike

Bocoggi

L. Sciala

Sciasciamanna

Cotole

R Billate

Avela

Dalle

Uondo
Hula

Lake
Abaya

Giabassire

Adola

Uaddara

Alghe

Soroppa

Neghelli

Yavello

Mega

west of Jimma, to the mountainous district east of the Lakes is about the same. This makes a round total of forty thousand square miles. The movement of troops within this area was not hindered inordinately by the lakes or the mountains but what halted all movement of vehicles at times, since metalled roads were few and far between, was mud, deep mud and heavy rain.

The net was to be tightened on all sides. Down south the Gold Coast Brigade and two East African Brigades were eager to push northward as soon as movement became possible when the rains slackened, and the 22nd Brigade was about to apply pressure in the north. The Italian forces were faced with inevitable defeat but were ordered to continue to struggle so that it would be impossible for us to release any troops to reinforce our army in North Africa. Their strategy was, therefore, as withdrawal became necessary, to concentrate behind the line of the Omo River in the Jimma area.

We must now return to the Awash River and the two demolished bridges. We had learnt from captured documents that General de Simone himself intended to escape down the road from Adama with a very mixed body of men including Blackshirt battalions, regular infantry, some Air Force men turned into infantry, customs officers and armed police. They had with them some medium and light tanks and a large amount of artillery, chiefly 65-, 75- and 105-mm. guns. Their route after crossing the bridge, the Ponte Malcasa, was to be through Aselle and Bocoggi, over a ten thousand two hundred-feet-high pass and down to Sciasciamanna via Cofole. The estimated time of arrival of this column at Sciasciamanna was 6 April according to the Italian document, but the road after Bocoggi was appalling due to rain, as we ourselves were shortly to find out, and they were not able to keep to the schedule.

When the task force from the 5th K.A.R. moved down this road from Adama they found the river crossing held by the enemy and the bridge demolished. They were fired on by small-arms, artillery and an anti-tank gun which knocked out our two leading armoured cars. Our infantry deployed, one company to clear and hold the north bank and put down mortar fire on the enemy positions across the river and the other to work its way downstream, ford the river and outflank the Italians. They did this successfully, capturing the anti-tank gun, and the enemy then withdrew but continued to shell the river banks.

By then the Nigerian Light Battery had arrived on the scene and proceeded to fire on to the road along which the enemy transport was retiring. But, some four miles away and out of range of our guns, were some Italian 105s which continued to harass our force and prevent repairs to the bridge being started. Not until the arrival of some South African 60-pounders a day later was the position rectified. Some of the South African gunners stoutly maintained that they had taken these big guns from the World War I memorial in Johannesburg. If this were true it would substantiate the old saying that many a good tune is played on an old fiddle!

By 9 April a temporary bridge had been erected by 54(EA) Field Company and, on the 11th, the 5th K.A.R. with armoured cars, 18 Mountain Battery, some anti-tank guns and a detachment of sappers crossed the river and went south to enter Aselle without opposition. They found a large number of armed and mounted Abyssinians there surrounding a group of farm buildings from which intermittent shots were being fired. On investigation they learned that about a hundred Italian men, women and children had barricaded themselves inside, had fought off an attack by the Abyssinians the day before and were awaiting a further assault. One knew what the outcome would have been had our troops not arrived at that moment because the dead and mutilated bodies of those who had failed to reach the farm in time were found nearby. Protesting hotly but with no alternative the Abyssinians departed. 'This is war,' they said. 'The Italians gave us no quarter when they took our country and now we will give them none.'

The Brigade Group then concentrated at Aselle on 13 April, Brigade Headquarters being in the same buildings that had so nearly been attacked and burnt to the ground, together with its occupants, by our Abyssinian allies. A small force with armoured cars, machine-guns and some of Henfrey's Scouts went on to occupy Bocoggi. (Some of Henfrey's men were by that time right down in the valley near Cofole watching the arrival of General de Simone's party!)

A motorized reconnaissance group went down to Cofole too. They brought back the Residente and six Italian civilians, refugees from the wrath of roaming bands of Abyssinians – and something more useful, some machine-guns and twenty thousand rounds of ammunition. The road was so bad that it took them eleven hours to cover the eighty-six miles from Bocoggi – and eighteen hours to get back. Motoring under such conditions played havoc with the vehicles and, a further major consideration, it increased petrol consumption to about only three to four miles per gallon. In view of this the Brigadier decided to switch his main advance on to the road south from Moggio.

The map showed a road leading from Aselle across to the Moggio road but the sappers had been to have a look at it and found it not passable. So, leaving small forces at Bocoggi and Aselle with orders to make their presence known to the enemy and cause a diversion on 26 April, he moved the Brigade Group back to Adama and thence on to the road south from Moggio. On 24 April the bridge over the Awash near Bole, the Ponte Machi, was ready for use and an advance party of the Brigade crossed over and reached Adamitullo without opposition. Defensive positions were established on the two roads going south from there, one on the east and another on the west side of Lake Abeita, while reconnaissance patrols went forward towards Sciasciamanna and to Butagira on the slopes of Mount Mugo to the west, where it was thought there might be some enemy forces. In fact there were none but the patrol had its second experience of operating with Patriots. On the second morning as they were going on foot to occupy Butagira, out of the early morning mist thundered a band of mounted Abyssinians apparently bent on destroying the village. Seeing our patrol, however, they pulled up and it was then seen that a large number of the riders were women. All were armed with lances and shields and looked like medieval Cossacks. After a moment's hesitation they galloped off. Were they chasing some Italians? But a little later our men, having taken to their troop carriers, found themselves embroiled in a battle between the horsemen (and women) and a neighbouring village or tribe that must have incurred their displeasure. The commander of the K.A.R. patrol decided that it would be unwise to become involved in family squabbles and went off to find quarters for the night. He found some empty houses in the village including that of the absent Residente. Part of this had been dismantled, presumably to provide building material for a Patriot house.

That evening a large body of Patriots under an Abyssinian army officer arrived in the village. British and Abyssinian flags were run up on an improvised staff and cups of tea were handed round. They were able to communicate sufficiently to arrange for information on enemy movements to be sent to our Brigade Headquarters, but the meeting was marred and, of necessity, adjourned when a thunderstorm and a strong wind proved too much for the weakened structure of the Residente's house and it collapsed on to the ground.

These incidents were food for reflection. We knew our Abyssinian Scouts and Irregulars but there were obviously Patriots — and Patriots! Whether they were Scouts, Irregulars, Patriots or freelance bandits they all had an inherent love of fighting; it was their national sport and their appetite for it had been whetted by their hatred of the Italians. Travelling light, generally with little but a rifle, ammunition and a blanket, they could live off the land and travel at will throughout the country. But there the similarity ends. The Patriots were not enrolled in any organization and, mostly, were not paid or fed. They just turned up at the bidding of their feudal lord and, there being no discernible discipline, disappeared and returned home when they felt like it. In north and west Abyssinia where they were to a great extent organized and generally led by British officers, they played a major part in the defeat of the Italians and the restoration of the Emperor. But to our forces operating south of Addis Ababa they were of doubtful value. In a military operational area such as the Lakes, Patriots could not be keyed into the army organization: they were just 'unkeyable'.

The Irregulars and Scouts on the other hand were enlisted, paid and disciplined soldiers who, when led by British or allied officers, became highly enterprising and efficient, not only in obtaining information but in ambushing and attacking enemy convoys and patrols. When, therefore, information was needed about the Italian strength at Sciasciamanna, Henfrey's Scouts were the men to get it. Whilst doing this in the last few days, they had ambushed a convoy near Faggi destroying five lorries and killing three Italians. Then, on the 29th, they ambushed another convoy, killed sixteen Italians and nineteen of their Askaris and captured eight 65-mm. guns, two machine-guns and four lorries. These men were indeed valuable allies.

While the 5th K.A.R. patrol was away in the Mount Mugo area, two smaller patrols from the 5th and 6th K.A.R. went forward, one on each side of Lake Abeita. Both located enemy with artillery on a hill-top at Fike. This position dominated the road south of the lake and would have to be cleared before an attack on Sciasciamanna could be made. So, on 29 April, the one remaining company of the 5th K.A.R. made a close reconnaissance of the Fike position. To reach this they had to cross the Gidu River, a difficult matter because it was in flood and a wide area on each side of it had become a swamp. They managed to get over, however, and spent the night on some high ground. There, at 2 a.m., the company from Mount Mugo found them. In view of this reinforcement, the C.O. signalled to Brigade Head-quarters for permission to attack the hill position. This was given but, as they were moving on foot through the swamp, the attack was called off by Brigade and the two companies were ordered to return to their base on the main road to defend it against an imminent attack by an Italian armoured column.

Warning of this attack had been sent to Brigadier Fowkes from

General Cunningham's headquarters where an enemy signal had been intercepted ordering General Bertello, the one who had escaped to Diredawa from British Somaliland on a mule, to move north from Sciasciamanna with his infantry and armour to cut our lines of communication at Moggio. This Italian general had the reputation of being a determined and courageous fighter and, as the 22nd Brigade was very much under strength at the time, the Brigadier decided to be prudent and pull in his horns. Our positions on the Adamitullo road were then wired in and mined and the onslaught was awaited. Next morning, 30 April, our armoured cars scouting in front of these defences saw some enemy medium tanks and engaged them. Three of our cars were knocked out and the remainder withdrew. So, luckily, did the Italian tanks! Then, as the expected attack did not materialize, the Brigadier sent the two companies, with a detachment of the 18th Mountain Battery, back to take the hill at Fike. The attack is described in the official account of the operations of the 22(EA) Brigade as follows:

On the morning of 1 May, 5 K.A.R. supported by 18 Mtn. Bty. crossed the River Gidu and almost immediately came under heavy fire from the enemy positions on the western slopes of Mount Fike. Lieut.-Colonel Hurt delivered a feint frontal attack with one of his companies sending his only other company round the upper slopes of the hill to deliver an attack on the enemy's left flank. In spite of hard going the flank attack, under command of Capt. D.H. Kemble, was entirely successful. With a final bayonet charge at dusk the enemy resistance was completely overcome. Some thirty Italians and twenty Africans were killed and 65 Italians and 94 Africans captured. Booty included three 65/17-mm. guns and two 20-mm. Breda guns and 11 medium and 13 light machine-guns. Our casualties were one officer and two Askaris wounded.

The officer was Douglas Draffan, the Adjutant, who got a bullet in his stomach. But, due to the prompt and skilful work of the M.O., he recovered.

One further incident during the attack should be recounted. One of our stretcher-bearers was so carried away by the excitement of battle that he joined in the final assault. He had, of course, neither rifle nor bayonet — but he had his stretcher. With this he bashed one of the enemy on the head and knocked him out. Then, calling up his assistant, they carefully laid the unconscious man on the stretcher and carried him back to the first-aid post.

This brisk little action exemplifies the aggressive spirit which enabled the small K.A.R. force to defeat the larger and better equipped one of the Italians. It was not a solitary incident, there were many. The advantage gained from them lay not so much in the prisoners taken, the casualties inflicted and the guns and equipment captured as in the erosion and gradual destruction of the morale of the enemy.

After this success the way was open for an attack on Sciasciamanna. This small town was important mainly because, by taking it, the 22nd Brigade would be in control of one of the roads to the west and then move on to Dalle, thirty miles farther south, to block the only other one. The Italian divisions being gradually driven northward by our 12th Division would then be sandwiched between it and the 22nd Brigade and unable to escape through Soddu to Jimma — except by going across country.

But the 22nd Brigade was not at that time strong enough to mount a major attack. It had had to relinquish the whole of the 1st K.A.R. for L. of C. protection and half of the 5th Battalion were at Aselle and Bocoggi. The drain on the fighting strength of the Division to guard its lines of communication was a serious problem. The road link with Kenya must continue to be secured as all the army's requirements could not come by sea — and this link was some one thousand seven hundred and fifty miles long. Garrison battalions with older and less highly trained men than those in the first-line battalions were being equipped to send up from Kenya, but this took time — more of it than General Cunningham had used in getting to Addis Ababa.

However, on 3 May, the 1st Natal Mounted Rifles* were sent to reinforce the Brigade and the two companies of the 5th K.A.R. returned from Aselle and Bocoggi. This immediately doubled the strength of the Brigade and the capture of Sciasciamanna was then planned.

Whilst an attack along the line through Bubissa and Colito would have the advantage of cutting the enemy line of retreat to Soddu, there was a big disadvantage in the flooded and swampy ground by the

---

* When the 1st (South African) Division was relieved by General Godwin-Austen's 12th (African) Division early in March 1941 after the capture of Mega in southern Abyssinia, H.Q. 1(S.A.) Division, the Divisional Troops and the 5th (S.A.) Brigade went up to the Middle East. The 2nd (S.A.) Brigade, comprising the 1st Natal Mounted Rifles and the 1st and 2nd Field Force Battalions, was held in reserve for the operation of retaking British Somaliland. In the event this was unnecessary and 1 N.M.R. and 1 F.F.B. were sent to assist the 22nd Brigade at Sciasciamanna and Dalle.

Gidu River. It was decided, therefore, that the major attack should be down the main road: only a small force should go across country to Bubissa on this difficult flanking route with the object of causing a diversion and preventing reinforcements being sent to Sciasciamanna from there. Accordingly the 1st N.M.R. with the 22nd Mountain Battery, the 5th South African Field Battery, armoured cars and light tanks moved down the road on 9 May, crossed the Auada and Dadaba Rivers unopposed but came in contact with the enemy next day when they were fired on by small-arms and artillery from positions on the south bank of the Dadaba Piccolo River.

In the meantime the 5th K.A.R. with the 18th Mountain Battery, armoured cars and a detachment of Engineers managed to cross the Gidu River with considerable difficulty on 9 May and reached Lokole. The local people reported that the Italian garrison at Bubissa had some guns and tanks. Next day, after further trouble with swampy ground, they reached a point about three miles short of Bubissa and halted to reconnoitre the ground. Their orders were not to get heavily involved there but to harass the garrison and contain it. Early on 10 May, therefore, one company with the guns attacked the east side of the village whilst a small tank hunting-party went round to the west side with three armoured cars, one (captured) anti-tank gun and some infantry.

The attack from the east appeared to be succeeding until some enemy medium tanks arrived on the scene. The situation was then very difficult. Three armoured cars went forward from the Reserve in an endeavour to draw the tanks away but two of them sank in the mud and had to be abandoned. But, just as the guns were preparing to fire at the tanks over open sights, they inexplicably withdrew and the company was able to extricate itself without serious casualties.

Meanwhile the tank hunting-party was stuck in a swamp about a mile away and had to abandon one of their armoured cars. They eventually returned to their base without having fired a shot. They had, however, taken some eighty prisoners who had run out of the village as soon as our guns started firing. One of our officers was taken prisoner but he, and the three sunken armoured cars, were all recaptured later.

During this mêlée when tanks were hunting men and men hunting tanks, Lance-Corporal Kiprono had both his legs smashed. However, he could just crawl and, indeed, that was the safest form of locomotion in the tricky situation. He and two officers pretended to be dead when an Italian tank passed five yards away — then they started to crawl again. Shortly, however, it became necessary to carry Kiprono and, by alternate crawls and carryings, they travelled a mile or more until they encountered some Abyssinians. These timely allies quickly made a rough stretcher out of branches and carried the wounded man, with a coat thrown over him and a cigarette in his mouth, back to the bivouac area.

When the M.O. had fixed Kiprono up as well as he could in the bush, the two officers went over to see him. He then solemnly and apologetically proffered a five-shilling note saying 'Please take this, *bwana*, it's all I've got. I have always said that the *bwanas* would never leave us behind on the battlefield — now I know.'

At that stage in the somewhat unsatisfactory little action the C.O. signalled to Brigade for permission to 'have another go', but the Brigadier firmly and wisely ordered the force to withdraw behind the line of the Gidu River pending the result of the main attack on Sciasciamanna across the Dadaba Piccolo River. A text book model battle was being staged there. The 6th K.A.R. were holding the south bank of the river facing the enemy while the 1st N.M.R. forded the river on the night of 12 May three miles to the west. Our guns harassed the enemy that night and, next morning, while the 6th K.A.R. and Henfrey's Scouts made a feint attack on the Italian left flank, the South Africans attacked the other and swept round to their rear. The battle was over. The bag was eight hundred prisoners, ten tanks and eighteen guns. On 14 May our armoured cars entered Sciasciamanna and collected a further one hundred and fifty prisoners. A mobile force consisting of one company of the N.M.R. and the 6th K.A.R. with light tanks and armoured cars was sent forward at once to take and occupy Dalle, thirty miles to the south, and block the second and last escape road towards Jimma for the Italian divisions in the south. This force captured the small town of Avela on the 16 May taking five hundred prisoners, and then went on to Dalle where they picked up three hundred more. Divisional Headquarters then ordered two South African battalions, the 1st N.M.R. and the 1st Field Force Battalion, which were on temporary loan to them, to hold Dalle while the A.F.V.s returned to the 22nd Brigade for their next task.

We must now, for a time, leave the 22nd Brigade resting on its laurels and look at contemporary events in the south. General Godwin-Austen's 12th Division, which had replaced the 1st South African Division in southern Abyssinia shortly after the fall of Mega on 18 February, was having an uncomfortable and sticky time in the mud. The Gold Coast Brigade, after moving up the line of the Juba River through Bardera, Lugh Ferrandi and Dolo where they met with only slight opposition, reached Neghelli during the last week of March. The 21st Brigade, which had been holding the whole front, then wisely, following the example of the Roman legions, went into winter quarters. Their base was at Yavello and, from there, they planned to attack an Italian post at Soroppa when weather permitted and, subsequently, the very strong enemy positions at Giabassire on the road northward through Alghe to the Lakes. But, from February to May, it was not a question of whether they could take the offensive but whether supplies from Kenya could even reach them where they were. The roads behind them as well as in front were becoming worse and worse, and the future prospect was no less grim: the rains always moved gradually northward – where they wanted to go – and the peak period around Addis Ababa was in August.

The forested mountainous area of south-west Abyssinia had never been developed and the few roads that existed were only unmetalled tracks which became quagmires when it rained and unfit for motor vehicles. The difficulties with which the drivers, many of whom were the ever-cheerful Cape Coloured from South Africa, had to contend were described at the time by an officer of the K.A.R.:

Day after day it rained and the lorries, about a hundred of them, sank deeper into the mud every time we tried to move them forward. We couldn't go back, for one thing we couldn't have turned the convoy round and for another we realized that it was probably worse behind than it was in front. The ruts became deeper, with the result that lorries sat fast on their axles, and in order to make any progress at all it was necessary either to cut away the middle of the road or fill up the ruts with bundles of brushwood. Hours were spent cutting brushwood and laying it in the tracks for the sake of moving the convoy a few hundred yards.

It now became apparent that no further supplies of food would reach us till the rains stopped, so every man went on to half rations, hardly sufficient to support a full day's work.

Daily progress varied from a few hundred yards to perhaps two miles for the whole convoy, but it was slow work manhandling every one of the odd hundred trucks. On occasions, river-beds normally dry became roaring torrents as much as ten feet deep which split up sections of the convoy and men from their food and bedding for hours and sometimes days.

But conditions were equally bad, perhaps worse, for the Italians where they were – and, so long as they stayed where they were, our 12th Division was achieving its object.

Despite these conditions, however, the Gold Coast Brigade from Neghelli and the 21st Brigade from Yavello managed to send out patrols to make contact with the enemy and spy out the land. The 21st Brigade succeeded in floundering through the mud to capture Soroppa after an action which has been described as a model of good planning and efficient execution. Their road north was worse than that from Neghelli and at one period they were only able to cover forty-seven miles in ten days. It was then decided that one battalion should continue the advance on foot with improvised pack transport whilst the other two churned their way back to Yavello with the motor transport. There, at least, they could be fed.

Another part of the Divisional plan which had to go by the board was that for the interchange of supporting arms between the brigades. There were insufficient for both of them so guns and A.F.V.s were to be switched from one line of advance to the other. The only road between Neghelli and Yavello, however, could not be used as a river bridge was continually being submerged and carried away by the floods. Luckily, as things turned out, this did not matter.

The Gold Coast Brigade was able to move on its road north with less difficulty and an advance force went up to reconnoitre the approaches to the renowned and redoubtable fortified positions at Uaddara on 19 April. It was there that the Abyssinians had withstood Italian attacks for eleven months in their war of 1936. The small Gold Coast force went bald-headed at this formidable defensive network, quickly captured some of the enemy outposts and then, with praiseworthy confidence and guts but inadequate appreciation of the situation, attempted to storm one of the main defences. This failed and they had to withdraw on the 22nd. Thereafter it took ten days to make a thorough investigation and exploration of the whole area.

The natural features alone presented great difficulties. There were precipitous cliffs, deep ravines and near impenetrable thick forest which prevented the use of A.F.V.s or any other type of vehicle. On and among these obstructions were cleverly placed gun and machine-gun positions covering a three-mile front and an area four miles in depth. The Italian right flank and front were protected by guns on a prominent feature with an excellent field of fire and their left flank was in dense forest. The Italian force holding this natural fortress consisted of five Colonial battalions containing a high proportion of tough and experienced Eritreans.

Apart from the cold, wet conditions, the Gold Coast Askaris were in their element in the forest. For ten days they pushed and hacked their way through it by day and by night, locating enemy positions and possible ways around them. Sometimes they were only able to feel their way forward in the dark and then find their way back by compass after hand-to-hand scraps with enemy patrols.

As a result of this work a plan was made and the main attack started on 3 May. It lasted a week. One battalion was to make a feint attack on the main promontory on the Italian right flank while another, in conjunction with some Irregulars, was to worm its way through the forest on the other flank and up and around the enemy's forward positions. Fighting was heard but could not be seen in the forest and, by noon that day, it seemed that the venture had failed. Later in the afternoon, however, it was learnt that one company had managed to reach a point behind the Italians and had cut the road. On this occasion the Italians, though separated from their main body, did not then submit but fought on for four more days before they were finally driven from the last of their posts.

The Gold Coasters – and the Italians – had fought magnificently. A Sergeant-Major who had been in the fighting in Libya said: 'Bardia was a skirmish compared to this.'

In the meantime the battalion of the 21st Brigade which had temporarily discarded its motor transport after the Battle of Soroppa, had gone ahead on foot to reconnoitre a very formidable obstacle on their front. This was the fortified area at Giabassire where the Abyssinians had resisted all attempts by the Italians to drive them out in the earlier war. Since then the Italians had strengthened the defences still further for their own use. However, it was found that, as a result of the Gold Coast victory at Uaddara, the enemy forces had pulled out, the more courageous of them to make their way across country to Soddu and Jimma and the others to Uondo and Dalle – into the net.

The Gold Coast, too, had swept on northward through Adola and Hula to the road junction at Uondo, taking prisoner Italian laggards and rearguards and driving the rest into the maw of the South Africans awaiting them at Dalle. The pursuit was hot and they received no time to reorganize and offer resistance – even if they had the will to do so at that time.

Descriptive of the speed with which the Gold Coasters followed up the enemy withdrawing after Uaddara is the story which has been told and re-told, but which I am certain is substantially true, of the captain (or major) who, with a platoon (or three) and some armoured cars, splashed their way through the mud from Adola to Hula on 20 May. Taking many Italian troops by surprise, he left a thousand (or two) prisoners of war along the road with a few Askaris to guard them. At dusk he reached the important town of Hula with its one thousand-strong garrison commanded by an Italian brigadier-general who offered no resistance – except to the indignity of surrendering to such a junior officer. But the junior officer insisted and said the only alternative would be for him to attack the town with his platoon (or two) whereat the Brigadier-General saw his point and accepted the indignity with fair grace.

This enterprising adventure by the advanced elements of the Brigade was followed up immediately by the remainder of the 1st Battalion of the Gold Coast Regiment which, on 22 May, captured Uondo. This operation was graphically described by an officer in the Gold Coast Regiment at the time:

The 22 May dawned a fine day, and we made ready for our move, hoping for a good road. The Battalion started off at 7 o'clock with a section of South African armoured cars in front. The Intelligence had told us that a famous Cavalry regiment was defending Uondo and would probably take up a position about five miles outside the town, which was fifteen miles away. The road was good but we had to proceed carefully wondering if the enemy would put up a fight.

The advance was continued steadily, but nothing happened, and no sign was seen of enemy troops except small parties wending their way under cover of a white flag to lay down their arms at Hula. Scant notice was taken of them – there were bigger fish to fry that day – and they were left to keep on walking.

It was an interesting journey; the road climbed for the first five or six miles, until the summit of the escarpment overlooking the Rift Valley was reached, and there were some magnificent views of the valley below and of Lake Margherita.* We had climbed to an altitude of somewhere around 9,000 feet and the vegetation was noticeably different from any we had seen before. Giant Lobelia, hypericum and feathery bamboo groves all made a change, brightened by clumps of red-hot pokers growing magnificently. At a hill called Garbitcha the real descent begins and the road drops steadily about 2,000 feet into Uondo.

There was a fair chance that the Italians did not mean to fight, and Captain Styles decided to make a dash into the town and not give them an opportunity to think twice about it. So the armoured cars speeded up to their maximum for safety. Swinging round a corner they came upon two

* Abyssinian name Lake Abaya.

Italian armoured cars equipped with vicious-looking cannons. Their crews were trying frantically to traverse their turrets to get the guns into action – fortunately, for some reason, the guns had been pointing in quite the wrong direction – but our cars got by them in time and the Italian crews then decided to surrender, in spite of their superior armament.

Just a little further on a company of Colonial Infantry was caught napping and they gave in without any show of resistance. It had been their duty to guard that particular approach into Uondo but their Commander had not organized a scheme of defence and he found himself overrun before he knew what was happening. He had, no doubt, thought that the Italian armoured cars would cover him long enough to give him time to organize something when the time came. He gave in without bother or fuss and lined up his company so that they could lay down their arms. He excused himself to Colonel Bruce for his lack of resistance on the grounds that he suffered from a weak heart and really didn't feel like fighting that morning. He was very serious about the apology and Colonel Bruce was just as serious when he assured him that it didn't matter a bit. Anyway, he seemed glad enough to pack his hand in and, if any of his officers or men had any regrets, they were remarkably adroit in hiding the fact. This bunch was left for 'C' Company to look after, Colonel Bruce ordering the fastest possible advance for the last lap. The column went on right into the town and didn't halt until the far edge was reached. Not a single shot was fired. It was obvious that the Italians had decided to give in without any attempt at resistance.

It became known later that the orders to the garrison were to resist and fight if the 'English' came before noon that day but, if they didn't come by then, they were to leave Uondo and make their way to Jimma. Further light was thrown on the situation from the diary of an Italian war correspondent who was in Uondo at the time. He wrote:

UONDO. 21 May. The Divisional Commander gathers all his troops together and explains the position to them, and what must be done. Most of the force will try to reach the Bottego (the Omo), and so open up for themselves the only possible line of retreat. Here, at Uondo, a garrison and the hospital staff is to remain. A part of the Colonial troops is to wait for a portion of the 30th Brigade which has escaped through the jungle from the British forces coming up from Hula.

UONDO. 22 May. At 3 a.m. the Divisional column has left. They will have to face a long and dangerous journey. Men and officers know what task lies before them.

At this point the diary ends with the entry of the Gold Coast troops into Uondo – and the capture of the war correspondent.

In the centre of Uondo there stood a monument on a triangle of grass. Surmounted by a treble eagle, two of its sides recorded the entry of Italian forces in the Abyssinian war. The third side was empty until 26 May 1941 when on it was recorded the entry of the 1st Battalion, The Gold Coast Regiment, on 22 May 1941.

Once again success was due to the rapidity of the advance, a certain amount of bluff, the unpreparedness of the Italian forces and their disintegrating morale. The net was now rapidly being closed — but there were still some big fish to be caught at Soddu and Jimma.

14

The Italian Retreat to the West

MAY TO JUNE 1941

After the successes of the 21st East African and the 24th Gold Coast Brigades in their battles at Soroppa and Uaddara, and the pursuit of the Italians through the mud to join up with the South Africans at Dalle, the net was closed. But we had captured more country than prisoners, and more country was the last thing General Cunningham wanted: it meant more transport/miles. Before the Italian army could be written off as a fighting force many more men had to be taken — dead or alive.

The Gold Coast Brigade had taken about four thousand prisoners between Uaddara and Uondo and about one thousand more were accounted for at Fike and Sciasciamanna. Therefore there were still, possibly, around thirty-five thousand enemy troops in the country west of Sciasciamanna. It was known that a considerable but unknown number of their African troops had deserted after Uaddara, but most of their 21st Division, after abandoning their defences at Giabassire, were trying to reach Soddu across country. So were the remainder of their 25th Division after the Battle of Sciasciamanna and some of their 24th Division after being chased north by the Gold Coasters. The total of these could be about twelve thousand men and, if we add to that figure the 101st Division stationed at Soddu, the 22nd Division at Jimma, and the 23rd and 26th Divisions in the Lechemti area, the estimate is approximately correct.

The chase for these men, numbering between thirty and thirty-five thousand, was on. But, unlike the usual hunt, the hares outnumbered the hounds by four to one! The 'hounds' were in two packs, the 22nd Brigade with the 5th and 6th K.A.R. and the 2nd Nigerians in the Sciasciamanna area, and the 23rd Brigade with the 1st K.A.R. and the 1st and 3rd Nigerians at the Omo River near Abalti on the road to Jimma. The task of each brigade was to cross the Omo River, and whichever succeeded first was to assist the other.

At first sight it would seem that it was unnecessary to undertake both of these difficult operations to cross the river and that one would have sufficed. For operational requirements this may have been so but there were then weightier considerations. The defeat of the enemy forces in the Galla Sidama was turning out to be an easier matter than that of supplying and maintaining our troops in the field. The Line of Communication by road from Kenya, by which the 12th Division had been supplied, was in a most precarious condition; the primitive equipment at the port of Berbera limited its capacity to supplying only two brigades beyond Addis Ababa; and the road from Addis Ababa going south past the lakes, by which the 22nd Brigade was being supplied, was rapidly becoming impassable with the increasing rain throughout Abyssinia. So, in order to circumvent some of the serious and threatening complications, it was necessary to have two river crossings. Then, with a bridge at each, all our forces could be supplied from Addis Ababa down the good road to Jimma.

However, there were several hurdles to get over before the 22nd Brigade could even reach the Omo. Their first job was to capture the important town of Soddu where there was a large Italian garrison force and to which all the Italian troops fleeing west from three divisions were making their way across country in order to be able to get from there to their concentration point at Jimma by road. But there were battles to be fought before they could tackle Soddu.

It had been planned that General Godwin-Austen's 12th Division should carry out the operation against the town of Soddu and cross the Omo River to take Jimma, but the delay in their arriving on the scene due to bad weather and worse roads necessitated a change and the task was allotted to the 22nd (EA) Brigade. Preparatory to this the enemy had to be removed from the villages of Bubissa, where the 5th K.A.R. had had trouble with their tanks, and from Colito. The 5th K.A.R. were, therefore, ordered to return across the flooding Gidu River which had caused them so much trouble, drive any enemy out of Bubissa and then join the rest of the Brigade in the Colito area on 19 May. They found that the Italians had withdrawn from Bubissa so they went on their way.

The 6th K.A.R., moving up the road from Sciasciamanna, ran into the enemy near Colito. They were holding positions each side of the road in thick bush and some of their medium tanks had been seen. So, while the 6th K.A.R. held the road front, the 2nd Battalion of the Nigerian Regiment, which had just rejoined the Brigade, attacked round the left flank before dawn next morning while it was still too dark for the tanks to operate – only to find that the enemy had gone. Our armoured cars and light tanks pursued them followed by the 6th K.A.R. and found them defending the Billate River where they had destroyed the bridge. Two factors against taking quick action were that the 5th K.A.R. had not arrived from Bubissa and the Nigerians had been marching all night. However, our artillery and machine-guns blasted and swept the Italian positions whilst a company of the 6th K.A.R. managed to ford the river and put in a determined bayonet attack on to the enemy left flank which cleared their whole forward position. But, just as the battle appeared to be over, the Italian tanks emerged from the bush and once again, as at Bubissa, the situation became critical. It was then that Sergeant N.G. Leakey of the 6th K.A.R. attacked and captured one of the tanks single-handed, for which gallant action he was awarded the V.C., unfortunately posthumously. Leaping on to the leading tank he shot the occupants, one of whom was the commander of the Tank Unit. He then tried to get it going but, when he could not manage to do that, went after the others on foot and was last seen climbing on to another of them. As a result of his action and the concentrated fire of the 6th K.A.R., who held their ground well, the enemy withdrew and our force took six hundred and thirty-five prisoners, ten field guns and three medium tanks.

There seems to have been a serious omission in that 22nd Brigade had no anti-tank guns at that time – with the exception of one captured Italian one the 5th K.A.R. had during their first attack on Bubissa on 10 May. (But, as the enemy tanks elected to attack on the other side of the village from where the solitary anti-tank gun was sited, it never came into action!) The 5th K.A.R. Task force at Aselle had a section of 1 Anti/Tk Battery but this seemed to have disappeared. The 12th Division had two batteries of anti-tank guns, one South African and one Rhodesian, but, while the 6th K.A.R. were fighting on the Billate River, these were still down the road south near Hula.

The bridge over the Billate was soon made fit to use and, on 22 May, the 2nd Nigerian Battalion with A.F.V.s crossed over and went on towards Soddu. The Italians tried again to halt their advance about six miles short of the town but, with the aid of one of the captured medium tanks and another bayonet charge, this time by the Nigerians, their resistance was broken and our small force captured eight 75-mm. anti-aircraft guns mounted on lorries, some field guns and about a thousand more prisoners. While the booty was being collected three of our tanks and two armoured cars went on to Soddu which surrendered that evening without a shot being fired. One company of the Nigerians was sent forward that same night to occupy the town.

The surrender was certainly not due to the inadequacy of the captured garrison which consisted of General Liberati and the Staff of the 25th Division, General Baccari and the Staff of the 101st Division and about seven thousand officers and men. We had also captured six medium and four light tanks and vast quantities of arms, transport and stores.

The remnants of another Italian division, the 21st commanded by General Gaffarati, were reported to be approaching Soddu from the east having come across country from the road near Dalle. Light tank patrols were sent down to Cencia to intercept them and prevent their getting through to Jimma and he surrendered with some one thousand seven hundred troops on 27 May. Elements of yet another division, the 24th commanded by General Pralormo, were trying to make their way to Jimma after their withdrawal from Giabassire. He was contacted south of Soddu by a few of our armoured cars and called upon to surrender but had refused to do so to such a small force. Subsequently he found it not possible to cross the Omo River, was cornered and being repeatedly attacked by Patriots. The next part of the episode is probably unique in military history. The following message was broadcast from Jimma:

> Italian column commanded by General Pralormo near Kindo on the river Bottego [Omo] is in desperate condition because attacked by rebels. We beg the English H.Q. to help that column. We will be grateful. [from] Commander of the city of Jimma General Bisson Milio.

A small force from the Gold Coast Regiment which was garrisoning Soddu brought him and the remnants of his troops in on 17 June.

In the meantime the 22nd Brigade had moved on to cross the River Omo. Considerable work had to be done on the fifty-mile stretch of road between Soddu and the river before it was passable. Demolitions had to be cleared, two wrecked bridges replaced and hundreds of land-mines removed. But, by 30 May, almost the whole of the Brigade Group had concentrated on the high ground east of the river near a village called Sciola. The road from Soddu goes over a plateau at five thousand five hundred feet above sea level and through some of the most beautiful, fertile and densely populated country in Abyssinia. The river flows through a deep gorge and, to reach it, the road twists and turns whilst dropping some two thousand feet. The view across this valley to the mountainous country through which the road to Jimma passes is spectacular.

For the military point of view the river and the gorge were major obstacles. Every move on our side of the valley could be observed by the enemy, the road down into the valley had been blown up and demolished in several places and liberally mined and every likely target on the east side from the river upward had been registered by the Italian guns. But the river itself presented the greatest problem. It was then in flood and about one hundred yards across. It was flowing at around six miles an hour and was ten to fifteen feet deep in the middle.

The Italians had never made a bridge across it but ferried vehicles over on a cable-operated pontoon. A small footbridge had been destroyed just as our force arrived on the scene and, unfortunately, access to where the ferry had operated was completely blocked by wrecked Italian vehicles which had been bombed by our aircraft a few days before. But, in any case, the cable had gone and we were, for the time being, short of most of the equipment needed to make such repairs.

The Engineers and Askaris achieved the near-impossible by having the road down to the river open to traffic on 1 June. A battalion of the Nigerian Regiment then went down to reconnoitre each side of the ferry and look for alternative crossing-places but, due to accurate shelling and machine-gun fire from enemy positions in a belt of thick forest running parallel to the river, this was not feasible. It was clear that, before a large-scale crossing could be effected, the enemy gun-fire must be neutralized – or the crossing made at night. It was known that the Italians had both 75-mm. and 105-mm. guns, the latter being very formidable weapons. Our 22nd Brigade had the 22nd and 18th Mountain Batteries, the 1st and 7th South African Field Batteries and a section of medium artillery. The two light mountain batteries were sited down the slopes of the escarpment and the bigger guns on top of it. The machine-guns of the 1/3 K.A.R. had been cleverly placed well down near the river from where they would be able to fire on the enemy 105s high up on the west bank. The stage was set.

On the night of 2 June the 5th K.A.R., assisted by experienced Nigerian watermen, managed to get three platoons across the river at a point about a mile below the ferry. But this hazardous operation had to be suspended when all but one of the assault craft had either been swept away downstream or too severely damaged for further use. However, the small party that had reached the west bank managed to retain its precarious foothold there for three days although attacked repeatedly by enemy patrols and periodically shelled. During the next two days and nights further efforts were made to find a better crossing-place elsewhere and get over by means of ropes, swimming or assault boats, but these were thwarted either by the current or by enemy fire. It was, therefore, decided to try again at the original crossing where the small bridgehead was being held. This succeeded. During the late afternoon of 4 June, and all that night, troops were ferried across in the three remaining assault boats and, by dawn, three companies of the 5th K.A.R. and two of the Nigerian Regiment were across.

The plan was to capture the enemy guns, all of which were sited well up the escarpment. The task of the 5th K.A.R. was to make a wide encircling march round the Italian right flank and up the cliff to attack the gun positions from the rear. That of the Nigerians was to clear the river bank as far as the footbridge and contact the 5th K.A.R. on their return journey. No one had much rest that night. A few who managed to lie down in the long grass for a bit were disturbed by puzzled hippo wandering about. At first light the K.A.R. started their long trek. It was difficult, broken country and they had to cross a number of deep gullies as they climbed higher and higher. They could not signal progress to Brigade as the batteries of the wireless transmitter sets had petered out but they were able to indicate their position from time to time by helio.

By noon they were above the site of the enemy 75-mm. guns. It was half expected that this battery, or what was left of it, would have been moved. (It had been unwise enough to open fire at dusk on 2 June, three days before, so disclosing its position, and had consequently been both shelled by our guns and bombed from the air the next day.) This turned out to be the case and the K.A.R. swept through the gun positions finding only two Italian gunners there who immediately surrendered.

After a brief halt they went on and arrived at a point above the site of the 105-mm. battery at 5 p.m. They were tired after the ten-hour climb so it was fortunate that these guns too were almost undefended: they charged down on to a few unresisting Italians who had been under fire from our machine-guns on the other side of the river. Leaving a party to guard the guns, the battalion started to move down towards the road to contact the Nigerians – but were then attacked. It was dusk and the official report that the situation at that time became rather involved was almost certainly an understatement. Small-arms and even mortars were being used in the mêlée that ensued and then, as is the way in Africa, in a matter of minutes darkness fell and confusion was complete. Several platoons of the K.A.R. became separated from the main body and were surrounded by Italians. It turned out, however, that most of them were asking to surrender and, when the C.O. decided that the situation was too obscure for further action and managed to collect and extricate his force, they followed him to the bivouac area as prisoners.

In the meanwhile the Nigerians had moved up the road and, by midday, were a mile beyond the footbridge. The going was difficult as they were periodically under fire from enemy troops in the belt of forest on their left. At 3 p.m. they stopped and held positions astride the road two miles west of the river. They beat off a determined attack made late in the afternoon and remained there overnight. Soon after daylight they and the 5th K.A.R. found that they were in complete possession of the battlefield. Captain C.P.B. Moggridge, who had commanded the machine-gun detachment of the 1/3 K.A.R., was awarded the M.C. for his excellent work in this action.

This had been a victory over natural hazards – the river, the mountain and the mud and rain – rather than over human ones. The numbers of prisoners captured and the quantity of arms and equipment taken had begun to mean little and even to pall. Nevertheless, statistics are now a part of one's life so it must be recorded that, in this battle, we took prisoner one thousand and ninety-one Italians and one hundred Africans while seventy Italians were killed. Our losses during the week's fighting were two officers and six Africans killed and three officers and twenty-one Africans wounded.

The sappers had a ferry working by 7 June and the remainder of the Brigade Group then started crossing the river. By the 12th they also had a pontoon bridge in use. Demolitions along the road up the west side of the valley were tremendous. At one place the road along a precipitous cliff had been blown away for a distance of a hundred yards – together with three Italian cars and four lorries which had tried to cross too late. However, this and other demolitions were cleared by 9 June, due in great part to help given by the local people.

In the meanwhile the 23rd (Nigerian) Brigade, which then included the 1st K.A.R., one of the original battalions of the 22nd Brigade, had been searching for possible places where they too could cross the swollen and flooded river some fifty miles upstream. Their crossing and that of the 22nd Brigade were to be, as nearly as possible, at the same time.

The Nigerians were luckier than the 22nd Brigade in two respects. They managed to find a crossing-place which was not spotted by the enemy, and they had a bridge waiting to be erected by the sappers as soon as a bridgehead had been secured. At that time the Engineers had only one bridge available. They had already erected or made seventy since leaving Kenya and they were running out of material. It was much easier to transport a bridge to Abalti than to Sciola, so Abalti had it.

The unobserved crossing-place was of great value as the operation was a slow and highly precarious one. They had managed to get a rope across the hundred-yard-wide river, and the men had to hang on to this to avoid being swept away by the torrent. Their task was made more difficult by each man having to carry three days supplies and ammunition since it would be some time before vehicles could get over. There were casualties by drowning but, during the night of 5 June, the whole of the 3rd Nigerian Battalion and a company of the 1st K.A.R. managed to cross — and were unseen. The Nigerian contingent moved forward from the river bank and turned upstream to attack known Italian positions in the rear. This succeeded after they had fought off several counter-attacks.

The task of the company of the 1st K.A.R. was to advance upwards the escarpment which rose steeply some six miles from the river. On top of this was the village of Abalti and the main Italian defences. Somehow they reached this without being seen and then hid in the bush until dusk. The enterprising company commander then used the Trojan horse tactic. Placing his troops astride the road at the base of the cliff he ambushed and captured an Italian truck from its unsuspecting driver. He then filled it with Askaris and drove it back up the escarpment. There he found the wires for detonating road demolitions, cut them and kidnapped an Italian lieutenant-colonel who was supervising the work. During the night the rest of his company marched up the road and, by dawn, were in two commanding positions on the plateau. By 10 a.m. on 6 June they had taken two thousand eight hundred surprised Italian prisoners of war who found it difficult to realize what had happened.

By 9 June, elements of the 23rd Brigade had reached the road junction on the way to Jimma at which a road led down to the 22nd Brigade crossing at Sciola. A company of the 1st K.A.R., which was leading the field, signalled to their old brigade, no doubt with secret glee, that they had crossed the Piccolo Ghibbie River and accepted the surrender of the Italian garrison. It was a sort of 'Wish you were here' message. But had they beaten the 22nd Brigade to it? Another source of information reveals that Brigadier Fowkes was at Piccolo Ghibbie in person that afternoon! A drawn match, I think.

General Cunningham's next problem was to decide what should be done about Jimma. Information was coming in that General Gazzera was withdrawing the remains of his 22nd, 23rd and 26th Divisions to the west side of the Didessa River and he wanted to concentrate on administering the *coup de grâce* to the remaining parts of these formations rather than assume responsibility for the town with its large civilian population. He, therefore, moved the Nigerian Brigade to the good road between Addis Ababa and Lechemti in order to be able to get at them more easily in their refuge in the extreme west of Abyssinia.

There was no danger of any interference in these plans by the garrison at Jimma as the town, at the request of the British, was being invested by a force of some eight thousand Patriots with British officers. However, General Bisson, who had been left in command of the town, sent an emissary to Brigadier Fowkes stating that the town had been declared open and requesting him to send a force to protect the civilian population from the Abyssinians surrounding them. By then the number of 'Patriots' had swollen to an estimated twelve thousand by the arrival of hordes of prospective looters and were out of control. The Emperor sent a representative to deal with them but he had no success, so the Brigadier sent a battalion-strong force with tanks and guns to observe the situation and only act if absolutely necessary. This show of force was sufficient, and the town was left to its own devices until 21 June when it suited the British force to take over. Once again it was clear that the Italian garrison had been over-anxious because on the day of the take over some eight thousand prisoners surrendered to the 22nd Brigade, including a corps commander (General Scala), the Commander of the Air Force in Somaliland (General Sabatini), the Vice Governor-General of Ethiopia (General Daodiace), three divisional commanders (Generals Sabatini, Tissi and Maynardi) and eight brigadier-generals. There was also, of course, the usual vast amount of matériel and equipment including some five hundred vehicles.

The day after the occupation of Jimma a strong force under Lieut. Col. Macnab consisting of his 1st K.A.R., a section of 1 (SA)

Medium Brigade with 6-inch Hows, a field and a mountain battery, two sections of light tanks, a troop of East African armoured cars and a detachment of sappers was sent to hunt down the enemy forces fleeing towards the Didessa River. They then had very little space in which they could manoeuvre, and no chance at all of escaping, as Sudanese forces and a Belgian Contingent were pressing in on them from the west.

The Italians were reported to be in the vicinity of Agaro. Agaro itself was known to have been taken by Patriots but the enemy was located holding the line of the Didessa River. There, after a brief gun battle, the Italians capitulated. They were ordered to remove mines they had laid on the road and a token force of one platoon crossed the river in a bosun's chair. A box girder bridge was then erected and part of the main force moved across to occupy Dembi where the surrender of the Italians was formally accepted. But General Gazzera himself was still not present and had to be sought farther afield.

The general who had threatened to cut our Line of Communication at Moggio with his armoured column, General Bertello, was still at large too. When it was heard that he was at Belletta on the road to Bonga with a large force, a message was dropped on him by air, together with a warning bomb, calling on him to surrender – or else more bombs. He surrendered and he and General Tosti were collected on 28 June together with over two thousand Italian and eight hundred and fifty troops.

Information also came in that some Italians were holding out at Gore, so a small party was ordered to go there via Bedelle to investigate. The road condition, however, was too bad for them to get there and no further contact was made with Gore until General Gazzera, the Supreme Commander of the Italian forces, surrendered to General Gilliart, the Belgian Commander at Dembi on 4 July.

The Italian armies in Abyssinia had been liquidated – with the sole exception of General Nasi and his force at Gondar in the north.

Tailpiece

If there has to be a war it is some small comfort if the enemy are made to pay for it. So, when Financial Advisers and Custodians of Enemy Property hovered around our headquarters like vultures and then pounced, we hoped they had found a rich seam of Italian gold which would help to reduce the burden on the wretched tax-payers at home –

and sometimes they did. They did pretty well, for example, at Jimma.

It was known that General Gazzera had taken many truckloads of bullion from the bank in Addis Ababa when he moved with the remainder of his army into western Abyssinia. And, as his head-quarters were at Jimma, it seemed likely that he would have hidden it somewhere there rather than carry it around. At least that is the conclusion reached by the said financial 'vultures' who decided to hunt for it. The Staff Captain of the brigade in Jimma who assisted them gave the following account of the search:

One day a measly little padre arrived at my office and said, 'The Bishop wants to see you on an important matter.' I went down to see the bishop and he said he'd got some barrels which were awfully heavy. He couldn't think what was left in them, but he was terribly afraid of putting a foot wrong with the British, and he wanted to be honest about everything, and he was a Godly man and had three barrels to disclose to me. I went and looked at the three barrels, which were so heavy you couldn't shift the damn things at all, and I arranged for a lorry to collect them. Just then he said he'd got another eleven barrels but they were hidden somewhere else, not by him, of course. We went into a garage, chock full of tyres and spares, and unearthed a further eleven barrels, and took them all up to my office.

When we were taking them off the lorry, one barrel fell and burst, and a lot of half-dollar pieces fell out. We opened another barrel and another lot of half dollar pieces fell out. Some expert came along and said they were only nickel and were worth practically nothing, so in view of this, and the fact that a lot of spectators were trying to take souvenirs, I shut the barrels up and rather lost interest in them.

Next day the custodian of enemy property arrived and said he'd like to have a look at the barrels as they were really his concern. We opened some new ones up and found they were chock full of gold bars. We then opened another and found packets of rings, necklaces and the like. In fact, as the custodian said to me, 'It is rather like a super sort of bran tub.'

When I next went to the Mission, I said to the bishop, 'You have been very stupid to produce these drums so late in the day. You really must realize you have been a little unwise. I don't want to search your Mission, but I have got to have an assurance from you there's nothing else, or I'll have to search the place.' He immediately said, 'There's nothing else. This is all I know about.'

I was scared stiff at having all this gold about the place so I packed off the fourteen barrels to Addis Ababa.

Sometime later the bishop admitted to the financial adviser that he had a few East African shillings and about half a million Maria Theresa dollars buried in the garden as well as some U.S. dollars and Egyptian pounds, but these, he explained, were for buying necessities for the Mission such as chickens and eggs. So, in the end, the bishop was a great help. It is obviously bad policy to kill a goose that lays golden eggs, but there is certainly no harm in giving it a bit of a squeeze occasionally.

15

The Duke of Aosta's Last Stand

APRIL TO MAY 1941

With the capitulation of Addis Ababa and Asmara in the first week of April it might well have seemed that the war was over. But this was far from being the case. The story has just been related of how it took three months after that date to round up the seven Italian divisions south and west of the capital – a month more than it took General Cunningham to get from Kenya to Addis Ababa. In addition there remained three enemy strongholds in the north where the Italians had gone to ground; Gondar, Dessie and Amba Alagi.

While the Italians held Dessie and Amba Alagi they controlled the main arterial road to the north, so separating General Platt's and General Cunningham's forces and constituting a threat to each. This had to be removed. The enemy force at Gondar could be left to languish for a while. It was isolated in the far west and could do no harm since it was surrounded by swarms of Patriots who were gradually eating into its outer defences. General Nasi, the commander, was a fighter and he had plenty of good fighting material. It would be easier to topple him later when the morale of his troops had been sapped by the corroding influence of a virtual siege. The first objective must be to open the road up to Eritrea, and the first step towards this was to drive the Italians from their strong positions in the mountains near Dessie, two hundred and thirty miles north of Addis Ababa. It was a matter of urgency, too, because General Wavell needed the 1st South African Brigade in the Middle East and this could be moved by sea from Massawa more easily than from any other port. It was logical, therefore, that Brigadier Pienaar and his brigade should be deputed to tackle the job – and so fight their way out of the country!

It was not going to be a push-over by any manner of means; the Italians had their backs to the wall and were in great strength. They had twelve battalions against three South African ones – which were appreciably under strength after two months hard campaigning – and more than fifty guns as compared with the South Africans' fourteen. It was, therefore, a measure of the esteem in which the South African troops were held by General Cunningham that this one brigade was given the responsibility for driving the Italians from Dessie.

The country to the north of Addis Ababa was vast, mountainous and inclement – but it had one great advantage, a good macadamized road all the way up to Asmara, a distance of about six hundred miles. For the first hundred miles this highway, known as the Strada Vittoria, followed the edge of a mountain shelf which, in parts, was over ten thousand feet above sea level. Further to the east, the Awash River flowed parallel to it in a deep gorge, finding its way down to the hot, arid Danakil Desert. A wild country indeed; easier to defend than to invade. The Strada was a fine example of Italian road-making skill but, since it clung in places to steep mountainsides and then dived and turned round innumerable built-up hairpin bends, it would be easy to block by demolitions. It was anticipated that this would be a major problem during the advance north.

The Brigade Group rolled out of Addis Ababa on 13 April and met no opposition until reaching the Mussolini Pass, a hundred miles to the north. At the highest point the Italians had drilled tunnels for the road to pass through two mountain peaks. This was a great engineering feat but a costly one. During their construction, three hundred lives were lost through accidents or attacks by Abyssinians. It had been fully expected that major demolitions would be carried out in these tunnels but, surprisingly, this was not the case. Having a greater interest and pride in making tunnels than in making war, the Italians did not blow them up. So the grateful South Africans drove through them – and, during one brief attack by Italian planes, used them as air-raid shelters. A mile north of the tunnels there was a road block and some opposition, but this was soon brushed aside and the Brigade moved on, winding down into the valley where they occupied the village of Debra Sina on 14 April.

They encountered no stiff resistance until, on 17 April, they reached the Combolcia Pass, some two hundred miles from Addis and thirty miles south of Dessie. They were then confronted by strongly fortified enemy defences on the hills and mountain slopes on each side of the road. Dessie, with its even stronger fortifications, was straight ahead of them and up in the clouds. The enemy guns had registered on every approach and the numerous road blocks were all mined – and covered by accurate gun-fire, a thing they had seldom bothered to do in the past. It was a daunting prospect for all but the staunchest of gunners and sappers.

The South African artillery immediately went into action and tried to outshoot the Italian guns but, skilful and courageous though the gunners were, this was just not on. They were shooting from open ground against guns in hidden fortified positions − and with only a quarter of the number of weapons the enemy had. The Italians could not be blasted from their holes in the ground; they would have to be winkled out.

So, on 19 April, the South Africans climbed up into the mountains to stalk and outwit the enemy. They were assisted by a large body of European-led Patriots known as Campbell's Scouts who undertook to operate on each flank and harry the Italians wherever they could. It was tough going, particularly as every man had to carry food and ammunition: there were neither pack animals nor air-drops. After climbing more than three thousand feet, they reached the upper ridges held by the Italians and, there, the 'Dukes' stayed for four days and nights facing a biting cold wind and driving rain. They gradually worked their way forward, located enemy defences, drove them from some of the hills and seized and occupied others that had commanding positions. The Italians made several spirited counter-attacks in which they sustained great losses, but the pressure on them was unrelenting.

Every spare man, were he driver, cook, stretcher-bearer or clerk, was detailed to carry food, water, ammunition or greatcoats up to these men in the mountains each night. Sometimes this entailed a seven-mile trek followed by an arduous climb up into the clouds. The climax came on 22 April when the Royal Natal Carbineers attacked a series of hilltop positions at dawn after a night approach on a compass-bearing. They pounced on a line of enemy machine-guns almost before they had time to open fire and then carried on, driving the Italians farther and farther back. At the same time the Transvaal Scottish were attacking in the centre of the front and rapidly gaining ground.

After the successful advances by the 'Carbineers' and the 'Jocks', the 'Dukes' again took over the lead on the 23rd. Scrambling and fighting their way over and around the hilltops they, together with Campbell's Scouts, drove the Italians gradually back and, by the 26th, had captured key positions overlooking Combolcia. That evening Italians were seen pulling out of the area around the village at the foot of the escarpment and making their way up through the pass to Dessie. Reinforcements had been sent to them from Dessie, but it seemed that they too were on their way back. After this withdrawal, the sappers were able to remove a road block in front of the village during the night. It was an unusual obstacle consisting of over a hundred derelict trucks piled up and held in place by concrete pillars and barbed wire. Nevertheless it was soon removed, mainly by hauling the trucks apart and dropping them over the edge of the road into the valley below. Next morning the 'Jocks' took Combolcia, and many prisoners, in their stride and went on towards Dessie.

Combolcia was important for two reasons. First, a road led down from there to the port of Assab on the Red Sea which could be used as an escape route for the Italians. They had, in fact, started to use it as such but found that Campbell's Scouts were there before them and had blocked it. Secondly, there was a good air-strip there and the S.A.A.F. started to use it almost as soon as the last of the Italian guns in the area had been silenced.

A little way up the hill from Combolcia, the leading troops had a surprising find. Forty-six good trucks and six splendid medium guns, neatly parked on the roadside, had been abandoned by the enemy. This was due, once again of course, to someone having blown a demolition too soon and so making their withdrawal impossible. The demolition in question was nearby but, when a start was made to clear it, the enemy artillery opened up from Dessie. Soon after the Brigade's guns replied, however, and got at least one direct hit on the fort, white flags started to flutter from the walls and a deputation came out to ask for terms. Unconditional surrender was demanded and given and the Transvaal Scottish moved up into the town – in enemy transport since a destroyed bridge prevented the use of their own.

The ten-day battle was over – a triumphal success for the South Africans. But it was not a triumph just because they had gained a victory – it was the manner in which it had been fought and won which was remarkable. Their tactics were not those of the First World War; there were no blind and senseless charges against machine-guns on the pattern of the battles of the Somme. After a silent night-approach and a brisk bayonet charge at first light, the position was taken and held until mortars or, if possible, guns had silenced the next line of enemy defences. Any post which then still held out was stalked and the gun crew killed at short-range before the advance was resumed. Their peacetime skill in hunting brought a rich reward. The South Africans were no longer, as I wrote some months before, 'good but inexperienced material'. They were seasoned, tough fighting soldiers, comparable with the Gurkhas. That is why, after a week of

battles around Dessie, their casualties were no more than twelve killed
and fifty wounded, whilst the Italians are known to have had some four
hundred men killed during the same period.

When the fighting was over, the fabulous tonnage of stores,
supplies, arms and ammunition hidden away in caves in the mountains
had to be collected and guarded, as also the artillery and vehicles of all
descriptions. Then, too, there were over eight thousand prisoners and,
as the last straw on the camel's back, forty-four trunks of clothing and
personal possessions belonging to the Duke of Aosta.

But this task did not delay the onward move and the 'Carbineers'
left Dessie on 30 April to reconnoitre the way to the north: the
Brigadier had an appointment at Amba Alagi, one hundred and fifty
miles away. On 1 May they occupied Waldia, taking more prisoners.
But further road blocks, the bogey and bugbear of the Brigade, held
them up there for three days. This time a tunnel had been blown up, a
more than usually difficult thing to clear. But even this did not halt the
move north and Campbell's Scouts went skirmishing ahead towards
Alomata which was occupied on 5 May. The remainder of the Brigade
Group arrived there on 8 May and, on that date, came under
command of Major-General Mayne of the 5th (Indian) Division for a
joint attack on the Duke of Aosta's stronghold at Amba Alagi.

The mountain fortress of Amba Alagi is a most impressive feature,

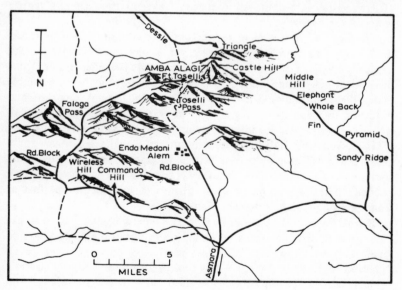

towering above the surrounding countryside and dominating the two valleys through which pass two roads which link northern and central Abyssinia. Over a period of many months, Italian engineers had been drilling tunnels and passages through the mountain, blasting out caves for men to live in and vaults for storing everything the defenders could possibly need from ammunition and food to clothing and Chianti. They had also carved out of the rock many impregnable gun-pits, machine-gun sites and infantry positions. In addition, every hill round about the main fortress had its own defences with entrenchments for infantry with machine-guns, all of which were surrounded and protected by picketed barbed-wire entanglements and minefields. Then the two approach roads were blocked by demolitions which were covered by gunfire. In fact everything that human ingenuity could devise was done to create a stronghold that would be invulnerable and secure against any attack that could be launched at that time.

The fortress was manned by five thousand well-armed and equipped men, for the most part from the cream of the Italian forces in Africa. General Frusci, the commander, had managed to bring part of his army from Eritrea after the Battle of Keren to join the garrison, which had also recently been reinforced by two battalions of white troops of the 211th Infantry Regiment and the Savoia Grenadier Machine Gun Battalion plus the artillery of the Savoia Division. Their orders were: 'Resist to the last man; no man may leave his post for any reason whatsoever, even if surrounded.'

The body of men sent to reduce and overcome this Goliath could well have been named 'Davidforce'. As a joint operation by the 5th (Indian) Division and the 1st (South African) Brigade, it sounded a great deal better than it actually was. Very few troops were available from General Platt's Sudan force. The 4th (Indian) Division had returned to Egypt after Keren and at least a brigade from the 5th Division was needed for internal security and garrison duty in Eritrea. This left only the 29th Brigade, a motorized Cavalry Regiment and a Jewish-Arab Commando plus Royal Engineers and the Divisional Artillery. From the south, an overworked and under-strength South African Brigade was hurrying northward to join them — as fast as road blocks and demolitions permitted.

Before the operation could be started, General Mayne had to stock-pile the supplies and stores he would need, dump them ahead — and protect them. Working from his base at Khartoum, over seven hundred miles away by road, this took a fortnight. The mobile force which was screening this operation had been patrolling and reconnoitring the approaches to Amba Alagi. When General Frusci heard of its proximity, he interpreted this as indicating an imminent attack and detonated his main road demolition near Enda Medani Alem. This cost them a further two hundred vehicles as, with their usual carelessness and impetuosity, it was done before the trucks could be withdrawn behind the road block.

Our greatest error, a perennial one throughout the whole campaign, was our lack of pack-animal transport. Before the era of air-drop and helicopters this was a real necessity in mountain warfare. There were, certainly, two Cypriot Mule Companies on the strength, but they had arrived in the country too late to serve at Keren. On this occasion General Mayne had insufficient transport to bring them up into Abyssinia – but he did manage to improvise a small supply unit with local animals.

When the General moved his comparatively small force southward he knew, of course, that the project was an ambitious one and that he would have to use guile since he lacked brute strength. The defences of Amba Alagi had been planned in the expectation that any attack would come from the north – which was where he was. He couldn't get round the enemy, and his Brigade on the south side could not reach him for a week – or two. He decided, therefore, to make several thrusts and feint attacks and move gradually nearer to the mountain by driving the enemy from some of their outer defences on the surrounding hills. This would give him good observation for his guns, and a better conception of the main problem – where a major attack or attacks would be most likely to succeed.

The tactics he adopted were exactly those used by a pack of hunting-dogs when attacking a lion at bay. One of them would dart in and then swerve away as the lion struck at it, while another dog would jump into the fray on the opposite flank. Others would follow suit until the lion was exhausted and the pack could then finish him off. Accordingly a small part of the British force comprising Skinner's Horse, the Commando and elements of a Frontier Force Battalion made a demonstrational feint advance towards the Falaga Pass and took possession of Commando Hill on 1 May. During this action some of the men and their supplies had to be hauled up cliffs by rope. They then beat off several Italian counter-attacks and, next day, shot the enemy troops from the next hill, Wireless Hill. To give credence to the belief that the main attack was being mounted from that, the east side, a further small force, with Bren carriers, went down the main road through Enda Medani Alem. Men of the Garhwal Rifles then demonstrated for the benefit of the Italians in Fort Toselli that they were occupying the whole valley as well as picketing the hilltops. That night a show of continually moving headlights and the hum of engines indicated the concentration of a large force. Meanwhile, however, the whole of the 29th Brigade, with its guns, had been quietly moving to the opposite flank behind Sandy Ridge and, at 4 o'clock in the morning of 4 May, they swept forward past Pyramid, Fin, Whaleback and Elephant Hills to Middle Hill. At one point some of the Worcesters went farther and managed to get under the wire defences. But they would have been annihilated had they tried to cross the open ridge leading to Little and Amba Alagi and were recalled. The Brigade remained holding Middle Hill. From there a battalion of the Frontier Force Rifles with a company of the Worcesters slithered down into a valley two thousand feet deep on the night of 8 May, scrambled up the other side and attacked the enemy on Castle Hill. They were then on the south side of Amba Alagi. When they were in possession of the greater part of the hilltop, a white flag was displayed by the Italians. But, when the Frontier Force men went forward to accept their surrender, fire was opened on them and their casualties were heavy. A thick mist then came down which enabled the Italians to organize a counter-attack and our force withdrew.

Meanwhile General Mayne had reinforced the drive through the Falaga Pass and captured Gumsa Ridge from which there was direct observation on to Fort Toselli. The 5th Division then held the centre hill on Castle Ridge, Middle Hill and Gumsa, so investing the enemy position on three sides. The advantage gained from this was not that these places would be springboards for infantry attacks on the mountain but observation posts for the guns. Unlike the situation at Dessie, it was improbable that the Italians could be winkled out of their holes on Amba Alagi, they would have to be blasted out. From the positions they then held, the guns were able to put heavy and accurate fire on to Fort Toselli and on to the main fortress. Some of the enemy guns were put out of action and an ammunition magazine was blown up.

However technically impregnable a fortress may be, its human garrison can never be impervious to incessant day and night bombardment. Harassed as they were, even in their strongly constructed defences, by steel and stone splinters and by the continuous roar of gun-fire and bombs, their morale was ebbing.

In the meantime troops from the Sudan Defence Force and the Patriots of Ras Seyoum were closing in on the west and Brigadier

Pienaar was approaching from the south. On 11 May General Mayne flew down to Alomata to discuss plans with him for a final assault and, when his Brigade arrived hot-foot on the 14th, they, and the Patriots, drove the Italians from Triangle Hill. This was a good site for their guns and, on the 14th, they joined in the general bombardment.

The Duke of Aosta indicated on the 16th that he wished to discuss terms of surrender. So great was the turmoil, however, that he could only do this by signalling to General Nasi at Gondar asking him to send a plane to drop a message for General Mayne. This was done and receipt of the request was acknowledged by a temporary cease-fire to allow an Italian envoy to come to Divisional Headquarters. The Duke sent General Volpini, but he was unwise enough to come without an adequate armed escort and was killed by Abyssinians before he had even left his own defended area. A British officer was, therefore, sent into Amba Alagi.

There followed a series of somewhat histrionic incidents. The Duke wanted to retain a token non-combatant garrison in the fort until the end of hostilities, but this, of course, was wholly unacceptable to General Mayne.

Was this to placate Mussolini for their not having resisted to the last man? To have done so would have caused the death of thousands of men and served no useful purpose. This was no siege of Mafeking, no rearguard action to cover a withdrawal, no Verdun to ensure that *ils ne passeront pas*.

So, after total capitulation and the evacuation of the fort was demanded and agreed, the garrison was granted the honours of war. Some five thousand Italians, with their arms, filed out past a Guard of Honour while the pipes played 'The Flowers of the Forest'. The Duke came out last and was given a Royal Salute. He then thanked the South Africans for bringing his forty-four uniform trunks from Dessie and was driven off to meet General Platt. It was all over.

16

The Last Lap

When I flew to Addis Ababa in October 1941 on posting to Headquarters of the 12th Division, there was scarcely any sign in the capital that there had ever been a war. Peace reigned and life proceeded normally. The Emperor, Haile Selassie, was in residence in his palace, important-looking Abyssinian gentlemen strutted about in elegant long cloaks and many Italian civilians were shopping as usual, some of them driving little two-seater pony buggies around the town. The banks, hotels and shops were all doing a brisk business and even the theatre was open and a concert advertised. Under the surface, however, there was a great deal of hardship. The Italians were selling their cameras, watches and jewellery at about a quarter of their real value in order to buy the necessities of life at the inflated prices.

Addis Ababa is up in the mountains at over eight thousand feet. It has not, therefore, the sort of warm, kindly climate one expects near the equator, but a cold, damp one. The scenery, to match, is harsh and craggy and only relieved by the trees, planted in his wisdom at the command of the former Emperor, Menelik, to arrest erosion and provide fuel. But even these failed, in my eyes, to add charm to the countryside — through sheer monotony: no one had thought of planting any tree other than eucalyptus.

On the lower slopes of the mountains and in the valleys the soil was sufficiently fertile to sustain subsistence agriculture for a large peasant population whose life was similar to that of the feudal tenant farmers in Europe in the heyday of the Norman kings. They owed fealty to the Emperor, but even he had little if any influence throughout the country as a whole and was only in complete control of a limited domain around his capital. Beyond that other feudal lords held sway.

The country around Addis Ababa is not typical of Abyssinia: no one place could claim to be that since the diversity at different altitudes is so great. Almost every crop known to man can be grown somewhere in Abyssinia; from sugar, maize and sorghum to coffee, wheat and tea. Being a farmer myself I wanted to see more of the country but, for the time being, I was tied to my desk.

I found that my job at Headquarters was that of D.A.Q.M.G. which I interpreted as Dogsbody to the Adjutant and Quartermaster General. The only member of the staff I knew was Jack Fisher who held the exalted post of G.S.O.1. He took me under his wing and showed me around. I was in 'B' Mess with the other juniors. That was in town whilst 'A' Mess, I gathered, was 'in the country'. 'It's an easy walk to the office for you,' he said, 'only takes about ten minutes.' I began to feel that, for this job, I should be wearing a bowler hat and carrying a rolled umbrella. I had to get some new clothes anyway as I'd had rather an unlucky break. Awaiting me at Headquarters were two signals from Nairobi, one telling me that my house in Tanganyika had been burnt to the ground, and the other that the ship carrying a uniform case of mine back to Mombasa had been sunk. But that wasn't all. That very night our Mess was burgled and all the clothes I had brought with me were taken – except my pyjamas.

I quickly settled into the routine work but I missed my old friends in the 22nd Brigade. One day, however, to my surprise, Sam suddenly appeared in my office. 'My General will be along tomorrow,' he announced, 'and please don't refer to me again as the orderly officer, I'm an A.D.C. now.' The Brigadier had become a Major-General and was coming to take over the Division from General Godwin-Austen who was being elevated to the War Office as Quartermaster General. His brigade had been slogging it out in the mud and rain for over three months since reaching Addis Ababa, and fighting battle after battle. The new general deserved a comfortable office chair for a bit if anyone ever did – but I knew he wouldn't be happy in it for long.

I found there was time for other things than work for a peacetime soldier. Those handymen, the sappers, had improvised a squash court and occasionally, per kind favour of Jack, I had a ride. He and the other lieutenant-colonels on the staff lived in some state with the General in the Duke of Aosta's ex-residence. It was a lovely country house with well-kept gardens and fine stables for the Duke's hunters. These, to match his height, were all around seventeen hands.

As we seemed to have settled down comfortably for the duration of the war, I bought a pony of my own. I first saw him in the main shopping centre, harnessed to one of the little buggies. He was an ugly but spirited beast and the owner was having some trouble with him, so I asked if he would sell him to me. I should have been warned by his very eager reply of '*Si, si, Signor*' but I was keen to buy something to ride and ponies were not easy to come by, so I asked him to bring it up to the race-course that afternoon for me to try.

When I met them there a few hours later the pony gave me a nasty look, bared his teeth and laid his ears back; but I managed to mount him. After that he took charge and went off like a rocket. I gave him his head – he would soon tire going flat out round the track. But neither he nor I saw it in time. No races had been held since the war started and, right across the course, there was a triple Dannert barbed-wire fence. He couldn't stop in time, nor could I, and we slid into it at speed. I went clean over his head and, luckily, over the wire too. I walked back to the owner who looked dejected thinking the sale was off. But he cheered up when I paid him. The beast, including saddle and bridle, was not too expensive, I thought, at £15.

There were occasional parties and, from time to time, the Emperor gave one. We knew about these well ahead because an equerry would come over to my office to ask if we could let him have a few cases of whisky. The alternative was that we should get nothing to drink except the local Tej and, as most of us found it difficult to acquire a taste for this, I always, with the approval of my A.A.&Q.M.G., gave gracious assent and an order was duly sent to NAAFI. An hour or two later the equerry would return bearing a number of enormous, gold-embossed cards, not inviting but commanding us to attend the party in question.

I can't say they were a riot but they were interesting. After advancing down the length of the ballroom at the Palace, then bowing to His Imperial Majesty the King of Kings, one did one's best to retire backwards against the probable opposition, and a butt in the bottom, from one of his Great Danes. Then came refreshment – per kind favour of NAAFI. The Emperor spoke fluent French and preferred speaking it to English. So, when he found that my French was a little better than ordinary schoolroom stuff, he summoned me on several occasions to have a chat with him. Before I left Addis Ababa for other fields, he offered to give me a citrus plantation at Diredawa after the war. That this did not materialize was my fault and not his.

Then there were the *bôites de nuit*. The two best were, in strictly correct parlance, brothels. But this ugly word ill-describes the *clubs de joie* that they were, joyful congregations of wine, women and song. And, with the typical British idea of fun rather than the Latin one, most of the patrons went there for the wine and the song rather than the girls.

One had the odd worry from time to time. NAAFI, for which I had a responsibility, gave me a headache or two. The breakage rate, particularly of bottles of whisky, became so high as to threaten the ration we were each allowed to buy. The NAAFI staff naturally blamed the transporters who, in turn, blamed the roads. There could be no fault on the part of NAAFI because the sealed tops of the broken bottles were produced as evidence that they had not been opened but smashed by some act of God. This turned out to be the case, except that the blow had not been administered by God but by a member of the NAAFI staff — with the bottle held over a tin bath to catch the whisky for straining through a towel later on! No doubt this trick had been tried out in the Peninsula and Crimean Wars, but it was new to me.

Apart from minor contretemps such as this, life went by peacefully, pleasantly and calmly until, one day, the General announced that he was going to attack Gondar. We had been expecting this for some time, but I should have been disturbed had I known the manner in which it was to affect me a week later. The General had decided that his force should move up the main north road as far as Dessie and then turn north-westward past Magdala and through Debra Tabor to Lake Tana. The staff got to work and every detail was calculated to the last gallon of petrol, round of ammunition and bite of food. I played my part in this which consisted mainly of totting up columns of figures, adding on ten per cent for luck and handing the answers to my boss, the A.A.&Q.M.G. He then, poor chap, went sick.

Two days later, and four days before we were due to move, the General said: 'The Intelligence people tell me that the road from Dessie to the west is impassable due to heavy rain. We shall now have to change the plan, go further north up to Aduwa, turn left there on to the road from Asmara to Gondar. We shall be able to get some supplies from Asmara but the whole administrative order will have to be altered. You,' said he pointing to me, 'had better get cracking.'

I had been caught like this once before so I knew what to do: I hastily summoned the best brains I could find to pick. These were from Supply and Transport, Ordnance, Signals and our own head-quarters and, between us, they soon had the job done.*

---

* Extract from a despatch by Lt.-General Sir William Platt dated 31 March 1943:

'The change of plan brought about by the unexpected fall of Wolchefit in September had necessitated a change of line of supply, but the necessary administrative changes had been carried out satisfactorily and worked well.'

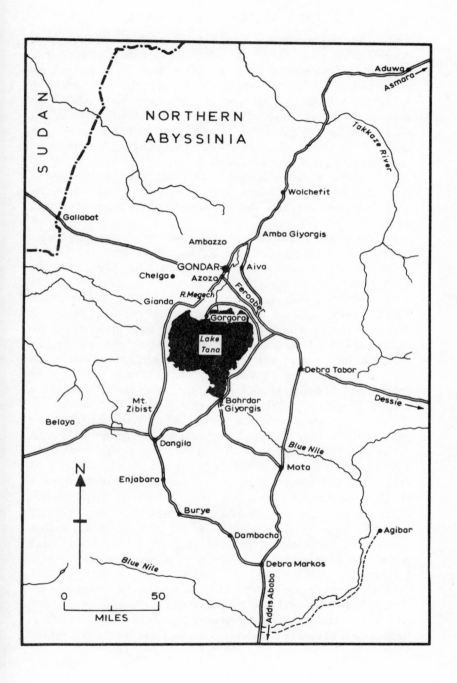

It was then October and five months since the fall of Amba Alagi, yet General Nasi, undoubtedly the best of the Italian commanders, remained in his stronghold at Gondar. At the time this seemed strange and almost as if he had been forgotten. During the recent months all the South Africans and the two brigades from West Africa had departed for other theatres of war and we were almost down to just garrison strength. We should be able to rake up sufficient manpower to do this job, but it would be a case of scraping the bottom of the barrel to find enough guns and transport.

The delay in dealing with Gondar was not due to an oversight. It had been appreciated before the operations against Dessie and Amba Alagi that time was on our side and General Nasi's force was getting weaker, not stronger.

For many months Sudanese and Ethiopian regulars and Abyssinian Patriots, organized by Brigadier Sandford, had been worrying at General Nasi's outposts south and west of Lake Tana, gradually forcing him back towards Gondar itself.

The operation had started in September 1940 when Brigadier Sandford, with two other British officers and wireless equipment, set up a small post on Mount Zibist on the west side of the lake. The two chiefdoms in the area, under Dejasmatches Mangasha and Nagash, supported the Emperor and, together, they organized and carried out small-scale raids on Italian outposts. Colonel Torelli, who commanded an Italian brigade at Dangila, made several attempts to capture them but, by dodging from place to place, they managed to elude him. On one occasion the Banda who were searching for them passed over the cave in which the imperturbable brigadier was hiding. It was a hard life. Only once during the first three months was a small mule convoy able to reach them with supplies. They lived mainly off the country and, when they ran out of money, borrowed from one of the Dejasmatches until some bags of the shiny, new Maria Theresa dollars, recently minted in Bombay, could be sent to them. Through his unwavering confidence, unfailing cheerfulness and apparent uncapturability, Brigadier Sandford established a presence which encouraged other local chiefs to give, at least, their tacit support to the Emperor.

In the meanwhile an expeditionary force was being equipped in the Sudan to join them and this, together with the Emperor, crossed into Abyssinia at the beginning of February 1941. The Emperor made his headquarters at Belaya – in a cave. The main part of the force went on to occupy a fortress at Enjabara which had recently been evacuated by the Italians.

There were no roads up from the Sudan in this area which could carry motor transport, so it was planned to use mules which would take over the loads of stores and supplies from the camels when the hill country was reached. Appeals were made to the Abyssinians throughout the Gojjam to sell mules, but the response was so poor that the force was compelled to use the camels to complete the trek into the mountains. The poor beasts were completely out of their element in the cold, wet mountainous conditions and died like flies on the journey. Twelve thousand out of the original fifteen thousand were lost.

The British force consisted of one Sudanese and two Kenya trained Ethiopian battalions* with seventy British and Australian officers and NCO's. For artillery they had four 3-inch mortars. The Italians had in the Gojjam, the district on the south and west sides of Lake Tana which was to be invaded, sixteen Colonial and four Blackshirt battalions, two groups of Banda and six batteries of guns. The British were outnumbered by eight to one.

It seemed a highly ambitious plan containing a number of imponderable factors. Had one propounded such an unrealistic scheme at the Staff College, one would immediately have been sent down to the bottom of the class. Success depended too much on luck, bluff and an unknown amount of support from the local people – and therein lay the biggest gamble of all.

Ras Hailu, who commanded a large force of Banda, was the most influential of them. He was an important member of the Gojjam dynasty, which was hostile to the Imperial one, and the Italians planned to hand over the control of the Province to him. A few others, less confident and audacious than Mangasha and Nagash, began to pay lip-service to the Emperor but were hesitant in supporting him openly. Most, but not all, of those who offered help to the British force in those difficult early days were unreliable in any active role, whilst a few proved themselves to be staunch and courageous allies. This, of course, substantiates the old adage that all generalizations, including this one, are dangerous.

Brigadier Sandford knew the worth and the weakness of the

---

* One of these battalions, the 1st Ethiopian Battalion, was divided into a number of 'Operational Centres', each about 180 strong, and attached to different Patriot chiefs.

Patriots better than anyone; he had lived among them. He understood how utterly perplexed and confused most of them were by the
political scene. It was incomprehensible to them and incompatible
with their traditional parochial life. They were aware that the Italians
had captured Gallabat and Kassala in the Sudan and had taken
possession of British Somaliland. So, while hating them for taking
their country from them, they had come to regard the Italians as
invincible and many, therefore, got on to their bandwagon which, so
clearly, was carrying the biggest guns. Then there was an even more
cogent — and personal — reason for hesitation in backing the British;
the haunting fear of reprisals by the Italians on their families and
villages.

However, the expeditionary force, which was commanded by a
colonel named Wingate, was unaffected by such hypothetical
conjecture and undaunted by a shortage of supplies. They could live
on the country and capture from the enemy what the country could
not provide. They just wanted to get on with the job. But, with so
much uncertainty and so many unknown factors, how could a small,
heterogeneous, lightly armed and equipped and poorly supplied force
such as this defeat heavily armed and well trained troops eight times
their number? But they did — and with a degree of skill, pertinacity
and resolution over a period of many months which, I believe, has
never been surpassed in our history.

Towards the end of February the situation had improved. News
came that General Cunningham's offensive against Italian Somaliland
was moving fast and that General Platt was advancing into Eritrea;
R.A.F. bombers had made several attacks on key enemy positions in
the Gojjam before their full-time services were required over Keren,
and rumour had greatly magnified the size and strength of the small
British invading force. As a result of the changing conditions, the
Italians decided to withdraw their troops from all the smaller stations
and concentrate at two major points, Bahrdar Giyorgis on the south
shore of Lake Tana at the source of the Blue Nile, and Debra Markos.
As a further consequence, prudence began to overcome the long-
standing traditional jealousy between the Imperial and the Gojjam
dynasties and several more of the local chiefs proclaimed their
allegiance to the Emperor.

Colonel Wingate divided his force into two main operational
groups. The larger 'Gideon Force' he commanded himself and the
other 'Beghemder Force' he put under Major Simonds. The latter
group, comprising one company of the Sudanese Frontier Battalion

and part of the 1st Ethiopian Battalion, a total of about 350 men, was given the task of investing Colonel Torelli's nine battalions at Bahrdar Giyorgis in order to prevent them from breaking back and attacking 'Gideon Force', which was busy harassing the major Italian concentration at Burye. The Emperor's nominee as governor of Beghemder, a Province on the east side of the Blue Nile, was Fitaurari Birru. He arrived to assist Major Simonds with five hundred of his Patriots – but four hundred and fifty of them deserted the following day. (Perhaps they went home to harvest their crops!)

In the event this default did not affect the position. The garrison was successfully contained and when, on two occasions, Colonel Torelli attempted sorties, he suffered heavy losses. The first time, he brought out five of his Colonial battalions with guns and mortars but he was stopped by two hundred and fifty Sudanese and seventy-five Patriots after losing one hundred and seventy-five men. At his second attempt he lost one hundred and fifty killed and wounded whilst our losses were two killed and three wounded. General Platt pinpointed the reason for these successful little operations when, in his despatch dated 11 September 1941, he said: 'As usual the Sudanese soldier set a high example of coolness and discipline.'

Towards the end of March Colonel Wingate decided that he could bluff Colonel Torelli and maintain the siege of his garrison with no more than half the small force then being used for the task. So he ordered Major Simonds to cross the Nile with one hundred and eighty of his men to deal with the Italian garrison at Debra Tabor which was blocking the road between Dessie and Gondar. Wingate's stratagem was successful. Torelli made no further attempt to break out until 2 May when he evacuated his whole force across Lake Tana to the north shore near Gondar. Having no navy, Wingate could not in any case have prevented this.

Fitaurari Birru and seventy-four of his followers accompanied Major Simonds across the Nile where they were joined by two other chiefs. These two were believed to have the support of about a quarter of their Province, another quarter was found to be neutral and the rest actively hostile. Nevertheless, they raised a considerable force which fought a successful action against Italian troops resulting in the isolation of the Debra Tabor garrison from any further contact with, or reinforcement from Gondar.

At the time when he sent 'Beghemder Force' to confine Colonel Torelli's legions to Bahrdar Giyorgis, Colonel Wingate started to harass Colonel Natele's five thousand-strong garrison at Burye. It was a difficult proposition as there were a number of small forts surrounding the town. However, 'Gideon Force' worried and prodded each one of these in turn by mortar and machine-gun fire, mainly at night – the time when morale is most destructible. He then used another weapon, a loudspeaker which shrieked adjurations at the enemy to desert – which many did – and encouraged and inspired his own men.

Colonel Natale had been undecided whether to move his force back to Debra Markos: he realized that earlier precipitate withdrawals in the Gojjam had discouraged his troops and increased desertions from his Colonial battalions. This period of indecision gave Colonel Wingate time to move the 2nd Ethiopian Battalion into position to cover the Italian line of retreat to Debra Markos and, when Colonel Natale, under pressure from the R.A.F. as well as ground attacks, finally broke out from Burye on 4 March, his column was ambushed near Dambacha. His dilemma was increased by being attacked at the same time in the rear by two companies of the Sudanese Frontier Battalion.

The Italian casualties were around the thousand mark, of whom one hundred and eighty were killed. The Ethiopian Battalion, which was eventually smothered by sheer numbers, lost a British officer and ninety men. They also lost all their transport camels but, at the same time, captured sufficient trucks to solve their supply problem.

After this fiasco General Nasi replaced Colonel Natale by Colonel Maraventano who assumed command over all the Italian troops in the Debra Markos area. They were estimated to number about twelve thousand. Lieut.-Colonel Boustead* could not, of course, contain such a force with his Frontier Battalion and a mortar platoon – but he held a watching brief over it. Wingate was determined that this huge body of men, though being diminished by about a hundred deserters a day, should not get away to reinforce another front. (General Cunningham had then only just reached Jigigga and General Platt had been temporarily checked before Keren.) So he sent a small party to block the road between Debra Markos and the crossing of the Nile. The local chief, Lij Belai Zelleka, agreed to assist in preventing the Italians from getting across the river and three platoons of troops and a section of mortars were sent to help him. In addition, Azaj Kabada, the Emperor's representative, added some of his irregulars to the force.

---

* Later to become Colonel Sir Hugh Boustead, K.B.E., C.M.G., D.S.O., M.C.

A few days before Addis Ababa capitulated on 6 April, the Italian High Command ordered Colonel Maraventano to evacuate Debra Markos and take his whole force across country to Dessie. This was a formidable task – but he was a formidable man. His long column moved off southward towards the Nile bridge on 4 April and, before long, fell into the trap. The ambushers were then, however, at only half their original strength because Lij Belai and his followers had reneged. It appears that his ambition to marry into the distinguished family of Ras Hailu had taken precedence over his promise to Wingate. Nevertheless, the reduced force inflicted considerable damage and many casualties on Maraventano's column before he was able to move forward again and cross the river. He then turned north up the east bank, planning to cut off eastward later on and follow one of the valleys across to Dessie.

The South African Air Force found him and bombed the column on 8 April and, as he was being harassed continually by Patriots, the going was slow and difficult. Then came the news that the fall of Dessie was imminent: the last haven of refuge was closed to him. But he still refused to surrender and, when he was again bombed, he left his motor transport and took to the hills where he could construct defences and get food.

Wingate caught up with him in the middle of May and, when the old Patriot leader, Ras Kassa, joined him with some two thousand of his followers, they launched a combined attack on the Italians. Maraventano again refused to give in, turned to bay at Agibar and fought it out for three days before ultimately surrendering on 22 May. By that time his effective force had been reduced to seven thousand by desertions and the sick and wounded. Among the incidental booty of arms and equipment were seven hundred camels, two hundred horses and mules – and seven hundred anxious and unhappy civil servants.

In his despatch dated 22 July, General Cunningham wrote: 'So ended what must have been for the whole of his column an exhausting and desperate flight through mountainous country full of hostile Ethiopians.'

After the Italian withdrawal from Debra Markos there remained only two enemy garrisons in the Gojjam, that on the lake shore at Bahrdar Giyorgis and a smaller one at Mota. This was an isolated place up in the Chokey (Ciocche) Mountains, some of the peaks of which are almost 14,000 feet high, and the pass across the range not much less. It was held by a Colonial battalion and this had to be removed.

So three hundred undauntable Sudanese and their British officers marched over the mountains – carrying their precious artillery, one 3-inch mortar and a lot of bombs. They had only their cotton tropical uniforms and a blanket apiece to protect them from the ice-cold blizzards: those were acceptable acts of Allah, but what puzzled them, no more than that, was mountain sickness.

Soon after they had taken up positions around Mota, orders were received, for some unrecorded reason, for all but two platoons and the mortar to return to their base. The remaining handful of sixty men and their colonel then proceeded to paste the garrison, at night of course, with mortar and Bren gun-fire. Next morning a British lieutenant, having borrowed the crowns from his C.O.'s shoulder badges in order to appear as a major, went into Mota with a letter demanding the surrender of the garrison. After a mild show of resistance, the Italian C.O. agreed. I expect the four hundred Italians were a little dismayed when the victors, two platoons of Sudanese, marched in to take over.

The month of May was drawing to a close. Addis Ababa, Asmara, Dessie and Amba Alagi had all fallen and the Emperor was back on his throne. Patriots who had been slow off the mark were raising their standards all over the country, declaring their loyalty, offering to fight – and hoping for loot. No Italian troops remained in the Gojjam Province, but General Nasi still controlled the two main roads to Gondar with his garrisons at Debra Tabor and Wolchefit. Debra Tabor had been under siege by Patriots ever since 'Beghemder Force' had cut its line of communication with Gondar almost a month earlier. But time was becoming important and steps had to be taken to raise the blockade and drive the enemy out. A small British force, two hundred and fifty strong, was, therefore, sent out from Dessie to help the Patriots to bring the matter to a head. This consisted of a squadron of Skinner's Horse, a company of the Punjabi Regiment and a detachment of sappers. They were armed with light machine-guns and (captured Italian) 81-mm. mortars. The Italian garrison was believed to be about two thousand five hundred strong.

The rains had started and they had to plough their way through the mud for one hundred and fifty miles. On arrival they were warmly welcomed by the Patriots, who must have numbered some eight thousand men, and a plan was made for a joint attack on the town. However, none of the Patriots turned up for this, nor, almost unbelievably, did they put in an appearance on any one of four subsequent appointments! The British force abandoned hope of co-operation after that and carried out harassing tactics on their own against the garrison. As a result the Italians asked for terms of surrender and the British force took over the town on 3 July. The enemy strength was found to be four thousand four hundred and they had six guns and enough motor transport to lift one thousand two hundred men.

The stronghold at Wolchefit was a very different kettle of fish. It is scarcely possible to imagine a more formidable military undertaking then the capture of the fortified positions on the summit of that escarpment. In his despatch reporting the operation, General Platt assessed the natural strength of Wolchefit at double that at Amba Alagi and five times that at Keren.

The road, winding round ninety-nine hairpin bends from the valley up the cliff face, could be blocked with the greatest of ease at a score of different places, and every movement in the valley could be observed from the top, an easy target for the thirty well-sited guns on the summit. There was another way up to the Wolchefit plateau, by a long and tortuous mule track which meandered up a gorge for about eighteen miles and reached the top at a point about the same distance again from the fortifications. Any force arriving there would then have to contend with the garrison of five thousand well armed and equipped men. Several brave attempts to get at the garrison through this back door were made by Major Ringrose and his Patriots who, on one occasion, captured one of the outer posts at night, only to be driven back by an Italian counter-attack.

In the middle of July a further attack was made by them in conjunction with a battalion of the Punjabi Regiment. One of the main objects of this was to establish an artillery O.P. on top. Extensive reconnaissance had failed to find any feature from which observation could be obtained on to this ten thousand-feet high fortress against which no guns less than 25-pounders would have been effective – except perhaps anti-aircraft guns! But this expedition, too, was repulsed. However, the undaunted Major Ringrose successfully attacked an Italian post near Wolchefit at the end of August and the South African and Royal Air Forces continued their periodical raids on the stronghold. But to hit a target such as Wolchefit was like trying to drop a bomb on a knife edge.

In the end this policy of attrition prevailed and, somewhat surprisingly, the apparently impregnable fortress surrendered on 27 September. The way was then open for a strong force to move up for an assault on Gondar.

Patriots had been moving progressively closer to Gondar as the

Italian forces pulled back into their defended positions at Gorgora, Chelga, Kulkaber and Ambazzo. These outposts were maintained to defend the road approaches to Gondar and to protect the army's sources of supply, the lake for fish and the countryside for grain. But, being far apart and each some twenty miles from the town, they were liable to siege or attack one by one.

The 2nd Ethiopian Battalion from 'Gideon Force', commanded by Lieut.-Colonel Benson, had marched up from Debra Markos, captured Gianda on 11 November and then isolated Gorgora and Azozo. Patriots and regulars from the Sudan had cut all communications between Chelga and Gondar and Major Douglas' Patriots had surrounded Kulkaber. Bimbashi Sheppard, in normal times a professor of poetry, had been carrying on a little war of his own with his followers against two of the local chiefs who were supporting the Italian cause. After three days of jousting and *feu de joie* in a valley just north of Gondar known as the 'Bad Lands', they agreed to change sides and support him. So, with their help, he then occupied the important village of Amba Giyorgis which overlooked Gondar.

It seemed that they had left little for General Fowkes to do except administer the coup de grace — but it was to be more difficult than that.

When General Fowkes' 12th Division moved north from Addis Ababa in November there were still some loose ends to tie up at Headquarters, so I was told to stay behind and tie them. When this was done a Wellesley bomber would fly me up to Asmara and, from there, I should find my way to Advanced Divisional H.Q. by road, some three hundred miles. The day came and I went to the airport. The Wellesley did not look as splendid as I had imagined it would. It was spattered with oil and obviously overworked and very tired. As I arrived, the pilot and navigator were putting on their parachute harness.

'Have you got one of those for me?' I asked. His reply was disappointing.

'No, because you wouldn't be able to get out anyway from where you'll be lying.'

He was quite right; I think I was in the bomb rack — but wherever it was, it was very cramped and uncomfortable.

The old plane went well to begin with. So it should, we had started at eight thousand eight hundred feet and were going down-hill. But, soon after the navigator had handed me a note saying we had passed

Dessie, even I knew we were in some difficulty: the aircraft was flying round and round in circles. His explanation was far from encouraging. 'We are at Alomata and trying to make enough height to get into The Pass of Death.' Eventually we managed to get through the ominously named gorge, clear the escarpment by a few feet and, some two hundred anxious miles later, land safely at Asmara.

My Italian farmer friend, Davico di Quittengo, a prisoner of war on parole, met me. With his usual cunning he had found out that I was on the way there. Through his influence with the manager of the hotel, we had an excellent dinner that night and he told me how he had picked up my indiscreet wireless message to Beles Gugani, what he was then doing to resuscitate agriculture in Eritrea and what he planned to do after the war. He did not tell me about his last stand at Amba Alagi with the Duke of Aosta: the future interested us more than the past.

Next day I went on towards Gondar. After passing through Aduwa and Axum we climbed the fabulous Wolchefit escarpment which rises four thousand feet from the valley. In places the road had been carved out of the sheer rock face by men suspended on ropes. The tableland at the top is ten thousand feet and one of the peaks fourteen thousand feet above sea level but, although the countryside there is bleak and wind-swept, there were wild roses and primroses on the roadside and heather on the hills, all of which gave it a homely look.

I found Divisional Headquarters tucked away just off the road at Amba Giyorgis, about the highest and coldest spot on that roof of Africa. From it one could look down into the valley and see some of the villages around Gondar. After the usual caustic pleasantries such as 'Had a good leave?' and 'Nice and warm down there, isn't it?', Jack put me into the picture about the operations taking place.

'Irregulars and Patriots are worrying away at the defences on the west side,' he said, 'and "Southforce" is prodding along their front at different points to try and find a weak spot but, so far, without any luck. It's not going to be easy. The sappers are now making a road southward behind the crest of a ridge over there which screens them from observation so that we can get the 25-pounders into a good position. We tried one small frontal attack near Kulkaber but had to pull out: the "Itos" are obviously not going to let us have Gondar without a stiff fight.'

He added that they had had no trouble from enemy aircraft, but he spoke too soon. The very next day the General had to dive into a ditch to escape the attention of an Italian fighter which was machine-gunning the road from far too low an altitude for everybody's safety.

The town of Gondar lies within a horseshoe-shaped chain of hills and mountains, open at the southern end where the plain slopes down to Lake Tana, twenty miles away. The old fort in the town was built by the Portuguese in the sixteenth century. Four roads lead from the outer world to this mountain fastness, but only two of them have any claim to be called that, the other two being little more than mule tracks. Of the two sometimes motorable roads, the better was the one I had taken from Asmara, and the other came from Dessie through Magdala and Debra Tabor. One of the others winds and twists its way up through the mountains from Gallabat in the Sudan and the last runs up the west side of the lake from the south. There, in the wild north-west corner of Abyssinia, General Nasi, a good soldier and a stern but just disciplinarian, elected to make the last stand. He had a strong force both in numbers and quality. Out of a total of thirty-four thousand men, eighteen thousand of them were white Italians, many of them the braver ones who had made their way down to him after the fall of Keren rather than surrender. They were well armed with machine-guns, mortars and artillery – he had sixty guns of various calibres.

The defences of Gondar covered a very large area – too large for them to be efficient and effective. The garrisons at Gorgora and Chelga were being contained and Kulkaber, also, was surrounded by Patriots. Nevertheless, although they were not parts of an integrated defence system, their own defences were intact and they were by no manner of means out of the fight. Their role was to hold fast – which they were doing – and the possibility of their breaking out could not be discounted.

The mountain of Ambazzo on the north side of the town probably held the strongest force of them all: it certainly was in the strongest position, and it was in no way invested or cut off from Gondar. It would, however, almost certainly be expecting an attack from the direction of Amba Giyorgis and could be relied upon, therefore, to stay put while General Fowkes concentrated on the capture of Kulkaber, the key to his whole strategy. Had he been able to use the road to Gondar from Dessie, as he had originally planned, his approach would have been from the south and across fairly open country in which a large force could be deployed. But, as circumstances had obliged him to come round from the north, he was in hilly country in which there was no room for manoeuvre. He had to move out of it and get down south by hook or by crook – but the Italians were blocking his way at Kulkaber.

He had, of course, been aware of this problem and had sent a small force over the appalling road from Dessie to deal with it. This, known as 'Southforce', consisted of the 6th K.A.R., the 1st (EA) Pioneer Battalion, the 51st Gold Coast Light Battery and a machine-gun company of the 1/3 K.A.R. They slogged their way through the mud to Kulkaber and then, supported by Major Douglas's Patriots, attacked the very strong and extensive enemy defences on the Kulkaber-Feroaber ridge. They clambered gallantly up steep hills under rifle and machine-gun fire from enemy positions protected by wire and mines whilst, at the same time, they were being shelled by several Italian batteries which their light guns were unable to locate, never mind silence. At one time it seemed that they would succeed, but the odds were heavily against them and, finally, they were driven back, largely due to physical exhaustion. That day two platoons of the 1/3 K.A.R. carried their machine-guns twenty-five miles. It was November 13.

The 25th and 26th Brigade Groups had arrived in the vicinity of Amba Giyorgis during the first week of November and a battery of 25-pounders was expected daily from Massawa. This delay was exasperating but, even if these guns had arrived earlier, there would have been, as it happened, no really suitable site from which they could have been used against the main Gondar defences. But, when an old, disused track was found running the right way, southward from Amba Giyorgis through some rocky defiles, all available hands were put to work on opening it up. In a few days it was cleared and fit to use for a distance of two or three miles and, when the guns did arrive, they went straight into a good position. By then it had been found that the old track went on to join the road from Dessie at a point west of Kulkaber. So, working by night, and also by day where the operation was screened from the enemy's view by a ridge, it was quickly made passable throughout the whole length and the 25th Brigade went down it. The next assault on Kulkaber was to be a joint one by them and 'Southforce' on 21 November. It was a hard fight but, after two separate attacks and several counter-attacks by the Italians, the whole ridge was captured. Troops and supplies could then move across to the southern front and attack Gondar through the open end of the horseshoe.

General Nasi's force was numerically stronger than that of General Fowkes who had some twenty thousand regular troops and about six thousand Patriot allies. He also had more than double the number of guns the British possessed — sixty as against our twenty-five. But the Italian force was dispersed in a number of isolated positions, long distances apart, which were, one by one, captured or put out of action by siege. This policy undoubtedly contributed to his eventual defeat.

General Fowkes' plan was to attack on the broadest possible front in order to reduce the effect of the Italian advantage in guns by not presenting any troop concentration as a target. He, therefore, placed the 25th Brigade well over to the left flank to attack northward in the direction of Azozo, Major Douglas' Patriots in three groups under Captains Pilkington, McLean and Nurk on a ten-mile front in the centre, and the 26th Brigade on the right flank to attack across the Megech River. The country this brigade would have to cross was rough and hilly, making the task of supply difficult, so each man carried three days rations. Then, for the first time in the whole campaign and in its last battle, a company of pack-animal transport, formed by requisitioning local horses, mules and donkeys, carried the machine-guns, mortars and ammunition. The initial move by the infantry was a tricky one as it had to be down a bare, open slope in full view of the enemy. However, they overcame this problem with great ingenuity by cutting bush and 'planting' it on the open ground at night and this covered their advance next morning.

The attack was launched at dawn on 27 November and was supported by bombers and fighters of the S.A.A.F. and R.A.F. The 26th Brigade had a sticky time from mines and booby traps as well as from well-registered gun-fire, but they took these, and several counter-attacks, in their stride and went steadily forward. The 25th Brigade had easier terrain for their advance but it was not all easy going and they had to stem some counter-attacks too. The tanks and armoured cars were held up for a time while a bridge was put across the river – but nothing stopped the three groups of Patriots for long. They were certainly not impervious to shot and shell but appeared heedless of it. They broke through wire defences, stormed and captured strong-point after strong-point and, by early afternoon, had started fighting the battle scheduled for the next day.

The final outcome of the battle had been clear shortly after midday when the Italians started blowing up ammunition dumps and burning stores in Gondar. One heard later that, at that stage, General Nasi had sent envoys to ask for terms. He had an understandable apprehension that, if thousands of wildly excited Abyssinians entered Gondar first, there could be chaos and carnage. I don't know what happened to the envoys; I only hope they were not trampled underfoot in the rush. Of course there wasn't a hope of anyone being able to stop the fight at that juncture. In the old days a bugle call was sufficient to start or stop a battle – but nothing could have stopped this one. The roar and thunder of guns and bombs, the chattering of machine-guns, the savage cries of angry men and the resonant wailing of the Shoan war-horns would have drowned the sound of a thousand bugles.

By late afternoon the Patriots were in Gondar — after covering twenty miles in ten hours, fighting most of the way. But there was no catastrophe: the armoured cars arrived hot on their heels and General Nasi surrendered to them in person. The Union Jack then flew over the town.

When some four thousand hostile Abyssinians, excited by the heat of battle and filled with hatred of the Italians, poured into Gondar, some disorder and destruction was inevitable. In the circumstances it was remarkable that order was restored so quickly. By the evening of 30 November all troops except a garrison force were out of the town and, thereafter, one only knew that occasional acts of lawlessness and looting were being attempted by the sound of shots fired in the night by vigilant guards and patrols. This speedy return to normal, or should one say normal Chicago-style life, was due to the sternest of measures ordered by the General and to the presence of the Crown Prince who had been staying at our headquarters and had assumed the governorship of the Province.

One of my first discoveries in Gondar was that the old Portuguese castle had been converted into a good hotel. Divisional Headquarters, therefore, moved into far better quarters than the tents we had been in on the cold, windy, blasted heath above. It made a change in other ways, too. We had Italian instead of Argentine bully beef and, as far as I remember, some macaroni with it. One officer, however, led by the orderly numbering of the rooms and the general atmosphere of tourism into expecting full hotel service, put his boots outside his bedroom door to be cleaned. When, bootless, he complained next morning, we pointed out that it was not, of course, a case of looting but merely someone hunting for souvenirs.

It was then that the question of looting raised its ugly head. The army could take anything belonging to the Italian government which could be of use or value to it, whether it be arms, supplies, petrol, stores or cash and bullion. But the individual soldier could take nothing. Again I had to say to a dejected Jackson: 'Wars ain't what they used to be.' But what was to happen to the personal property abandoned by Italian army officers and civilians who had gone; the glass, silver, cutlery, clothing, cameras, field-glasses, furniture, carpets, saddles and bridles, fishing rods, guns and even cars, bicycles, etc., etc.? The circumstances were exceptional. When we left the town in a few days, the wild men from the hills would flock in like locusts and, in all probability, indulge in an orgy of destruction. Would they appreciate the glass, silver, cutlery, etc., etc.? I think the honest answer was 'Yes, but not so much as we should.'

So, whilst the law had to be obeyed, a blind eye was turned to souvenir hunting – within reason. I don't think any man, with the exception of the General, came away empty-handed. I myself could not resist a beautifully made Italian saddle that was lying around, and a friend of mine, more enterprising than me, managed to take away a large double bed and a radiogram. But, as he said, 'The bed will make the journey back to Asmara more comfortable for one of the wounded, and the radiogram will advertise the high quality of Italian goods.'

I was glad the General came away with one trophy: a congratulatory signal from the Prime Minister.

I myself should have sent a signal – to the Governor of Tanganyika. It would have read: 'Ref your number 213 of 3 September 1939 stop the war here is now over rpt over stop'.

Wavell's objective had been achieved. With a total force of some 100,000 men he had invaded Italian East Africa, a country as large as Britain, France, Spain, the Low Countries and Italy put together, and routed a well trained army of 300,000 men equipped for modern warfare with aircraft, armour and guns. His success was due to fine generalship, good leaders at all levels and the fact that the majority of his men, both white and black, were skilled in bushcraft.

The conclusion of this epic achievement was scarcely noted at the time: it was insignificant in comparison with the battle for survival which Britain was then preparing to fight on her shores. Now that historians can examine the campaign dispassionately and objectively, however, it could well be rated as a military masterpiece of its time.

Epilogue

The Italians lost the war in East Africa mainly because they saw no good reason for having one and, when it came, their hearts were not in it. Their chief interest was in making new homes and developing their large colony comprising Somalia, Abyssinia and Eritrea.

However, after Dunkirk and the occupation of France, Mussolini was convinced that Germany would overrun Britain in a matter of weeks and, therefore, declared war in order to have an easy ride to victory and a share of the spoils with no great effort on his part. So sure was he of this that he ordered his armies in East Africa not to take the offensive but to await the inevitable and imminent victory. Thus the Duke of Aosta was prevented from launching an immediate attack on Kenya which he could then have done with every chance of success. Thereafter their military situation gradually deteriorated in comparison with that of Kenya.

The development which had taken place in Italian East Africa between 1936 and 1940 was phenomenal as compared with any other colonial enterprise in history. The first capital provision by the Italian government was £133,000,000 plus a further annual sum of £10,000,000 − vast amounts in relation to real value at that time. Teams were quickly set to work in the fields of agricultural, veterinary and medical science and in the exploration for minerals, sources of energy and the establishment of industries. There was enormous scope in agriculture: since the altitude of the fertile areas of the country ranged from two thousand to ten thousand feet about sea level with a corresponding rainfall of thirty to eighty inches a year, almost every crop known to man could be grown.

Communications were of first priority so sixty thousand Italians and fifty thousand Abyssinian workmen made two thousand miles of road in the first two years. (Their ultimate target was six thousand seven hundred miles.) The increase in the population of Addis Ababa is a good indication of the massive growth in all spheres. In 1936 it was five hundred and fifty, in 1937 it had increased to five thousand and, in 1939, to thirty thousand. That year there were one hundred and thirty thousand Italians in the colony.

Comparisons are said to be odious. The following one may well be that — but it is true. Before the 1914 war Britons were being encouraged by their government to settle in Kenya — in order to add another jewel to the Empire's Crown. More realistically, it was to develop the country's agricultural potential and thus make the railway economically viable and enable the British government to reduce income tax by a farthing or two in the pound. Development was slow: there were no all-weather roads but many animal and plant diseases with which the farmers had to contend.

Nevertheless, the total European population of Kenya struggled up to ten thousand by 1920 and thirty thousand by 1949. 1943 and 1944 were notable years in Kenya's development. During those two years the country's first tarmacadam road outside the towns was constructed. It was between Nairobi and Nakuru — and was made by Italian prisoners of war!

It is interesting to speculate how the great Italian plan would have fared if they had not entered the war. It is quite possible that the surge of development would have continued in all fields — provided the national aspirations of the Abyssinian people had been harnessed, directed and satisfied. The obsolete medieval governmental structure of the Emperor and the Rases had been swept away and a large section of the population was reconciled to Italian rule — and benefiting from it. If the Italians had educated Abyssinian youth to participate in a new, democratic and multiracial form of government, it is possible that they could have succeeded in maintaining long-term harmony where other colonial powers failed. They were operating on a more propitious basis than any other in that there were no European landed gentry, sahibs or bwana mkubwas; the Italian settlers came out with their wives and children and worked manually side by side with the indigenous people.

All things are possible but, as crystal balls are still not available in transistor form and we cannot put the clock back, we shall never know for certain what would have happened.

Bibliography

1. History of the 1/3 Bn King's African Rifles in Abyssinia, Somaliland and Eritrea.
2. War Journal of the 5th King's African Rifles.
3. War Diary of the 22nd (EA) Brigade.
4. The Abyssinian Campaigns. (War Office)
5. The London Gazette. (11 June 1946)
   13.6.46. Operations in the Middle East, Aug. '39 to Nov. '40.
6. The London Gazette. (9 July 1946)
   10.7.46. Operations in East Africa, Nov. '40 to July '41.
7. The London Gazette. (16 July 1946)
   17.7.46 Operations of East Africa Command, 12.7.41 to 8.1.43.
8. Abyssinian Patchwork. (Kenneth Gandar Dower)
9. Springbok Victory. (Carel Birkby)
10. Wavell. (John Connell)
11. History of the Second World War. (Winston Churchill)
12. Hope in Africa. (C.J. Alport)

Index

Index

GENERAL INDEX

INDEX TO FORMATIONS AND UNITS